Bloom's Modern Critical Views

Bloom's Modern Critical Views

WILLIAM SHAKESPEARE: TRAGEDIES
New Edition

Edited and with an introduction by
Harold Bloom
Sterling Professor of the Humanities
Yale University

BLOOM'S
LITERARY CRITICISM
An imprint of Infobase Publishing

Bloom's Modern Critical Views: William Shakespeare: Tragedies—New Edition

Copyright © 2010 by Infobase Publishing

Introduction © 2010 by Harold Bloom

Bloom's Literary Criticism

An imprint of Infobase Publishing

132 West 31st Street

New York NY 10001

Library of Congress Cataloging-in-Publication Data

William Shakespeare. Tragedies / edited and with an introduction by Harold Bloom.—New ed.

    p. cm. — (Bloom's modern critical views)

  Includes bibliographical references and index.

  ISBN 978-1-60413-637-1 (hardcover)

  1. Shakespeare, William, 1564–1616—Tragedies. I. Bloom, Harold. II. Title. III. Series.

  PR2983.W488 2009

  822.3'3—dc22   2009022849

Contributing editor: Pamela Loos

Cover designed by Alicia Post

Composition by IBT Global, Troy, NY

Cover printed by IBT Global, Troy, NY

Book Printed and bound by IBT Global, Troy, NY

Date printed: November, 2009

Printed in the United States of America

10 9 8 7 6 5 4 3 2 1

Contents

Editor's Note

My extensive introduction examines the five major tragedies and then adds *Coriolanus* as a coda. The emphasis throughout is on what Samuel Johnson called "Shakespeare's skill in human nature."

The late A.D. Nuttall contrasts *Julius Caesar* and *Coriolanus* as powerful and different modes of mimesis, while E.A.J. Honigmann stresses the uniqueness of *King Lear*'s double plot.

"The passions of the mind" in the tragic protagonists are engaged sensitively by Arthur Kirsch, after which Nicholas Grene accurately demonstrates the secular cosmos of *Antony and Cleopatra*, where varying human perspectives exclude transcendence.

Maynard Mack's *Hamlet* certainly is not my own, but then no single vision can encompass all of Shakespeare's "Poem Unlimited," and limitation (stressed by Mack) is a possible apprehension of Hamlet's final acceptance.

The tragic mad scenes receive a thorough survey from Peter Wenzel, while Nancy Cluck confronts deathly beginnings in labyrinthine Shakespeare.

An elegantly balanced analysis of language in *Othello* by Sir Frank Kermode is followed by Werner von Koppenfels's rather original depiction of imaginative sexual passion in several of the tragedies, in the light of Burton's *Anatomy of Melancholy*.

HAROLD BLOOM

Introduction

Shakespeare's five major tragedies are widely recognized as among the supreme achievements of Western literature. One can think of the J Writer's strand of Genesis-Exodus-Numbers, of the *Iliad*, of Dante's *Comedy*, as comparable eminences, together with the principal surviving dramas of Aeschylus, Sophocles, and Euripides. Though it is customary to group Shakespeare's major tragedies, *Hamlet* clearly is in a class of one, since its inwardness is unique and enigmatic, while *Antony and Cleopatra*, at the other chronological extreme of these masterworks, also stands apart. *Othello, King Lear*, and *Macbeth* have more affinities with one another than with *Hamlet* or *Antony and Cleopatra*.

Hamlet is a radical theatrical experiment, perhaps the most radical we have known. Shakespeare cuts a gap into the play, from act 2, scene 2, through act 3, scene 2, that ought to destroy any audience's belief in the reality of what is being represented. Since the play co-opts us as accomplices, we accept every bewilderment we are shown. Hamlet himself is displayed as an authorial consciousness and also as a great hero-villain, loved but unloving and perfectly capable of acting as a casual slaughterer. Yet, despite the well-founded cavils of a few critics, audiences tend to love Hamlet the more intensely even as he demonstrates that he neither wants nor needs such love. William Hazlitt, speaking for the audience, said that we were Hamlet, a fusion that has been endemic for two centuries, and that may never depart. The drama is a "poem unlimited," of no genre really, and its protagonist, who has inspired so many imitators, continues to be an unique figure, the most isolated character in Shakespeare, perhaps indeed in all of Western literature.

1

Is Hamlet a tragic hero? So various are both the prince and his play that the answer may tell us more about you than about Hamlet. Something deeply personal, perhaps familial, enters into this play, whose lost original very likely was by the young Shakespeare himself (though some scholars, on dubious evidence, vote for Thomas Kyd, author of the celebrated *Spanish Tragedy*). Perhaps the deaths of Shakespeare's father and of Hamnet, his only son, are more relevant to *Hamlet* than we know, or perhaps Shakespeare is atoning for an earlier dramatic defeat, though that again is much more than we know.

Hamlet is all that is central to his play; even Claudius and Gertrude seem more peripheral than not. No other consciousness can assert much for itself in Hamlet's charismatic and overwhelming presence. Yet *Othello*, while the Moor's tragedy, is Iago's play, his triumphal march to the psychic and moral annihilation of his superb captain. Iago's malignity is anything but motiveless. He has been passed over for promotion by his war-god, Othello, and this partial rejection has been a vastation for the ensign or flag officer, loyally pledged to perish rather than permit Othello's colors to be taken in battle. John Milton, involuntarily Shakespeare's closest student, made his Satan into a disciple of Iago. Satan's sense of injured merit is precisely Iago's, but Othello is considerably more vulnerable than Milton's God. Othello falls, and only Emilia, at the price of her life, prevents Iago's absolute triumph.

Shakespeare wrote *King Lear*, *Macbeth*, and *Antony and Cleoptra* in a continuous burst of creativity for fourteen consecutive months. I cannot think of anything comparable in the history of literature. *King Lear*, though very oddly handled by recent politicized critics, is the most awesome poetic drama that I know. It is a great dance of contraries, a quarrel between sublimity and human clay. Whether the character of King Lear is too grand for the stage, as Charles Lamb argued, is hardly a popular question these days but remains pragmatically quite real to me, as I have never seen an actor wholly adequate to the role. Shakespeare risked a tragedy beyond limits, and yet we have no choice but to share in the play's extravagance. No other drama seems to me to make such large demands on an audience.

Macbeth emanates out of cosmological emptiness akin to *King Lear*'s. In both plays, we have been thrown into realms that touch the limits of nature. Macbeth himself, more even than Lear, becomes a theater open to the night sky and to the forces that ride the air. What is most surprising and most sublime about *Macbeth* is that we cannot separate ourselves from the hero-villain, no matter how deeply he recedes into his heart of darkness. Shakespeare lavished intellect upon Hamlet and spirit upon Lear, but no one else receives so vast an imaginative endowment as does Macbeth. The paradox, tragically ironic, is that this man of blood is Shakespeare's greatest poet.

After the enormities of *King Lear* and *Macbeth*, Shakespeare breaks out into the world that destroys Antony and Cleopatra, whose heroic era dies with them. Though a double tragedy, *Antony and Cleopatra* is also a joyous display of Shakespeare's art at its most comprehensive. The largeness of personality in both Cleopatra and Antony is answered by the psychic and representational largeness of the play. Shakespeare's superb panoply of gifts, as comprehensive and generous as ever has been offered to us, come together in *Antony and Cleopatra* with a splendor that Shakespeare never sought again.

Romeo and Juliet

Except for *Hamlet* and *Macbeth*, *Romeo and Juliet* seems the most popular of Shakespeare's tragedies, though it is necessarily dwarfed by the heroic sequence of *Hamlet*, *Othello*, *King Lear*, *Macbeth*, and *Antony and Cleopatra*. Some critics prefer *Coriolanus* to the High Romanticism of *Romeo and Juliet*, and I myself would rather reread *Julius Caesar* than turn again to *Romeo and Juliet*. Yet the massive, permanent popularity of *Romeo and Juliet* is well-deserved. Its appeal is universal and worldwide, and its effect on world literature is matched among the tragedies only by *Hamlet*. Stendhal, who with Victor Hugo is the great partisan of Shakespeare in equivocal France, wrote his own sublime tribute to *Romeo and Juliet* in his last completed novel, *The Charterhouse of Parma*.

I desire here to make some brief reflections on the relative aesthetic eminence of the play in the full context of Shakespeare's achievement. So prodigal was Shakespeare's inventiveness, particularly in the creation of personalities, that I myself, in earlier years, tended to undervalue *Romeo and Juliet* in the full panoply of Shakespeare. There are perhaps twenty plays by him that I rated higher, even if some of them lacked the enormous popularity of *Romeo and Juliet*. I do not know whether I merely have aged or have matured, but Juliet herself moves me now in many of the same ways that I find Desdemona and Cordelia to be almost unbearably poignant. What Robert Penn Warren called her "pure poetry" remains astonishingly vital and powerful, as when she wishes her lover's vow to Romeo could be inaugurated again:

> But to be frank and give it thee again; And yet I wish but for the thing I have. My bounty is as boundless as the sea, My love as deep: The more I give to thee The more I have, for both are infinite.

That is a transcendently persuasive utterance of love's reality, as rich as literature affords, so distant from vainglory or self-deception that Romeo is transfigured by receiving it. Shakespeare is reputed to have said that he had to kill off Mercutio lest Mercutio kill the play. I think it likelier that the full revelation of Juliet's greatness made it necessary to dispose of the pruri-ent Mercutio, whose lively blasphemies against the splendors of Juliet's love might well have wearied us.

Juliet's is a difficult role to play, for the curse of our theaters are "high-concept" directors, and some of them do not seem to know clearly the dif-ference between Juliet and the Cressida of *Troilus and Cressida*! Properly performed, or adequately interpreted by a sensitive reader, Juliet is an essential part of Shakespeare's unmatched invention of the human.

Hamlet

Hamlet is the most persuasive representative we have of intellectual skepti-cism, with the single exception of Montaigne's self-portrayal, which would appear to have had considerable effect on Shakespeare the dramatist. Montaigne's skepticism was so beautifully sustained that he very nearly could persuade us to share his conviction that Plato essentially was a skeptic. Hamlet's skepticism, though powerful and protracted, dominates the prince rather less than Montaigne's preoccupies the greatest of all essayists. In the mimesis of a consciousness, Hamlet exceeds Montaigne's image of himself as man thinking. Even Plato's Socrates does not provide us with so powerful and influential an instance of cognition in all its processes as does Hamlet.

Yet Hamlet is as much a man of action as he is an intellectual. His intellectuality indeed is an anomaly; by rights he should resemble Fortinbras more than he does those equally formidable wits, Rosalind and Falstaff, or those brilliant skeptics gone rancid, Iago and Edmund. We tend not to situate Hamlet between Rosalind and Edmund, since good and evil hardly seem fit antinomies to enfold the Western hero of consciousness, the role that Hamlet has fulfilled since he first was enacted. Harry Levin eloquently warns against sentimentalizing Hamlet's tragedy, against "the obscurantist conclusion that thought is Hamlet's tragedy; Hamlet is the man who thinks too much; inef-fectual because he is intellectual; his nemesis is failure of nerve, a nervous prostration." Surely Levin is accurate; Hamlet thinks not too much but too well, and so is a more-than-Nietzsche, well in advance of Nietzsche. Hamlet abandons art and perishes of the truth, even becomes the truth in the act of perishing. His tragedy is not the tragedy of thought but the Nietzschean tragedy of truth.

The character of Hamlet is the largest literary instance of what Max Weber meant by charisma, the power of a single individual over nature, and so at last over death. What matters most about Hamlet is the universality of his appeal; the only rival representation of a secular personality would appear to be that of King David in 2 Samuel, and David is both of vast historical consequence, and perhaps not wholly secular, so that Hamlet's uniqueness is not much diminished. David, after all, has the eternal blessing of Yahweh, while Hamlet's aura is self-generated and therefore more mysterious. No other figure in secular literature induces love in so universal an audience, and no one else seems to need or want that love so little. It may be that negative elements in Hamlet's charisma are the largest single component in our general psychological sense that it is easier to love than to accept love. Hamlet is the subject and object of his own quest, an intolerable truth that helps render him into so destructive an angel, so dangerous an aesthetic pleasure that he can survive only as a story able to be told by Horatio, who loves Hamlet precisely as the audience does, because we are Horatio. Remove Horatio from the play, and we would have no way into the play, whether now or later.

What are we to make of Horatio as a literary character? He is the character as playgoer and reader, passive yet passionately receptive, and necessarily the most important figure in the tragedy except for Hamlet himself. Why? Because, without Horatio, Hamlet is forbiddingly beyond us. The prince is an agonist who engages supernal powers, even while he attempts to see his uncle Claudius as his almighty opposite. Hamlet's contention is with forces within his own labyrinthine nature, and so with the spirit of evil in heavenly places. Like wrestling Jacob, Hamlet confronts a nameless one among the Elohim, a stranger god who is his own Angel of Death. Does Hamlet win a new name? Without Horatio, the question would be unanswerable, but the presence of Horatio at the close allows us to see that the new name is the old one but cleansed from the image of the dead father. Horatio is the witness who testifies to the apotheosis of the dead son, whose transfiguration has moved him, and us, from the aesthetics of being outraged to the purified aesthetic dignity of a final disinterestedness beyond ritual sacrifice and beyond the romances of the family and of society.

Why does Horatio attempt suicide, when he realizes that Hamlet is dying? I blink at this moment, which strikes me as the most negative of all the many negative moments in the play:

HAMLET: Horatio, I am dead,
  Thou livest. Report me and my cause aright
  To the unsatisfied.
HORATIO: Never believe it,
  I am more an antique Roman than a Dane.
  Here's yet some liquor left.

Are we to associate Horatio with Eros, Antony's follower who kills himself to "escape the sorrow / Of Anthony's death," or with other heroic sacrificers to a shame culture? The court and kingdom of the wretched Claudius constitute something much closer to a guilt culture, and Horatio, despite his assertion of identity, hardly has wandered in from one of Shakespeare's Roman tragedies. Horatio's desire to die with Hamlet is a contamination from the audience that Shakespeare creates as a crucial element in *The Tragedy of Hamlet, Prince of Denmark.* Even as Iago writes a play with Othello and Desdemona as characters, or as Edmund writes with Gloucester and Edgar, so Shakespeare writes with Horatio and ourselves. Freud's death drive beyond the pleasure principle is a hyperbolical trope that we barely recognize as a trope, and similarly, we have difficulty seeing that Horatio's suicidal impulse is a metaphor for the little death that we die in conjunction with the apocalyptic end of a charismatic leader. Horatio truly resembles not the self-slain Eros of *Antony and Cleopatra* but the self-castrating Walt Whitman who gives up his tally of the sprig of lilac in his extraordinary elegy for Lincoln, the best of all American poems ever. The most extraordinary of Hamlet's universal aspects is his relationship to death. Whitman's Lincoln dies the exemplary death of the martyred father, the death of God, but Hamlet dies the death of the hero, by which I do not mean the death so much of the hero of tragedy but of the hero of Scripture, the death of Jonathan slain on the high places. The death of Hamlet is on the highest of all high places, the place of a final disinterestedness, which is otherwise inaccessible to us.

Can we not name that highest of high places as Hamlet's place, a new kind of stance, one that he himself does not assume until he returns in act 5 from his abortive voyage to England? Strangely purged of mourning and melancholia for the dead father, Hamlet seems also beyond incestuous jealousy and a revenger's fury. In his heart there is a kind of fighting and a sense of foreboding, not of death but of the inadequacies of life: "Thou wouldst not think how ill all's here about my heart." Speaking to Horatio, and so to us, Hamlet announces a new sense that there are no accidents, or need not be:

> If it be now, 'tis not to come; if it be not to come, it will be now; if
> it be not now, yet it will come. The readiness is all. Since no man, of
> aught he leaves, knows aught, what is't to leave betimes? Let be.

"It" has to be the moment of dying, and "the readiness is all" might be regarded as Hamlet's motto throughout act 5. "To be or not to be" is answered now by "let be," which is a sort of heroic quietism and clearly is the prince's final advice to the audience. There is an ultimate skepticism in Hamlet's assurance that none of us knows anything of what we will leave behind us when we die, and yet this skepticism does not dominate the prince as he dies:

You that look pale and tremble at this chance,
That are but mutes or audience to this act,
Had I but time—as this fell sergeant, Death,
Is strict in his arrest—O, I could tell you—
But let it be.

What he could tell us might concern a knowledge that indeed he has achieved, which I think is a knowledge of his relationship to us and necessarily to our surrogate, Horatio. Hamlet's extraordinary earlier praise of Horatio (act 3, scene 2, lines 54–74) may seem excessive or even hyperbolical, but not when we consider it as being in what Emerson called the optative mood, particularly in regard to the audience or to the ideal of an audience:

... for thou hast been
As one in suff'ring all that suffers nothing,
A man that Fortune's buffets and rewards
Hast ta'en with equal thanks; and blest are those
Whose blood and judgment are so well co-meddled,
That they are not a pipe for Fortune's finger
To sound what stop she please. Give me that man
That is not passions' slave, and I will wear him
In my heart's core, ay, in my heart of heart,
As I do thee.

Hamlet himself is hardly one who, in suffering all, suffers nothing, but then Hamlet is the hero, beyond Horatio and ourselves and perhaps, at the close, so far beyond that he transcends the limits of the human. Horatio is the man that the wily Claudius would not be able to use, partly because Horatio, like the audience, loves Hamlet, but partly also because Horatio stands apart from passion, from self-interest, from life. We are Horatio because he, too, is a spectator at Elsinore, yet a spectator who has taken sides, once and for all. Hamlet does not need Horatio's love or ours, though he has it anyway. He needs Horatio to survive to tell his story and us to receive his story, but he does not need our passion.

To discuss Hamlet as a literary character is to enter a labyrinth of speculation, past and present, that is bewildering in its diversity and in its self-contradictions. The personalities of Hamlet are a manifold, a veritable picnic of selves. Excess is the mark of Hamlet as it is of Falstaff, but the Falstaffian gusto, despite all its complexities, does not compare either to Hamlet's vitalism or to Hamlet's negative exuberance. To be the foremost single representation in all of Western literature, you ought to be the hero of an epic or at least a chronicle but not the protagonist of a revenge tragedy. A consciousness as vast as Hamlet's ought to have been assigned a Faustian quest, or a journey to God, or a national project of renewal. All Hamlet has to do (if indeed he ought to do it) is chop down Claudius. Avenging the father does not require a Hamlet; a Fortinbras would be more than sufficient. What it was that could have inspired Shakespeare to this amazing disproportion between personage and enterprise seems to me fit subject for wonder.

The wonder is not that Hamlet should be too large for Elsinore, but that he may be too comprehensive for tragedy, just as Nietzsche may be too aesthetic for philosophy. We can envision Hamlet debating Freud or Nietzsche; hardly a role for Lear or Othello. Yet we do not think of Hamlet as running away from the play, the way that Falstaff takes on a mimetic force that dwarfs the action of *Henry IV, Part 1*. Rather, Hamlet transforms his drama from within, so that as its center he becomes also a circumference that will not cease expanding. Long as the play is, we sense that Shakespeare legitimately could have made it much longer, by allowing Hamlet even more meditations on the perplexities of being human. Indeed it is hardly possible to exclude any matter whatsoever as being irrelevant to a literary work centering on Hamlet. We welcome Hamlet's opinions on everything, just as we search the writings of Nietzsche or of Freud to see what they say on jealousy or mourning or art or authority or whatsoever. Hamlet, a mere literary character, seems the only literary character who has and is an authorial presence, who could as well be a Montaigne, or a Proust, or a Freud. How Shakespeare renders such an illusion persuasive has been illuminated by a rich tradition of criticism. Why he should have ventured so drastic and original an illusion remains a burden for critics to come.

Doubtless it is wrong to see Hamlet as a Shakespearean self-portrait, but though wrong it seems inevitable, and has a sanction in Joyce's witty interpretation, when Stephen expounds his theory of *Hamlet* in *Ulysses*. What is clear is that Shakespeare has lavished intelligence on Hamlet, who is not so much the most intelligent personage ever to be represented in language as he is a new kind of intelligence, one without faith either in itself or in language. Hamlet is the precursor of Schopenhauer and Wittgenstein, as well as of Nietzsche and Freud. The prince understands that each of us is her own worst enemy, unable to distinguish desire from playacting, and liable to create disaster out of her equivocal doom-eagerness, a drive against death that courts death. The diseases of consciousness, one by one, seem invented by Hamlet as defenses that contaminate and are contaminated by the drive. Hamlet invents Freud in the sense that Freud is always in

Hamlet's wake, condemned to map Hamlet's mind as the only route to a general map of the mind.

The consequence is that *Hamlet* is a Shakespearean reading of Freud that makes redundant any Freudian reading of Shakespeare. Hamlet is the theologian of the unconscious, anticipating Wordsworth as well as Freud. In the same way, Hamlet precedes Kafka and Beckett, by systematically evading every interpretation that might confine him to some reductive scheme that too easily transcends the realities of suffering. Hamlet, as an intelligence, is perpetually ahead of all later literature, which cannot deconstruct his dilemmas any more forcefully or overtly than he himself has done. Shakespeare makes all theorists of interpretation into so many instances of poor Rosencrantz and Guildenstern, who would pluck out the heart of the mystery yet cannot play upon Hamlet, call him what instrument they will. Historicizing Hamlet, whether in old modes or new, ends in reducing the exegete to an antiquarian, unable to separate past values from impending immediacies. There is a politics to Hamlet's spirit, but it is not our politics, though it remains our spirit.

The sickness of the spirit, in Hamlet as in our lives, is perhaps the most perplexing issue of the tragedy. Feigning derangement, Hamlet also becomes deranged and then returns, apparently self-purged of his alienations from reality. We never do learn the precise nature of his illness, except that it ensued from the trauma brought on by the murder of the father and the mother's fast remarriage. But for a moral intelligence that extraordinary, the squalors of the family romance, or even the king's murder, do not seem the necessary origins of the falling away from selfhood. Imaginative revulsion seems the source of madness in Shakespeare, whether in *Hamlet, Timon of Athens*, or *Macbeth*. Hamlet was as much a new kind of man as the King David of 2 Samuel had been: a figure who seemed to realize all of human possibility, an ultimate charismatic whose aura promised almost a triumph over nature. The biblical David has a superb pragmatic intelligence, but his changes are natural, or else presided over by the favor of God's blessing. Hamlet changes in the Shakespearean way, by overhearing himself, whether he speaks to himself or to others. His study of himself is absolute and founded upon a pondering of his own words. Divinity lies principally within himself and manifests itself in his fate, as in the fates of all connected with him. His character is his daimon, and overdetermines every event.

Literary character, like authorial presence, always returns, whatever the tides of critical fashion. Hamlet's particular union of representational force and linguistic authority has much to do with his universal appeal and makes it likely also that a return to the study of personality in literature must find one of its centers in this most radiant of all fictional consciousnesses.

Julius Caesar

The Tragedy of Julius Caesar is a very satisfying play, as a play, and is universally regarded as a work of considerable aesthetic dignity. We tend to read it first when we are in school, because it is so clear and simple a drama that our teachers find it suitable for us there. I have seen it only once onstage, once on television, and once as a film, and found none of these three presentations quite adequate, the problem in each case being with the actor who misplayed Brutus. Directors and actors seem to place more of Hamlet in Brutus than Shakespeare himself set there, and Brutus just cannot sustain Hamlet's aura. Hamlet scarcely can speak without extending our consciousness into the farthest ranges, but there is a narcissistic, rather spoiled quality to the perhaps excessively noble Brutus, and he does not achieve ghostlier demarcations, keener sounds, until his fortunes begin to fail.

Modern critics find somewhat problematical Shakespeare's supposed political stance in *Julius Caesar*. Presumably Shakespeare, as an Elizabethan royalist, is unhappy about the assassination of Caesar, and yet Brutus is the tragic hero. Caesar is in decay, a touch vainglorious, the conqueror dwindled into a ruler who accepts flattery. But however the politics of *Julius Caesar* are to be resolved, the play seems problematical in no other respect. Its characters, including even Brutus, are not endless to meditation, and its rhetoric does not reverberate so as to suggest a beyond. There is no Marlovian element in *Julius Caesar*, no hero-villains of Hermetic ambition or Machiavellian intensity, no surpassingly eloquent and outrageous overreachers. Whether from North's Plutarch or from Seneca, or more likely from a strain in his own nature, Shakespeare brings forth a stoic music with its own dying falls but without a grudge or bias against our given condition. Brutus essentially is a stoic, acutely self-conscious and self-regarding, with a touch of Virgil's Aeneas in him. But he has been too much admired in Rome, and he greatly admires himself. A.D. Nuttall is useful in contrasting Brutus and his stoicism to Antony's affective opportunism:

> Brutus, the aristocrat, his theoretic Stoicism borne on a foundation of shame-culture, on ancient heroic dignity, belongs to the Roman past. He can do the Stoic trick (rather like "isolating" a muscle) of separating his reason from his passions but he cannot exploit his own motivating passions with the coolness of an Antony. With all his fondness for statuesque postures Brutus remains morally more spontaneous than Antony.

Where is Cassius on this scale of moral spontaneity? He plays upon Brutus in order to bring him into the conspiracy, but then yields to Brutus both as to Antony's survival and on granting Antony permission to speak at Caesar's funeral. When he yields a third time and consents, against his will, to stake everything on battle at Philippi, he completes the irony of his own undoing, and Caesar's ghost is avenged. The irony could be interpreted as a dialectic of conscience and affection, since Cassius politically seduced Brutus by exploiting the stoic hero's moral spontaneity. Cassius is destroyed by Brutus's incompetent political and military decisions, to which Cassius yields out of affection, but also because he must accept the moral consequences of having seduced Brutus into leadership, the only role possible for Brutus in any enterprise.

Cassius is the one figure in the play who might have benefited by a touch of Marlovian force or antithetical intensity, but Shakespeare preferred to maintain his own stoic control in representing a stoic tragedy. We ought to marvel that Shakespeare, a year or so later, could venture on the infinite by writing *Hamlet*, where every current is antithetical and far beyond merely rational controls. *Julius Caesar* has more in common with *Henry V* than with *Hamlet*, just as the two parts of *Henry IV* reach out to *As You Like It* and *Hamlet*. What is excluded from *Julius Caesar* is the madness of great wit, the exuberance of Falstaff, of Rosalind, and of one of the endless aspects of Hamlet. As we miss Falstaff in *Henry V* so we miss someone, anyone, who could cause *Julius Caesar* to flare up for us. Shakespeare, with a curiously stoic forbearance, subdued himself to his subject, though we do not know why.

The results of this uncharacteristic *ascesis* are surely mixed. We receive clarity and nobility and lose nearly everything that makes Shakespeare unique. Dr. Samuel Johnson's summary speaks to this better than I can:

> Of this tragedy many particular passages deserve regard, and the contention and reconcilement of Brutus and Cassius is universally celebrated; but I have never been strongly agitated in perusing it, and think it somewhat cold and unaffecting, comparing with some other of Shakespeare's plays; his adherence to the real story, and to Roman manners, seems to have impeded the natural vigour of his genius.

Whatever the impediments, *Julius Caesar* is an anomaly among Shakespeare's mature plays in that it possesses his originality in language, to a fair degree, yet is almost wholly devoid of his principal originality in representation. Not even Brutus changes by listening to himself ruminate. How much difference can we hear between Brutus at the beginning of act 2 and Brutus near to the end of act 5? Brooding on the probable change in a crowned Caesar, Brutus takes the responsibility of prophesying the change:

It is the bright day that brings forth the adder,
And that craves wary walking.

Poor Brutus, once embarked on his venture, never encounters his own
bright day. Shakespeare subtly allows the stoic hero a continuous nobility
down to the end, while also allowing Brutus to be deaf to the irony of his
final self-praise:

Countrymen,
My heart doth joy that yet in all my life
I found no man but he was true to me.

We wince, however sympathetic we find Brutus, since he seems to have
forgotten Caesar's last words, with their shock that Brutus, of all men, should
have been untrue to his friend Caesar. Brutus's "As Caesar lov'd me, I weep for
him" does not linger in us, but we do remember Antony's bitter eloquence:

For Brutus, as you know, was Caesar's angel.

Perhaps Shakespeare's politics did inhibit his profoundest powers in
Julius Caesar. The tragedy of Brutus and the crime against the monarch could
not be reconciled with each other, and Shakespeare, divided against himself,
found he could not be wholly true to Brutus.

Othello

Dr. Samuel Johnson found in the representation of Othello, Iago, and Desdemona "such proofs of Shakespeare's skill in human nature, as, I suppose,
it is vain to seek in any modern writer." The High Romantic Victor Hugo
gave us the contrary formula: "Next to God, Shakespeare created most,"
which does not seem to me a remystification of Shakespeare's characters
but rather a shrewd hint in what might be called the pragmatics of aesthetics. Shakespeare was a mortal god (as Hugo aspired to be) because his art
was not a mimesis at all. A mode of representation that is always out ahead
of any historically unfolding reality necessarily contains us more than we
can contain it. A.D. Nuttall wonderfully remarks of Iago that he "chooses
which emotions he will experience. He is not just motivated, like other
people. Instead he *decides* to be motivated." Though Nuttall says that makes
of Iago a Camus-like existentialist, I would think Iago is closer to a god, or
a devil, and so perhaps resembles his creator, who evidently chose emotions
to be experienced and decided whether or not to be motivated. We do not
feel Othello to be a critique of Shakespeare, but in some sense Iago is just

that, being a playwright, like Edmund in *King Lear*, like Hamlet, and like William Shakespeare. Hamlet's "the rest is silence" has a curious parallel in Iago's "from this time forth I never will speak word," even though Hamlet dies immediately and Iago survives to die mutely under torture.

It is not that Iago is in Hamlet's class as an intellectual consciousness. No, Iago is comparable to Edmund, who in *King Lear* outplots everyone else in the royal world of the play. Othello is a glorious soldier and a sadly simple man, who could have been ruined by a villain far less gifted than Iago. A.C. Bradley's charming notion is still true: exchange Othello and Hamlet in each other's plays, and there would be no plays. Othello would chop Claudius down as soon as the ghost had convinced him, and Hamlet would have needed only a few moments to see through Iago and to begin destroying him by overt parody. But there are no Hamlets, Falstaffs, or inspired clowns in *Othello, The Moor of Venice*, and poor Desdemona is no Portia.

The Moor of Venice is sometimes the neglected part of the tragedy's title. To be the Moor of Venice, its hired general, is an uneasy honor, Venice being, then and now, the uneasiest of cities. Othello's pigmentation is notoriously essential to the plot. He is hardly a natural man in relation to the subtle Venetians, but the sexual obsessiveness he catches from Iago develops into a dualism that renders him insane. A marvelous monism has yielded to the discontents of Venetian civilization, and we remain haunted by intimations of a different Othello, as though Desdemona, even before Iago's intervention, has been loss as well as gain for the previously integral soldier. Many critics have noted Othello's ruefulness when he speaks in act 1 of having exchanged his "unhoused free condition" for his love of "the gentle Desdemona." When we think of him in his glory we remember his ending a street battle with one line of marvelous authority:

Keep up your bright swords, for the dew will rust them.

"Sheathe or die" would be the reductive reading, but Othello in his zenith defies reduction, and a fuller interpretation would emphasize the easiness and largeness of this superbly military temperament. How does so spacious and majestic an authority degenerate so rapidly into an equivalent of Spenser's Malbecco? Like Malbecco, Othello forgets he is a man, and his name in effect becomes jealousy. Jealousy in Hawthorne becomes Satan, after having been Chillingworth, while in Proust, first Swann and then Marcel become art historians of jealousy, as it were, obsessive scholars desperately searching for every visual detail of betrayal. Freud's delusional jealousy involves repressed homosexuality and seems inapplicable to Othello, though not wholly so to Iago. Jealousy in Shakespeare—parent to its presence in Hawthorne, Proust, and Freud—is a mask for the fear of death, since what the jealous lover fears is that there will not be time or space enough for himself. It is one of the peculiar splendors of *Othello* that we cannot understand Othello's belated jealousy without first understanding Iago's primal envy of Othello, which is at the hidden center of the drama.

Frank Kermode curiously says that "Iago's naturalist ethic . . . is a wicked man's version of Montaigne," a judgment that Ben Jonson might have welcomed, but that I find alien to Shakespeare. Iago is not a naturalist but the fiercest version in all literature of an ideologue of the reductive fallacy, which can be defined as the belief that what is most real about any one of us is the worst thing that possibly could be true of us. "Tell me what she or he is really like," the reductionist keeps saying, and means: "Tell me the worst thing you can." Presumably the reductionist cannot bear to be deceived and so becomes a professional at deception.

Iago is Othello's standard bearer, a senior officer skilled and courageous in the field, as we have every reason to believe. "I am not what I am" is his chilling motto and is endless to meditation. "I am that I am" is God's name in answer to the query of Moses and reverberates darkly and antithetically in "I am not what I am." God will be where and when He will be, present or absent as is His choice. Iago is the spirit that will not be, the spirit of absence, a pure negativity. We know therefore from the start why Iago hates Othello, who is the largest presence, the fullest being in Iago's world and particularly in battle. The hatred pretends to be empirical but is ontological and unquenchable in consequence. If Platonic eros is the desire for what one hasn't got, then Iago's hatred is the drive to destroy what one hasn't got. We shudder when the maddened Othello vows death to Desdemona as a "fair devil" and promotes Iago to be his lieutenant, for Iago superbly responds, "I am your own for ever," and means the reverse: "You too are now an absence."

Step by step, Iago falls into his own gap of being, changing as he hears himself plot, improvising a drama that must destroy the dramatist as well as his protagonists:

> IAGO: And what's he then that says I play the villain,
>   When this advice is free I give, and honest,
>   Probal to thinking, and indeed the course
>   To win the Moor again? For 'tis most easy
>   Th' inclining Desdemona to subdue
>   In any honest suit; she's fram'd as fruitful
>   As the free elements. And then for her
>   To win the Moor, were['t] to renounce his baptism.
>   All seals and symbols of redeemed sin,

His soul is so enfetter'd to her love,
That she may make, unmake, do what she list,
Even as her appetite shall play the god
With his weak function. How am I then a villain,
To counsel Cassio to this parallel course,
Directly to his good? Divinity of hell!
When devils will the blackest sins put on,
They do suggest at first with heavenly shows,
As I do now; for whiles this honest fool
Plies Desdemona to repair his fortune,
And she for him pleads strongly to the Moor,
I'll pour this pestilence into his ear—
That she repeals him for her body's lust,
And by how much she strives to do him good,
She shall undo her credit with the Moor.
So will I turn her virtue into pitch,
And out of her own goodness make the net
That shall enmesh them all.

Harold C. Goddard called Iago a "moral pyromaniac," and we can hear Iago setting fire to himself throughout the play but particularly in this speech. I think that Goddard, a profoundly imaginative critic, captured the essence of Iago when he saw that Iago was always at war, making every encounter, every moment, into an act of destruction. War is the ultimate reductive fallacy, since to kill your enemy you must believe the worst that can be believed about him. What changes in Iago as he listens to himself is that he loses perspective, because his rhetoric isolates by burning away context. Isolation, Freud tells us, is the compulsive's guarantee that the coherence of his thinking will be interrupted. Iago interposes intervals of monologue so as to defend himself against his own awareness of change in himself and thus ironically intensifies his own change into the totally diabolic. As with Shakespeare's Richard III, Iago's monologues are swerves away from the divine "I am that I am," past "I am not what I am," on to "I am not," negation mounting to an apotheosis.

The collapse of Othello is augmented in dignity and poignance when we gain our full awareness of Iago's achieved negativity, war everlasting. No critic need judge Othello to be stupid, for Othello does not incarnate war, being as he is a sane and honorable warrior. He is peculiarly vulnerable to Iago precisely because Iago is his standard bearer, the protector of his colors and reputation in battle, pledged to die rather than allow the colors to be taken. His equivalent to Iago's monologues is a stirring elegy for the self, a farewell to war as a valid—because confined—occupation:

OTHELLO: I had been happy, if the general camp,
  Pioners and all, had tasted her sweet body,
  So I had nothing known. O now, for ever
  Farewell the tranquil mind! farewell content!
  Farewell the plumed troops and the big wars
  That makes ambition virtue! O, farewell!
  Farewell the neighing steed and the shrill trump,
  The spirit-stirring drum, th' ear-piercing fife,
  The royal banner, and all quality,
  Pride, pomp, and circumstance of glorious war!
  And O you mortal engines, whose rude throats
  Th' immortal Jove's dread clamors counterfeit,
  Farewell! Othello's occupation's gone.

"Pride, pomp, and circumstance of glorious war!" has yielded to Iago's incessant war against being. Othello, within his occupation's limits, has the greatness of the tragic hero. Iago breaks down those limits from within, from war's own camp, and so Othello has no chance. Had the attack come from the world outside war's dominion, Othello could have maintained some coherence and gone down in the name of the purity of arms. Shakespeare, courting a poetics of pain, could not allow his hero that consolation.

Macbeth

Macbeth is the culminating figure in the sequence of what might be called Shakespeare's Grand Negations: Richard III, Iago, Edmund, Macbeth. He differs from his precursors in lacking their dark intellectuality and their manipulative power over other selves. But he surpasses them in imagination, in its High Romantic sense, even though that is hardly a faculty in which they are deficient. His imagination is so strong that it exceeds even Hamlet's, so strong indeed that we can see that it is imagination, rather than ambition or the witches, that victimizes and destroys Macbeth. The bloodiest tyrant and villain in Shakespeare, Macbeth nevertheless engages our imaginations precisely because he is so large a representation of the dangerous prevalence of the imagination. The tragedy *Macbeth* constitutes an implicit self-critique of the Shakespearean imagination and therefore also of a crucial element in your own imagination, whoever you are.

Not even Hamlet dominates his play as Macbeth does; he speaks about one-third of the text as we have it. Compared to him, the other figures in the drama take on a common grayness, except for Lady Macbeth, and she largely vanishes after the middle of act 3. No Shakespearean protagonist, again not even Hamlet, is revealed to us so inwardly as Macbeth. Shakespeare quite deliberately places us under a very paradoxical stress: We intimately accompany Macbeth in his interior journey, and yet we attempt to refuse all identity with Macbeth; an impossible refusal, since his imagination becomes our own. We are contaminated by Macbeth's fantasies; perhaps someday our critical instruments will be keen enough so that we will comprehend just how much Sigmund Freud's theories owe to precisely Macbethian contamination. I myself am inclined to place *The Tragedy of Macbeth*, foremost among Shakespeare's works, above even *Hamlet* and *Lear*, because of the unique power of contamination manifested by its protagonist's fantasy-making faculty. Everything that Macbeth says, particularly to himself, is notoriously memorable, yet I would assign a crucial function to a passage in act 1 that defines the exact nature of Macbeth's imagination:

> Present fears
> Are less than horrible imaginings.
> My thought, whose murder yet is but fantastical,
> Shakes so my single state of man that function
> Is smothered in surmise, and nothing is
> But what is not.

What does Macbeth mean by "single" here? Perhaps "alone" or "unaided," perhaps "total," but either way the word indicates vulnerability to phantasmagoria. To smother function or thought's ordinary operation by surmise, which is anticipation but not action, is to be dominated by what might be called the proleptic imagination, which is Macbeth's great burden and his tragedy. Though the murder of Duncan is still a pure prolepsis, Macbeth has but to imagine an act or event and instantly he is on the other side of it, brooding retrospectively. The negations of Iago and Edmund were willed nihilisms, but Macbeth's imagination does the work of his will, so that "nothing is / But what is not." Macbeth represents an enormous enhancement of that element in us that allows us to see Shakespeare acted, whether in the theater, or the mind's eye of the reader, without protesting or denying the illusion. It is not that Macbeth has faith in the imagination, but that he is enslaved to his version of fantasy. Brooding on Macduff's absence from court, Macbeth sums up his proleptic mode in one powerful couplet:

> Strange things I have in head that will to hand,
> Which must be acted ere they may be scanned.

He seems to know already that he seeks to murder every member of Macduff's family, yet he will not truly have the knowledge until the massacre

is accomplished, as though the image in his head is wholly independent of
his will. This is the burden of his great soliloquy at the start of act 1, Scene 7,
with its Hamlet-like onset:

> If it were done when 'tis done, then 'twere well
> It were done quickly. If th'assassination
> Could trammel up the consequence, and catch,
> With his surcease, success; that but this blow
> Might be the be-all and the end-all—here,
> But here, upon this bank and shoal of time,
> We'd jump the life to come.

"Bank and shoal of time" is a brilliant trope, whether or not it is Shakespeare's, since "shoal" there is a scholarly emendation, and perhaps Shakespeare wrote "school," which would make "bank" into a schoolbench. Scholars
tell us also that "jump" here means "hazard," but I think Macbeth means both:
to leap and to risk, and I suspect that Shakespeare actually wrote "shoal." The
metaphor is superbly characteristic of precisely how Macbeth's imagination
works, by leaping over present time and over a future act also, so as to land
on the other bank of time, looking back to the bank where he stood before
action. The soliloquy ends with the same figuration but now broken off by
the entry of Lady Macbeth. Vaulting and overleaping, Macbeth's ambition,
which is another name for the proleptic aspect of his imagination, falls on the
other side of his intent, which is to say the other bank both of his aim and
his meaning:

> I have no spur
> To prick the sides of my intent, but only
> Vaulting ambition, which o'erleaps itself
> And falls on th'other—

The intent is a horse all will, but Macbeth's imagination again falls on
the other side of the will and dominates the perpetually rapt protagonist, who
is condemned always to be in a kind of trance or phantasmagoria that gov-
erns him, yet also is augmented by every action that he undertakes. Though
Shakespeare doubtless gave full credence to his witches, weird or wayward
demiurges of the Gnostic cosmos of *Macbeth*, they may also be projections
of Macbeth's own rapt state of prolepsis, his inability to control the temporal
elements of his imagination. The witches embody the temporal gap between
what is imagined and what is done, so that they take the place of Macbeth's
will. We could not envision Iago or Edmund being sought out by the witches,

because Iago and Edmund will their own grand negations or indeed will to become grand negations of every value. Macbeth imagines his negations and becomes the grandest negation of them all.

Why then do we sympathize with Macbeth's inwardness, in spite of our own wills? He shares Hamlet's dark side but is totally without Hamlet's intellect. It is almost as though Shakespeare deliberately cut away Hamlet's cognitive gifts while preserving Hamlet's sensibility in the immensely powerful if purely involuntary imagination of Macbeth. Hamlet interests us for reasons very different from why we interest ourselves; Macbeth precisely is interesting to us exactly as we are interesting, in our own judgment. We know Macbeth's inwardness as we know our own, but Hamlet's vast theater of mind remains an abyss to us. Both Macbeth and Lady Macbeth are well aware that in murdering Duncan they are slaying the good father. We share their Oedipal intensity (which becomes her madness) if not their guilt. The primal act of imagination, as Freud had learned from Shakespeare, is the ambitious act of desiring the father's death. The first part of Macbeth's appeal to us is his rapt state of being or Oedipal ambition, but the second part, even more appealing, is his power of representing an increasing state of being outraged, outraged by time, by mortality, and by the equivocation of the fiend that lies like truth.

William Hazlitt shrewdly observed of Macbeth that: "His energy springs from the anxiety and agitation of his mind." I would add that, as the drama advances, the principal agitation is the energy of being outraged by the baffling of expectations. Increasingly obsessed with time, Macbeth fears becoming an actor who always misses his cue and constantly learns that the cues he was given are wrong. The energy that stems from an adroit representation of a state of being outraged is one that imbues us with a remarkable degree of sympathy. I recall watching a television film of Alec Guinness playing the last days of Hitler, portrayed accurately as progressing to a greater intensity of being outraged from start to end. One had to keep recalling that this was a representation of Hitler in order to fight off an involuntary sympathy. Our common fate is an outrage: Each of us must die. Shakespeare, implicating us in Macbeth's fate, profoundly associates the proleptic imagination with the sense of being outraged, nowhere more than in Macbeth's extraordinary refusal to mourn the death of his afflicted wife. All of Western literature does not afford us an utterance so superbly outraged as this or one that so abruptly jumps over every possible life to come:

She should have died hereafter;
There would have been a time for such a word.
Tomorrow, and tomorrow, and tomorrow
Creeps in this petty pace from day to day,

To the last syllable of recorded time;
And all our yesterdays have lighted fools
The way to dusty death. Out, out, brief candle!
Life's but a walking shadow, a poor player
That struts and frets his hour upon the stage
And then is heard no more. It is a tale
Told by an idiot, full of sound and fury
Signifying nothing.

Dr. Samuel Johnson was so disturbed by this speech that initially he wished to emend "such a word" to "such a world." Upon reflection, he accepted "word" but interpreted it as meaning "intelligence," in the sense that we say we send "word" when we give intelligence. Macbeth, outraged yet refusing to mourn, perhaps begins with the distancing observation that his wife would have died sooner or later anyway, but then centers ironically on the meaninglessness now, for him, of such a word as "hereafter," since he *knows* that quite literally there will be no tomorrow for him. In the grim music of the word "tomorrow," he hears his own horror of time, his proleptic imagining of all of remaining life and not just for himself alone. Recorded time, history, will end with the last syllable of the word "tomorrow," but that will refer to a tomorrow that will not come. If all our yesterdays have existed to light "fools" (presumably meaning "victims") the way to a death that is only ourselves (Adam being created from the dust of red clay), then the brief candle of Lady Macbeth's life just as well has gone out. By the light of that candle, Shakespeare grants Macbeth an outraged but astonishing vision of life as an actor in a Shakespearean play, rather like *The Tragedy of Macbeth*. The best in this kind are but shadows, but life is not one of the best, being a bad actor, strutting and fretting away his performance and lacking reverberation in the memories of the audience after they have left the theater. Varying the figurative identification, Macbeth moves life's status from bad actor to bad drama or tale, composed by a professional jester or court fool, an idiot indulged in his idiocy. The story is either meaningless or a total negation, signifying nothing because there is nothing to signify. Theatrical metaphors are more fully appropriate for Shakespeare himself than for the tyrant Macbeth, we might think at first, but then we remember that Macbeth's peculiar imagination necessarily has made him into a poetic dramatist. Iago and Edmund, nihilistic dramatists, manipulated others, while Macbeth has manipulated himself, leaping over the present and the actions not yet taken into the scenes that followed the actions, as though they already had occurred.

Critics of Macbeth always have noted the terrible awe he provokes in us. Sublime in himself, the usurper also partakes in the dreadful sublimity of the apocalyptic cosmos of his drama. When Duncan is slain, lamentings are heard in the air, great winds blow, owls clamor through the night and behave like hawks, killing falcons as if they were mice. Duncan's horses break loose, warring against men, and then devour one another. It is as though the daemonic underworld of the Weird Sisters and Hecate had broken upward into Duncan's realm, which in some sense they had done by helping to spur on the rapt Macbeth. Shakespeare's protagonist pays a fearful price for his sublimity, and yet as audience and readers we do not wish Macbeth to be otherwise than the grand negation he becomes. I think this is because Macbeth is not only a criticism of our imaginations, which are as guilty and Oedipal as his own, but also because Macbeth is Shakespeare's critique of his own tragic imagination, an imagination beyond guilt.

King Lear

In the long reaction against A.C. Bradley, we have been warned endlessly against meditating on the girlhood of Shakespeare's heroines or brooding on the earlier marital days of the Macbeths. Yet Shakespearean representation, as A.D. Nuttall observes, allows us to see aspects of reality we would not otherwise recognize. I would go beyond Nuttall to suggest that Shakespeare has molded both our sense of reality and our cognitive modes of apprehending that reality to a far greater degree than Homer or Plato, Montaigne or Nietzsche, Freud or Proust. Only the Bible rivals Shakespeare as an influence upon our sense of how human character, thinking, personality ought to be imitated through, in, or by language. No Western writer shows less consciousness of belatedness than Shakespeare, yet his true precursor is not Marlowe but the Bible. *King Lear* as tragedy finds its only worthy forerunner in the Book of Job, to which John Holloway and Frank Kermode have compared it.

A comparison between the sufferings of Job and of Lear is likely to lead to some startling conclusions about the preternatural persuasiveness of Shakespearean representation, being as it is an art whose limits we have yet to discover. This art convinces us that Lear exposed to the storm, out on the heath, is a designedly Jobean figure. To be thrown from being king of Britain to a fugitive in the open, pelted by merciless weather and betrayed by ungrateful daughters, is indeed an unpleasant fate, but is it truly Jobean? Job, after all, has experienced an even more dreadful sublimity: His sons, daughters, servants, sheep, camels, and houses all have been destroyed by Satanic fires, and his direct, physical torment far transcends Lear's, not to mention that he still suffers his wife, while we never do hear anything about Lear's queen, who amazingly brought forth monsters of the deep in Goneril and Regan, but also Cordelia, a soul in bliss. What would Lear's wife have said had she accompanied her royal husband onto the heath?

So went Satan forth from the presence of the LORD, and smote
Job with sore boils from the sole of his foot unto his crown.
And he took him a potsherd to scrape himself withal; and he sat
down among the ashes.
Then said his wife unto him, Dost thou still retain thine integrity?
curse God, and die.

That Shakespeare intended his audience to see Job as the model for
Lear's situation (though hardly for Lear himself) seems likely, on the basis
of a pattern of allusions in the drama. An imagery that associates humans
with worms and with dust is strikingly present in both works. Lear himself
presumably thinks of Job when he desperately asserts, "I will be the pattern
of all patience," a dreadful irony considering the king's ferociously impatient
nature. Job is the righteous man handed over to the accuser, but Lear is a
blind king who knows neither himself nor his daughters. Though Lear suffers
the storm's fury, he is not Job-like either in his earlier sufferings (which he
greatly magnifies) or in his relationship to the divine. It is another indication
of Shakespeare's strong originality that he persuades us of the Jobean dignity
and grandeur of Lear's first sufferings, even though to a considerable degree
they are brought about by Lear himself, in sharp contrast to Job's absolute
blamelessness. When Lear says that he is a man more sinned against than
sinning, we tend to believe him, but is this really true at that point?

Only proleptically, as a prophecy, but again this is Shakespeare's astonishing originality, founded on the representation of impending change, a
change to be worked within Lear by his own listening to and reflecting upon
what he himself speaks aloud in his increasing fury. He goes into the storm
scene on the heath still screaming in anger, goes mad with that anger, and
comes out of the storm with crucial change deeply in process within him, full
of paternal love for the Fool and of concern for the supposed madman, Edgar
impersonating Poor Tom. Lear's constant changes from then until the terrible end remain the most remarkable instance of a representation of a human
transformation anywhere in imaginative literature.

But why did Shakespeare risk the paradigm of Job, since Lear, early and
late, is so unlike Job and since the play is anything but a theodicy? Milton
remarked that the book of Job was the rightful model for a "brief epic," such
as his *Paradise Regained*, but in what sense can it be an appropriate model for
a tragedy? Shakespeare may have been pondering his setting of *King Lear* in
a Britain seven centuries before the time of Christ, a placement historically
earlier than he attempted anywhere else, except for the Trojan War of *Troilus and Cressida*. *Lear* presumably is not a Christian play, though Cordelia
is an eminently Christian personage, who says that she is about her father's

business, in an overt allusion to the Gospel of Luke. But the Christian God and Jesus Christ are not relevant to the cosmos of *King Lear*. So appalling is the tragedy of this tragedy that Shakespeare shrewdly sets it before the Christian dispensation, in what he may have intuited was the time of Job. If *Macbeth* is Shakespeare's one full-scale venture into a Gnostic cosmos (and I think it was), then *King Lear* risks a more complete and catastrophic tragedy than anything in the genre before or since.

Job, rather oddly, ultimately receives the reward of his virtue; but Lear, purified and elevated, suffers instead the horror of Cordelia's murder by the underlings of Edmund. I think then that Shakespeare invoked the book of Job in order to emphasize the absolute negativity of Lear's tragedy. Had Lear's wife been alive, she would have done well to emulate Job's wife, so as to advise her husband to curse God and die. Pragmatically, it would have been a better fate than the one Lear finally suffers in the play.

The Gloucester subplot may be said to work deliberately against Lear's Jobean sense of his own uniqueness as a sufferer; his tragedy will not be the one he desires, for it is not so much a tragedy of filial ingratitude as of a kind of apocalyptic nihilism, universal in its implications. We do not sympathize with Lear's immense curses, though they are increasingly related to his rising fear of madness, which is also his fear of a womanly nature rising up within him. Finally Lear's madness, like his curses, proceeds from his biblical sense of himself; desiring to be everything in himself, he fears greatly that he is nothing in himself. His obsession with his own blindness seems related to an aging vitalist's fear of impotence and so of mortality. Yet Lear is not just any old hero, nor even just a great king falling away into madness and death. Shakespeare allows him a diction more preternaturally eloquent than is spoken by anyone else in this or any other drama and that evidently never will be matched again. Lear matters because his language is uniquely strong and because we are persuaded that this splendor is wholly appropriate to him.

We can remark, following Nietzsche and Freud, that only one Western image participates neither in origin nor in end: the image of the father. Lear, more than Gloucester, more than any other figure even in Shakespeare, is *the* image of the father, the metaphor of paternal authority. Nature, in the drama, is both origin and end, mother and catastrophe, and it ought to be Lear's function to hold and safeguard the middle ground between the daemonic world and the realm of the gods. He fails, massively, and the ensuing tragedy engulfs an entire world, with a poignance unmatched in literature:

> *Enter* LEAR [*mad, crowned with weeds and flowers*].
> But who comes here?

The safer sense will ne'er accommodate
His master thus.

LEAR

No, they cannot touch me for [coining,] I am the King himself.

EDG

O thou side-piercing sight!

LEAR

Nature's above art in that respect. There's your pressmoney. That fellow handles his bow like a crow-keeper; draw me a clothier's yard. Look, look, a mouse! Peace, peace, this piece of toasted cheese will do't. There's my gauntlet, I'll prove it on a giant. Bring up the brown bills. O, well flown, bird! i' th' clout, i' th' clout—hewgh! Give the word.

EDG

Sweet marjorum.

LEAR

Pass.

GLOU

I know that voice.

LEAR

Ha! Goneril with a white beard? They flatter'd me like a dog, and told me I had the white hairs in my beard ere the black ones were there. To say "ay" and "no" to every thing that I said! "Ay," and "no" too, was no good divinity. When the rain came to wet me once, and the wind to make me chatter, when the thunder would not peace at my bidding, there I found 'em, there I smelt 'em out. Go to, they are not men o' their words: they told me I was every thing. 'Tis a lie, I am not ague-proof.

GLOU

The trick of that voice I do well remember. Is't not the King?

LEAR

Ay, every inch a king!
when I do stare, see how the subject quakes.
I pardon that man's life. What was thy cause?
Adultery?
Thou shalt not die. Die for adultery? No,
the wren goes to't, and the small gilded fly
does lecher in my sight.
Let copulation thrive; for gloucester's bastard son
was kinder to his father than my daughters
got 'tween the lawful sheets.

To't, luxury, pell-mell, for I lack soldiers.
Behold yond simp'ring dame,
whose face between her forks presages snow;
that minces virtue, and does shake the head
to hear of pleasure's name—
the fitchew nor the soiled horse goes to't
with a more riotous appetite.
Down from the waist they are centaurs,
though women all above;
but to the girdle do the gods inherit,
beneath is all the fiends': there's hell, there's darkness.
There is the sulphurous pit, burning, scalding,
Stench, consumption. Fie, fie, fie! pah, pah!
Give me an ounce of civet; good apothecary,
Sweeten my imagination. There's money for thee.

GLOU

O, let me kiss that hand!

LEAR

Let me wipe it first, it smells of mortality.

GLOU

O ruin'd piece of nature! this great world Shall so wear out to nought. Dost thou know me?

LEAR

I remember thine eyes well enough. Dost thou squiny at me? No, do thy worst, blind Cupid, I'll not love. Read thou this challenge; mark but the penning of it.

GLOU

Were all thy letters suns, I could not see.

EDG

[*Aside.*] I would not take this from report; it is, And my heart breaks at it.

LEAR

Read.

GLOU

What, with the case of eyes?

LEAR

O ho, are you there with me? No eyes in your head, nor no money in your purse? Your eyes are in a heavy case, your purse in a light, yet you see how this world goes.

GLOU

I see it feelingly.

LEAR

What, art mad? A man may see how this world goes with no
eyes. Look with thine ears; see how yond justice rails upon yond
simple thief. Hark in thine ear: change places, and handy-dandy,
which is the justice, which is the thief? Thou hast seen a farmer's
dog bark at a beggar?

GLOU

Ay, sir.

LEAR

And the creature run from the cur? There thou mightst
behold the great image of authority: a dog's obey'd in office.
Thou rascal beadle, hold thy bloody hand!
Why dost thou lash that whore? Strip thy own back,
Thou hotly lusts to use her in that kind
For which thou whip'st her. The usurer hangs the cozener.
Through tatter'd clothes [small] vices do appear;
Robes and furr'd gowns hide all. [Plate sin] with gold,
And the strong lance of justice hurtless breaks;
Arm it in rags, a pigmy's straw does pierce it.
None does offend, none, I say none, I'll able 'em.
Take that of me, my friend, who have the power
To seal th' accuser's lips. Get thee glass eyes,
And like a scurvy politician, seem
To see the things thou dost not. Now, now, now, now.
Pull off my boots; harder, harder—so.

EDG

[*Aside.*] O, matter and impertinency mix'd, Reason in madness!

LEAR

If thou wilt weep my fortunes, take my eyes.
I know thee well enough, thy name is Gloucester.
Thou must be patient; we came crying hither.
Thou know'st, the first time that we smell the air
We wawl and cry. I will preach to thee. Mark.
[LEAR *takes off his crown of weeds and flowers.*]

GLOU

Alack, alack the day!

LEAR

When we are born, we cry that we are come
To this great stage of fools.—

Kermode justly remarks of this scene that it is at once Shakespeare's
boldest effort of imagination and utterly lacking in merely *narrative*

function. Indeed, it strictly lacks all function, and the tragedy does not need it. We do not reason the need: Poetic language never has gone further. Edgar, who once pretended madness, begins by observing that "the safer sense" or sane mind cannot accommodate itself to the vision of the ultimate paternal authority having gone mad. But "safer sense" here also refers to seeing, and the entire scene is a vastation organized about the dual images of eyesight and of fatherhood, images linked yet also severed throughout the play. The sight that pierces Edgar's side is intolerable to a quiet hero whose only quest has been to preserve the image of his father's authority. His father, blinded Gloucester, recognizing authority by its voice, laments the mad king as nature's ruined masterpiece and prophesies that a similar madness will wear away the entire world into nothingness. The prophecy will be fulfilled in the drama's closing scene, but is deferred so that the reign of "reason in madness" or sight in blindness can be continued. Pathos transcends all limits in Lear's great and momentary breakthrough into sanity, as it cries out to Gloucester and to all of us, "If thou wilt weep my fortune, take my eyes."

Hardly the pattern of all patience, Lear nevertheless has earned the convincing intensity of telling Gloucester, "Thou must be patient." What follows however is not Jobean but Shakespearean, perhaps even the essence of the drama's prophecy: "we came crying hither" and "When we are born, we cry that we are come / To this great stage of fools." The great theatrical trope encompasses every meaning the play crams into the word "fool": actor, moral being, idealist, child, dear one, madman, victim, truth teller. As Northrop Frye observes, the only characters in *King Lear* who are not fools are Edmund, Goneril, Regan, Cornwall, and their followers.

Lear's own Fool undergoes a subtle transformation as the drama burns on, from an oracle of forbidden wisdom to a frightened child, until at last he simply disappears, as though he blent into the identity of the dead Cordelia when the broken Lear cries out, "And my poor fool is hang'd!" Subtler still is the astonishing transformation of the most interesting consciousness in the play, the bastard Edmund, Shakespeare's most intensely theatrical villain, surpassing even Richard III and Iago. Edmund, as theatrical as Barabas, Marlowe's Jew of Malta, might almost be a sly portrait of Christopher Marlowe himself. As the purest and coolest Machiavel in stage history, at least until he knows he has received his death wound, Edmund is both a remarkably antic and charming Satan and a being with real self-knowledge, which makes him particularly dangerous in a world presided over by Lear, "who hath ever but slenderly known himself," as Regan remarks.

Edmund's mysterious and belated metamorphosis as the play nears its end, a movement from playing oneself to being oneself, turns upon his complex reactions to his own deathly musing: "Yet Edmund was beloved." It is peculiarly shocking and pathetic that his lovers were Goneril and Regan, monsters who proved their love by suicide and murder or by victimage, but Shakespeare seems to have wished to give us a virtuoso display of his original art in changing character through the representation of a growing inwardness. Outrageously refreshing at his most evil (Edgar is a virtuous bore in contrast to him), Edmund is the most attractive of Jacobean hero-villains and inevitably captures both Goneril and Regan, evidently with singularly little effort. His dangerous attractiveness is one of the principal unexplored clues to the enigmas of Shakespeare's most sublime achievement. That Edmund has gusto, an exuberance befitting his role as natural son, is merely part of the given. His intelligence and will are more central to him and darken the meanings of *King Lear*.

Wounded to death by Edgar, his brother, Edmund yields to fortune: "The wheel is come full circle, I am here." Where he is not is on Lear's "wheel of fire," in a place of saving madness. Not only do Edmund and Lear exchange not a single word in the course of this vast drama, but it defies imagination to conceive of what they could say to each other. It is not only the intricacies of the double plot that keep Edmund and Lear apart; they have no language in common. Frye points out that "nature" takes on antithetical meanings in regard to the other, in Lear and Edmund, and this can be expanded to the realization that Lear, despite all his faults, is incapable of guile, but Edmund is incapable of an honest passion of any kind. The lover of both Goneril and Regan, he is passive toward both and is moved by their deaths only to reflect on what was for him the extraordinary reality that anyone, however monstrous, ever should have loved him at all.

Why does he reform, however belatedly and ineffectually, since Cordelia is murdered anyway; what are we to make of his final turn toward the light? Edmund's first reaction toward the news of the deaths of Goneril and Regan is the grimly dispassionate, "I was contracted to them both; all three / Now marry in an instant," which identifies dying and marrying as a single act. In the actual moment of repentance, Edmund desperately says, "I pant for life. Some good I mean to do, / Despite of my own nature." This is not to say that nature no longer is his goddess, but rather that he is finally touched by images of connection or concern, be they as far apart as Edgar's care for Gloucester or Goneril's and Regan's fiercely competitive lust for his own person.

I conclude by returning to my fanciful speculation that the Faustian Edmund is not only overtly Marlovian but indeed may be Shakespeare's charmed but wary portrait of elements in Christopher Marlowe himself. Edmund represents the way not to go and yet is the only figure in *King Lear* who is truly at home in its apocalyptic cosmos. The wheel comes full circle for him, but he has limned his nightpiece, and it was his best.

Antony and Cleopatra

Freud taught us that the therapy-of-therapies is not to invest too much libido in any single object whosoever. Antony at last refuses this wisdom and in consequence suffers what must be called an erotic tragedy, but then Cleopatra, who has spent her life exemplifying the same wisdom, suffers an erotic tragedy also on Antony's account, one act of the drama more belatedly than he does. *The Tragedy of Antony and Cleopatra* is unique among Shakespeare's plays in that the tragedy's doubleness, equal in both man and woman as it was with Romeo and Juliet, takes place between equally titanic personages. Each truly is all but everything in himself and herself and *knows* it, and neither fears that he or she is really nothing in himself or herself or nothing without the other. Both consciously play many parts and yet also *are* those other parts. Both are adept at playing themselves yet also at being themselves. Like Falstaff and Hamlet, they are supreme personalities, major wits, grand counter-Machiavels (though overmatched by Octavian, greatest of Machiavels), and supreme consciousnesses. They fall in love with each other, resist and betray the love repeatedly, but finally yield to it and are destroyed by it, in order fully to fulfill their allied natures. More even than the death of Hamlet, we react to their suicides as a human triumph and as a release for ourselves. But why? And how?

The crucial originality here is to have represented two great personalities, the herculean hero proper and a woman of infinite guile and resource, in their overwhelming decline and mingled ruin. A destruction through authentic and mutual love becomes an aesthetic redemption precisely because love's shadow is ruin. We have no representations of this kind before Shakespeare, since a Euripidean vision of erotic ruin, as in *Medea*, permits no aesthetic redemption, while Virgil's Dido, like Medea, is a solitary sufferer. Antony and Cleopatra repeatedly betray each other, and betray themselves, yet these betrayals are forgiven by them and by us, since they become phases of apotheosis that release the sparks of grandeur even as the lamps are shattered.

From act 4, scene 14 through to the end of the play, we hear something wonderfully original even for Shakespeare, a great dying fall, the release of a new music. It begins with the dialogue between Antony and his marvelously named, devoted follower Eros:

ANTONY

 Eros, thou yet behold'st me?

EROS

 Ay, noble lord.

ANTONY

 Sometime we see a cloud that's dragonish,

A vapor sometime like a bear or lion,
A [tower'd] citadel, a pendant rock,
A forked mountain, or blue promontory
With trees upon't that nod unto the world,
And mock our eyes with air. Thou hast seen these signs,
They are black vesper's pageants.

EROS

Ay, my lord.

ANTONY

That which is now a horse, even with a thought
The rack dislimns, and makes it indistinct
As water is in water.

EROS

It does, my lord.

ANTONY

My good knave Eros, now thy captain is
Even such a body. Here I am Antony,
Yet cannot hold this visible shape, my knave.
I made these wars for Egypt, and the Queen,
Whose heart I thought I had, for she had mine—
Which whilst it was mine had annex'd unto't
A million more (now lost)—she, Eros, has
Pack'd cards with Caesar's, and false-play'd my glory
Unto an enemy's triumph.
Nay, weep not, gentle Eros, there is left us
Ourselves to end ourselves.

There is a deliberate touch of the cloud-watching Hamlet in Antony here, but with Hamlet's parodistic savagery modulated into a gentleness that befits the transmutation of the charismatic hero into a self-transcendent consciousness, almost beyond the consolations of farewell. The grandeur of this transformation is enhanced when Antony receives the false tidings Cleopatra sends of her supposed death, with his name her last utterance:

Unarm, Eros, the long day's task is done,
And we must sleep.

The answering chorus to that splendor is Cleopatra's, when he dies in her arms:

The crown o'th'earth doth melt. My lord!
O, wither'd is the garland of the war,

The soldier's pole is fall'n! Young boys and girls
Are level now with men; the odds is gone,
And there is nothing left remarkable
Beneath the visiting moon.

Antony touches the sublime as he prepares to die, but Cleopatra's lament for a lost sublime is the prelude to a greater sublimity, which is to be wholly her own. She is herself a great actress, so that the difficulty in playing her, for any actress, is quite extraordinary. And though she certainly loved Antony, it is inevitable that, like any great actress, she must love herself all but apocalyptically. Antony has a largeness about him surpassing any other Shakespearean hero except for Hamlet; he is an ultimate version of the charismatic leader, loved and followed because his palpable glory can be shared, in some degree, since he is also magnificently generous. But Shakespeare shrewdly ends him with one whole act of the play to go, and retrospectively we see that the drama is as much Cleopatra's as the two parts of *Henry IV* are Falstaff's.

Remarkable as Antony is in himself, he interests us primarily because he has the splendor that makes him as much a catastrophe for Cleopatra as she is for him. Cleopatra is in love with his exuberance, with the preternatural vitality that impresses even Octavian. But she knows, as we do, that Antony lacks her infinite variety. Their love, in Freudian terms, is not narcissistic but anaclitic; they are propped on each other, cosmological beings who are likely to be bored by anyone else, by any personality neither their own nor one another's. Antony is Cleopatra's only true match, and yet he is not her equal, which may be the most crucial or deepest meaning of the play. An imaginative being in that he moves the imagination of others, he is simply not an imaginer of her stature. He need not play himself, he is herculean. Cleopatra ceases to play herself only when she is transmuted by his death and its aftermath, and we cannot be sure, even then, that she is not both performing and simultaneously becoming that more transcendent self. Strangely like the dying Hamlet in this single respect, she suggests, at the end, that she stands upon a new threshold of being:

I am fire and air; my other elements
I give to baser life.

Is she no longer the earth of Egypt or the water of the Nile? We have not exactly thought of her as a devoted mother, despite her children by Julius Caesar and by Antony, but in her dying dialogue with Charmian she transmutes the asps, first into her baby and then apparently into an Antony she might have brought to birth, as in some sense indeed she did:

CHARMIAN
  O eastern star!
CLEOPATRA
  Peace, peace!
  Dost thou not see my baby at my breast,
  That sucks the nurse asleep?
CHARMIAN
  O, break! O, break!
CLEOPATRA
  As sweet as balm, as soft as air, as gentle—O
  Antony!—Nay, I will take thee too:
  [*Applying another asp to her arm.*]
  What should I stay—*Dies.*

As Lear dies, Kent cries out "Break, heart, I prithee break!" even as Charmian does here, not wishing on the rack of this tough world to stretch Cleopatra out longer. When Antony's men find him wounded to death, they lament that "the star is fall'n" and that "time is at his period." Charmian's "O eastern star!" associates one dying lover with the other, even as her echo of Kent suggests that the dying Empress of the East is in something like the innocence of Lear's madness. Cleopatra is sucked to sleep as a mother is by a child, or a woman by a lover, and dies in such peace that Octavian, of all men, is moved to the ultimate tribute:

> she looks like sleep,
> As she would catch another Antony
> In her strong toil of grace.

Bewildering us by her final manifestation of her infinite variety, Cleopatra dies into a beyond, a sublime where actress never trod.

Coriolanus

William Hazlitt, writing in 1816, gave us what seems to me the most provocative criticism that Shakespeare's *Coriolanus* has received. Beginning with the observation that the play was "a storehouse of political commonplaces," Hazlitt sadly observed that Shakespeare, unlike himself, seemed a man of the right, if only because "the cause of the people is indeed but little calculated as a subject for poetry." It might be salutary if many of our contemporary students of literature, who wish to make of it an instrument for social change, would meditate on Hazlitt's profound reflections on poetry's love of power:

The language of poetry naturally falls in with the language of power. The imagination is an exaggerating and exclusive faculty: it takes from one thing to add to another: it accumulates circumstances together to give the greatest possible effect to a favourite object. The understanding is a dividing and measuring faculty, it judges of things not according to their immediate impression on the mind, but according to their relations to one another. The one is a monopolising faculty, which seeks the greatest quantity of present excitement by inequality and disproportion; the other is a distributive faculty, which seeks the greatest quantity of ultimate good, by justice and proportion. The one is an aristocratical, the other a republican faculty. The principle of poetry is a very anti-levelling principle. It aims at effect, it exists by contrast. It admits of no medium. It is everything by excess. It rises above the ordinary standard of sufferings and crimes. It presents a dazzling appearance. It shows its head turretted, crowned, and crested. Its front is gilt and bloodstained. Before it "it carries noise, and behind it leaves tears." It has its altars and its victims, sacrifices, human sacrifices. Kings, priests, nobles, are its train-bearers, tyrants and slaves its executioners.—"Carnage is its daughter."—Poetry is right-royal. It puts the individual for the species, the one above the infinite many, might before right. A lion hunting a flock of sheep or a herd of wild asses is a more poetical object than they; and we even take part with the lordly beast, because our vanity or some other feeling makes us disposed to place ourselves in the situation of the strongest party. So we feel some concern for the poor citizens of Rome when they meet together to compare their wants and grievances, till Coriolanus comes in and with blows and big words drives this set of "poor rats," this rascal scum, to their homes and beggary before him. There is nothing heroical in a multitude of miserable rogues not wishing to be starved, or complaining that they are like to be so; but when a single man comes forward to brave their cries and to make them submit to the last indignities, from mere pride and self-will, our admiration of his prowess is immediately converted into contempt for their pusillanimity. The insolence of power is stronger than the plea of necessity. The tame submission to usurped authority or even the natural resistance to it has nothing to excite or flatter the imagination: it is the assumption of a right to insult or oppress others that carries an imposing air of superiority with it. We had rather be the oppressor than the oppressed. The love of power in ourselves and the admiration of it in others are both natural to man: the one makes him a tyrant, the other a slave.

Even I initially resist the dark implications of Hazlitt's crucial insight: "The principle of poetry is a very anti-levelling principle." Wallace Stevens, who like Hazlitt and Nietzsche took the lion as the emblem of poetry, tells us that poetry is a destructive force: "The lion sleeps in the sun . . . / It could kill a man." Hazlitt, an unreconstructed Jacobin, writes with the authority of the strongest literary critic that the European left has yet produced. I prefer him to T.S. Eliot on *Coriolanus*, not just because Eliot writes with the grain politically, as it were, and Hazlitt against it, but because the romantic critic also understands the drama's family romance better than the poet of *The Waste Land* does.

Eliot certainly was fonder of Coriolanus than Hazlitt could find it in himself to be. I cannot quarrel with Hazlitt's account of the Roman hero's motivations: "Coriolanus complains of the fickleness of the people: yet, the instant he cannot gratify his pride and obstinacy at their expense, he turns his arms against his country." When Volumnia cries out for the pestilence to strike all trades and occupations in Rome, because they have defied her son, Hazlitt allows himself a splendidly mordant comment:

> This is but natural: it is but natural for a mother to have more regard for her son than for a whole city; but then the city should be left to take some care of itself. The care of the state cannot, we here see, be safely entrusted to maternal affection, or to the domestic charities of high life. The great have private feelings of their own, to which the interests of humanity and justice must courtesy. Their interests are so far from being the same as those of the community, that they are in direct and necessary opposition to them; their power is at the expense of our weakness; their riches of our poverty; their pride of our degradation; their splendour of our wretchedness; their tyranny of our servitude. If they had the superior knowledge ascribed to them (which they have not) it would only render them so much more formidable; and from Gods would convert them into Devils. The whole dramatic moral of *Coriolanus* is that those who have little shall have less, and that those who have much shall take all that others have left. The people are poor; therefore they ought to be starved. They are slaves; therefore they ought to be beaten. They work hard; therefore they ought to be treated like beasts of burden. They are ignorant; therefore they ought not to be allowed to feel that they want food, or clothing, or rest, that they are enslaved, oppressed, and miserable. This is the logic of the imagination and the passions; which seek to aggrandize what excites admiration and to heap contempt on misery, to raise power into tyranny, and to

make tyranny absolute; to thrust down that which is low still lower, and to make wretches desperate: to exalt magistrates into kings, kings into gods; to degrade subjects to the rank of slaves, and slaves to the condition of brutes. The history of mankind is a romance, a mask, a tragedy, constructed upon the principles of *poetical justice*; it is a noble or royal hunt, in which what is sport to the few is death to the many, and in which the spectators halloo and encourage the strong to set upon the weak, and cry havoc in the chase though they do not share in the spoil. We may depend upon it that what men delight to read in books, they will put in practice in reality.

Poetical justice is not political or social justice, because it ensues from the royal hunt of the imagination. Hazlitt is not concerned that this should be so; poetry and power marry each other. His proper concern, as a literary critic who would die for social change if he could, is that we protect ourselves not against literature but against those who would make a wrong, because literal, use of the poetics of power. Shrewd as Hazlitt's political insight is, his best insight into the play comes when he contrasts the attitudes toward Coriolanus of Volumnia, his mother, and Virgilia, his wife: "The one is only anxious for his honour; the other is fearful for his life." Glory indeed is Volumnia's obsession; Shakespeare makes her Homeric, a sort of female Achilles, while Coriolanus is more like Virgil's Turnus (as Howard Felperin notes), which may be why his wife is named Virgilia. What is most problematical in *Coriolanus* is the hero's relationship to his fierce mother, a relationship unique in Shakespeare.

Volumnia hardly bears discussion, once we have seen that she would be at home wearing armor in *The Iliad*. She is about as sympathetic as the Greek heroes in Shakespeare's *Troilus and Cressida*. Coriolanus himself sustains endless analysis and meditation; even the question of our sympathy for him is forever open. Neither a beast nor a god, he is a great soldier, far greater even than Antony or Othello. Indeed, to call him merely a great soldier seems quite inadequate. He is a one-man army, unique and pure, a sport of nurture rather than of nature, a dreadful monument to his mother's remorseless drive, her will to power. Perhaps he resembles Spenser's Talus, the iron man, more even than he suggests Virgil's Turnus. He has no military weaknesses, and no civilian strengths. Politically he is a walking and breathing disaster, in a play that persistently imposes politics upon him. The play would fail if Coriolanus were totally unsympathetic to us, and clearly the play is very strong, though its virtues do not make less weird Eliot's celebrated judgment that *Hamlet* was an aesthetic failure, while *Coriolanus* was Shakespeare's best tragedy. Hamlet contains us, while Coriolanus does not even contain himself. As several critics have remarked, he is a kind of baby Mars and is very nearly empty, a moral void. How can a baby nullity possibly be a tragic hero?

For Frank Kermode, *Coriolanus* is a tragedy of ideas, but Kermode is unable to tell us what the ideas are, and though he calls Coriolanus a great man, he also does not tell us in just what that greatness consists. I may be unjust to Kermode if the crucial idea turns out to be solipsism and if the greatness of Coriolanus is in his imperfect solipsism which cannot become perfect so long as Volumnia is alive. But solipsism, perfect or not, constitutes greatness in a poet, rather than in a tragic hero. Milton's Satan is an almost perfect solipsist, and that, rather than his splendid wickedness, is why he is a heroic villain and not the hero of a cosmic tragedy. Satan is a great poet, almost the archetype of the modern strong poet (as I have written elsewhere). Coriolanus has no imagination and is no poet at all, except when he provokes his own catastrophe.

Kenneth Burke's *Coriolanus* is a tragedy of the grotesque, which I translate as meaning that politics and the grotesque are one and the same, and that seems fair and true enough. Coriolanus is to Burke a master of invective, rather like Shakespeare's Timon, and the wielder of invective makes a convincing tragic scapegoat. That gives us still the question of this hero's eminence; is he more than a great (and prideful) killing machine? A.D. Nuttall, in his admirable study of Shakespearean mimesis, finds the warrior's aristocratic spirit to be both large and shallow, "at one and same time a sort of Titan and a baby." But how can we get at the Titanism, or is it actually a mockery of the old giants, so that Coriolanus is merely a prophecy of General George Patton? Nuttall shrewdly takes away everything he gives Coriolanus, whose "character is one of great pathos," but: "The pathos lies in the fact that he has no inside." Again, Nuttall salutes Coriolanus for one moment of "true Stoic grandeur," when he replies to banishment with: "I banish you." Nuttall then adds that we see a red-faced child in a temper tantrum. As Nuttall says, this is superb mimesis, but can we greatly care what happens to such a hero? In Homer, the answer would be affirmative, since Achilles is at least as much a spoiled child as Coriolanus is. Yet Achilles is a poet also, a powerful imagination brooding bitterly on its own mortality, and so we care what happens to him. His greatness is convincing not just because others reflect it to us, but because his eloquence is universally persuasive.

Harold C. Goddard, the most generous and perceptive of all Shakespearean critics, finds the one fault of Coriolanus to be that he "lacks unconsciousness of his virtue." Less generously, we could label Coriolanus an instance of "Mars as narcissist," rather than Goddard's "proud idealist" who is entirely a victim of his virago of a mother. Perhaps the ambivalence that Coriolanus provokes in us can be set aside if we contemplate his heroic death scene, wholly appropriate for a tragic protagonist in Shakespeare:

CORIOLANUS

  Hear'st thou, Mars?

AUFIDIUS

  Name not the god, thou boy of tears!

CORIOLANUS

  Ha?

AUFIDIUS

  No more.

CORIOLANUS

  Measureless liar, thou hast made my heart

  Too great for what contains it. "Boy"? O slave!

  Pardon me, lords, 'tis the first time that ever

  I was forc'd to scold. Your judgments, my grave lords,

  Must give this cur the lie; and his own notion—

  Who wears my stripes impress'd upon him, that

  Must bear my beating to his grave—shall join

  To thrust the lie unto him.

1. LORD

  Peace both, and hear me speak.

CORIOLANUS

  Cut me to pieces, Volsces, men and lads,

  Stain all your edges on me. "Boy," false hound!

  If you have writ your annals true, 'tis there

  That, like an eagle in a dove-cote, I

  [Flutter'd] your Volscians in Corioles.

  Alone I did it. "Boy"!

AUFIDIUS

  Why, noble lords,

  Will you be put in mind of his blind fortune,

  Which was your shame, by this unholy braggart,

  'Fore your own eyes and ears?

ALL CONSPIRATORS

  Let him die for't.

ALL PEOPLE

  Tear him to pieces! Do it presently!—

  He kill'd my son!—My daughter!—He kill'd my cousin
Marcus!—

  He kill'd my father!

2. LORD

  Peace ho! no outrage, peace!

  The man is noble, and his fame folds in

This orb o' th' earth. His last offenses to us
Shall have judicious hearing. Stand, Aufidius,
And trouble not the peace.
CORIOLANUS
O that I had him,
With six Aufidiuses, or more, his tribe,
To use my lawful sword!
AUFIDIUS
Insolent villain!
ALL CONSPIRATORS
Kill, kill, kill, kill, kill him!
Draw the Conspirators, and kills Martius, who falls.

This is Coriolanus at his worst and at his best, with the extremes not to be disentangled. His triple repetition of "Boy" reflects his fury both at Aufidius's insolence and at his own subservience to his mother, whose boy he now knows he will never cease to be. Yet his vision of himself as an eagle fluttering his enemies' dovecotes raises his legitimate pride to an ecstasy in which we share, and we are captured by his exultant and accurate "Alone I did it." There is his tragedy and his grandeur: "Alone I did it." If they have writ their annals true, then he is content to be cut to pieces by them. His death is tragic because it is a *sparagmos*, not Orphic, but not the death of Turnus either. What is torn apart is the last representative of the heroism that fights alone and wins alone and that can find no place in the world of the commonal and the communal.

A.D. NUTTALL

Shakespeare's Imitation of the World: Julius Caesar *and* Coriolanus

The eighteenth century was profoundly excited by the then novel intuition that Shakespeare's works conveyed the nature of the real world. This excitement lasted well through the nineteenth century and still rises, unbidden, in the untheoretical reader, even today. But in the twentieth century formalism came to Shakespeare criticism before it appeared elsewhere. The origins of this formalism, indeed, lie outside the twentieth century and outside England. Gustav Rümelin's *Shakespearestudien* (Stuttgart, 1866) is an important early essay in this mode. The translation in 1922 of Levin Schücking's *Die Charakterprobleme bei Shakespeare* brought the new approach to the attention of the English-speaking world. The consequent critical enterprise, powerfully led in the 1930s by E.E. Stoll, forms a distinct movement, quite separate from structuralism, but sharing with structuralism a hostility to the idea of mimetic veracity and a correlative impulse to substitute codes and schemata for verisimilitude. The identification of schemata was a positive gain. But the presumption that they must be treated as terminal objects of aesthetic apprehension rather than as formulations of further meaning entailed a very considerable loss. Stoll and others conceived their schemata as necessarily intransitive. At an opposite pole, every ordinary speaker of English treats the schemata of the English language as transitive, as conducting the user to a reality which exists beyond the linguistic forms. Similarly, ordinary

From *A New Mimesis: Shakespeare and the Representation of Reality*, pp. 99–119, 200–01.
© 1983 by A.D. Nuttall; 2006 by A.D. Nuttall for the preface to the Yale edition.

theatre-goers treat the very different stereotypes of drama as transitive, in so far as they pass through them into a world of probable inference.

L.C. Knights, following in the footsteps of Stoll,[1] would have us understand that Falstaff 'is not a man, but a choric commentary'.[2] In such statements the Opaque language of criticism rises up to condemn its former ally, the Transparent language. Knights's unguarded epigram expresses a hard formalist view and is as easily rebutted as such views always are. Falstaff is quite clearly presented, through fiction, as a human being. To strive to dislodge such fundamental and evident truths as this is a kind of critical idiocy. But the soft formalist position is a little more plausible. Falstaff, Everyman and Jack the Giant Killer are all fictional people but they are not realistic. The emphasis in realistic art is on *possible* people, but in none of these cases is any strong interest shown in the area of possibility and probability, while, conversely, a great deal of interest is lavished on story, image, motif. They are therefore only minimally mimetic and such minimal mimesis does not invite or reward critical scrutiny. Once again the 'weak thesis' is really the stronger one. Nevertheless, while they may be right about Jack and Everyman, they are wrong about Falstaff. The motifs and images are certainly there, but so is attentiveness to the world. The eighteenth-century critics were right. The poet of glorious, licentious imagination was also the poet of reverent and attentive perception. So long as we remember that fictions involve mediated truth to probabilities rather than immediate truth to specific facts, Shakespeare's plays may properly be seen as a continued feat of minute yet organized accuracy. So far in this book the literary examples have been simple illustrations, appropriate—I hope—to some twist or turn of the argument. Shakespeare's imitation of the world, on the other hand, is a complex thing and we must take it slowly.

How Roman are the Roman plays of Shakespeare? Teachers of literature used confidently to assert that Shakespeare had no sense of anachronism. Clocks chime in *Julius Caesar* (II. i. 192) and in *Coriolanus* the short-sighted wear spectacles (II. i. 196).[3] The notion that Shakespeare's Romans are really Elizabethans with specially sounding names persists. Students disparagingly observe that Shakespeare in *Antony and Cleopatra* betrays his complete ignorance of the most obvious and familiar of all Egyptian artefacts, the pyramids. In one sense they are quite right. The most ignorant student today probably has a better idea of the appearance of, say, a Roman senator or of the Roman forum than Shakespeare had. The reason for this is simple. Schoolchildren now grow up with lavishly illustrated history books, with classroom walls liberally decorated with posters showing the Colosseum and the like. Shakespeare had none of these things. But he read certain ancient authors. So it comes about that, while he will blunder in the physical detail of daily life—that is, over things like clocks and spectacles—when he comes to deal with a Roman suicide, as distinct from an English suicide, he leaves the average modern student light-years behind. In the study of history Shakespeare lacked the means to walk, but he saw a way to run and seized it. The more sophisticated conceptions of later historians are easily within his reach.

For example, it is commonly believed that it takes a modern anthropologist or cultural historian to see that human nature may itself evolve in time. Previously history was a tract of battles, legislation and migration, all presumably conducted by persons fundamentally like ourselves. This was the doctrine from which C.S. Lewis at last prised away his mind in 1942, in his celebrated rejection of 'the Unchanging Human Heart'.

> How are these gulfs between the ages to be dealt with by the student of poetry? A method often recommended may be called the method of the Unchanging Human Heart. According to this method the things which separate one age from another are superficial. Just as, if we stripped the armour off a medieval knight or the lace off a Caroline courtier, we should find beneath them an anatomy identical with our own, so, it is held, if we strip off from Virgil his Roman imperialism, from Sidney his code of honour, from Lucretius his Epicurean philosophy, and from all who have it their religion, we shall find the Unchanging Human Heart, and on this we are to concentrate. I held this theory myself for many years, but I have now abandoned it. I continue, of course, to admit that if you remove from people the things that make them different, what is left must be the same, and that the Human Heart will certainly appear as Unchanging if you ignore its changes.[4]

Could Shakespeare conceivably have discerned a change in the Human Heart, dividing the Romans from the people of his own time? Surely, it will be said, we can look for no glimmer of such a conception of human nature before, say, the novels of Sir Walter Scott; indeed, even tentatively to attribute such a conception to Shakespeare is historical solecism.

Yet Pope, who lived a hundred years before Sir Walter, saw some such thing in Shakespeare:

> In *Coriolanus* and *Julius Caesar*, not only the Spirit but Manners, of the *Romans* are exactly drawn; and still a nicer distinction is shown, between the manners of the *Romans* in the time of the former and of the latter.[5]

It may be thought that Pope's emphasis on something as superficial as 'manners' impairs my case. But by 'manners' Pope intends far more than the formalized shibboleths of social intercourse. The Latin word for what he has in mind is *mores*. The modern English equivalent is likely to be polysyllabic and pseudo-technical: 'sociocultural behaviour patterns'. In any case, Pope has already taken it as read that Shakespeare captured 'the spirit' of the Romans. But it is the extra discrimination proposed in the second part of his sentence that is especially challenging. Shakespeare did not merely distinguish Romans from English, he distinguished early Romans from later Romans.

Let us look first at Brutus, Cassius and Mark Antony, not as Romans, but less narrowly, as men having a culture which is, at least, different from ours, so that they may be conceived as belonging to an earlier phase in psychic evolution.

Brutus at once involves us in a large, though fairly standard question of cultural history. For Brutus, as is conceded on all hands, is obviously presented by Shakespeare as a conscious Stoic. Real-life Roman Stoicism is rather an aggregate of intellectual and social postures than the philosophy of a single, dominant thinker. Its common opposite, Epicureanism, is indeed derived from the teachings of one man, Epicurus, but few people can even name the master of the Stoics, Zeno. For the Elizabethans Seneca and, to a lesser extent, Plutarch and Virgil are the authoritative names. J.B. Leishman offers an admirable summary of the cult (I use the word in its modern, debased sense) in his book, *Translating Horace*:

> The central doctrine of Stoicism was that nothing mattered except virtue, that it was possible to detect in the world a divine purpose, guiding all things to their perfection, and that it was man's duty to try to identify himself with this purpose, and to train himself to feel indifference towards everything else, except towards any possibility, whether public or private, of helping others to become virtuous. About Stoicism there was much metaphor, much striking of attitudes, much of what the Germans call *pathos*: life was a battle, in which the Stoic's soul remained unconquerable and his head, though bloody, unbowed; life was a play in which each man had been given a part which he was to read and act at sight and to the best of his ability, without knowing what might happen in the last scene; the Stoic ate and drank from gold as if it were clay and from clay as if it were gold; amid the ruins of a falling world he would but involve himself the more impenetrably in his *virtus*, and his soul would finally ascend through the spheres to a region beyond the sway of fortune.[6]

Leishman catches admirably a certain duality which runs through Stoicism. There is, as he points out, much *pathos* about this philosophy of *apathia*, 'emotionless tranquillity'. The Stoics admired a condition of passionless indifference, but they also admired the heroic achievement of that condition. For the achievement to be spectacular or striking, some passion was after all required, if only as the material of moral conquest. Virgil's description, in Book iv of the *Aeneid*, of Aeneas shaken by Dido's plea that he stay with her, yet inwardly firm in his resolve, is one of the great images of Stoicism. Virgil likens his hero to a tree, tempest-torn yet firmly rooted, and ends his description with the famous, brief, enigmatic sentence:

> *lacrimae volvuntur inanes.*
> [the tears roll down in vain.]
>   (*Aeneid*, iv. 449)

The puzzle is: whose are the tears, Aeneas's or Dido's? Augustine, notoriously, thought the tears were Aeneas's (*City of God*, ix. 4). It is an interpretation entirely consonant with Stoicism: the suburbs of the personality rebel, but the virtuous will remains firm. Stoics are in one way like statues but it can be said with equal truth that the Stoic hero is typically wracked with strong emotions.

We must also notice that Stoicism is a 'postphilosophical philosophy'. Ancient philosophy falls roughly into two periods. The first (the only one which really deserves the name 'philosophical') is the period of Socrates, Plato, Aristotle. It is characteristic of this period that thinkers should see themselves as lovers of wisdom, as seekers after or purveyors of truth, as people trying to find the right answers to the most difficult questions. In the second period a strange alteration comes over the philosophers: they now present themselves as purveyors of mental health. It is as if some immense failure of nerve, a kind of generalized neurosis, swept through the ancient world, so that the most serious thinkers found that their most urgent task was not to inform or enlighten but to heal. They begin indeed to sound like psychiatrists. This is the period of Stoicism and Epicureanism, in which the philosophers say, again and again, 'Come to us and we will give you ἀταραξία, that is, *freedom from tumult, tranquillity.*' The great Epicurean poet Lucretius sought to free his hearers from the crushing fear of death by arguing—somewhat surprisingly to modern ears—that death is total annihilation. The Romans of the first century BC were terrified of torture after death.

The Stoic commendation of *apathia*, 'absence of feeling', is similar. Seneca wrote 'consolatory epistles', to comfort people in distress (notice how it has now become natural to expect *solace* from a philosopher—very soon books will appear with such titles as *The Consolation of Philosophy*, which would have seemed strange to Aristotle). Writing to people broken by bereavement and similar misfortunes, the Roman Stoic recommends a kind of withdrawal from the world:

> *Recipe to ad haec tranquilliora, tutiora, maiora.*
> [Recollect yourself, back to these things which are more tranquil, safer, more important.]
> (Seneca, *Ad Paulinum: de brevitate vitae*, xix. 1[7])

Contempt of life (and, by implication, of all one's most demanding personal relationships) must be supplemented by a proper egoism; the mind is its own place, and, though a man be banished from his beloved country, yet he can always reflect that over his own mind he is undisputed king. Thus the rational man is a citizen of the world, true to himself, exempt from emotional commitment to particular people and places. He cannot be banished.

> *Ideoque nec exulare unquam potest animus.*
> [And so the mind can never suffer exile.]
> (*Seneca, Ad Helviam de consolatione*, xi. 7)

> *Animus quidem ipse sacer et aeternus est cui non possit inici manus.*
> [The soul itself is sacred and eternal and on it no hand can be laid.]
> (ibid. xi. 7[8])

When, however, it is rational to leave this worthless life, the philosopher does so, with a steady hand.

It is clear that Senecan Stoicism worked by a systematic introversion of psychic patterns surviving from a much older, heroic culture, something like the shame-culture analysed by E.R. Dodds in *The Greeks and the Irrational*.[9] In a shame-culture no distinction is drawn between performing an action for the sake of glory and performing it out of virtue. Virtue itself is seen in strangely public terms, coinciding with elements which we think of as 'merely external', like beauty and physical strength. The greatest literary monument of a shame-culture is the *Iliad* of Homer. But it is by no means confined to archaic Greece. Anthropologists have traced it in cultures as remote as that of eighteenth-century Japan.[10] It is also vestigially present in our own culture. In Stoic philosophy the heroic ethic of pride, of glory in the sight of others, is cut off from its reliance on social esteem and made self-sufficient in each individual. The rational man is taught to fill the silence of his own skull with clamorous self-applause, with a majestically austere approbation of his own feats. Every man his own Achilles in his own, private Trojan War. Certain behavioural tricks of the old culture survive in Stoicism—the military strut, the strenuousness—but they have been strangely dehumanized. The vivid responsiveness of man to man has been deliberately dried up at its source and instead we seem to be watching a set of obscurely threatened statues. Truly for them, as Cicero said, *vita mors est*, 'Life is a state of death.'[11]

All this, note, is about real Stoicism. How much of it is 'noticed' in Shakespeare's Roman plays? I answer: pretty well all of it. Shakespeare knows that because Stoicism is an artificially framed philosophy, deliberately and consciously adopted by its adherents, any actual Stoic Roman will have within him un-Stoic elements. Your shame-culture hero Achilles, say, simply exemplifies that culture, but Stoicism is rather something at which you aim. The theory of shame-culture is posterior to and descriptive of the practice. The theory of Stoicism is prior to and prescriptive of practice. There are therefore elements of cultural tension present in Brutus which are absent from Achilles (and, one might add, from Othello, but more of that anon).

In the second scene of the first act of *Julius Caesar* Brutus is 'sounded' by Cassius, as to his willingness to kill Caesar. Cassius brings to his task a profound knowledge of Brutus's personality. He begins with the basis of that personality, which is the inherited and very ancient notion of self as essentially that which is presented to others. Cassius says,

> Tell me, good Brutus, can you see your face?
> (I. ii. 51)

Brutus answers that the eye cannot see itself except by reflection, in some other object such as a mirror. Cassius swiftly offers himself as a reflector:

> I, your glass,
> Will modestly discover to yourself
> That of yourself which you yet know not of.
> (I. ii. 68–70)

Notice what is happening. Cassius is, in effect, teaching Brutus what to think. But he contrives to use an image which both apprises Brutus of the opinion of others (a powerful primitive incentive) and yet evokes the private, self-regarding virtue of the Stoics (since the heart of his challenge is, 'Brutus, what do you think of yourself?'). All this is done with the image, carrying a simultaneous implication of self-absorption and external reference, of the glass. Such talk, we sense, is congenial to Brutus. Moreover the language of mirrors which Cassius uses to compass his end subtly apprises the audience that there may be something narcissistic in the Stoicism of Brutus. This note is struck again a little later when Brutus opens the letter in his orchard: 'Brutus, thou sleep'st. Awake, and see thyself' (II. i. 45).

But with all this Brutus is perhaps better than Cassius thinks him. In the orchard scene (II. i) we see his mind, not as it is when it is being manipulated by Cassius, but working alone, strenuously, struggling to determine what ought to be done:

> It must be by his death; and for my part,
> I know no personal cause to spurn at him,
> But for the general: he would be crown'd.
> How that might change his nature, there's the question.
> It is the bright day that brings forth the adder,
> And that craves wary walking. Crown him—that!
> And then, I grant, we put a sting in him
> That at his will he may do danger with.
> Th' abuse of greatness is, when it disjoins
> Remorse from power; and to speak truth of Caesar,
> I have not known when his affections sway'd
> More than his reason. But 'tis a common proof
> That lowliness is young ambition's ladder,
> Whereto the climber-upward turns his face;
> But when he once attains the upmost round,
> He then unto the ladder turns his back,
> Looks in the clouds, scorning the base degrees
> By which he did ascend. So Caesar may.
> Then, lest he may, prevent. And since the quarrel
> Will bear no colour for the thing he is,
> Fashion it thus—that what he is, augmented,
> Would run to these and these extremities;
> And therefore think him as a serpent's egg,
> Which, hatch'd, would as his kind grow mischievous,
> And kill him in the shell.
>   (II. i. 10–34)

Brutus sets out the case with scrupulous care. He knows nothing personally, here and now, against Caesar. The alpha and omega of the case against him is that he would like to be crowned King. That crowning might change a nature at present blameless. The case is not specific to Caesar, therefore. It is just that, commonly, when men are thus incongruously elevated, those who were not proud before become so. The case as Brutus puts it is tenuous and some critics have seen in this a sign that Brutus is feebly rationalizing a dark impulse which springs from the imperfectly repressed violence in him. In fact there are signs in the play of such a side to Brutus's nature, notably the strangely exultant 'red weapons' (III. i. 110), but I cannot think that the dominant tenor of this passage is mere rationalization. After all, rationalization usually aims at giving as powerful an appearance as possible of logical completeness. When Hamlet explains his sparing of Claudius at his prayers by observing that to kill a man in a state of grace would be to send him straight to heaven and hence would be no revenge (*Hamlet*, III. iii. 72–9), we have an argument at once watertight and insane, and there is therefore an excellent case for supposing that Hamlet is rationalizing his reluctance. Brutus is fairly close in conception to Hamlet, but the tone of this soliloquy, with 'there's the question' in line 13, is closer to the beleaguered but still operative sanity of 'To be or not to be' (*Hamlet*, III. i. 56f.) than to the faceless logic of 'Now might I do it, pat' (*Hamlet*, III. iii. 72) . Brutus goes out of his way to stress the *tenuousness* of his case, pauses on all the weak links in the chain, and this, surely, is almost the opposite of rationalization.

I suspect that many who say that such a chain of reasoning is an inadequate basis for any major political act cannot have reflected how much political action is necessarily founded on exactly this sort of 'lest he may, prevent' basis. I imagine that most people today would say that republicanism is better than despotism. If you ask them why, they are likely to say that it is right that a people should be, as far as possible, self-governing, rather than subjected to the will of a single individual. If you then point out that in any system which stops short of the total democracy of the (adult, male) ancient Athenians (we will set-aside the rigidly aristocratic character of real Roman republicanism!) the processes of government are in fact carried out by representative officers and not by the people at all, the answer is likely to be that as long as the officers remain answerable to the people they are more *likely* to act in the interest of the people—and now, notice, we have begun to speak in terms of *probability*.

Now let us make the situation concrete. Imagine yourself a citizen of France, wondering whether to vote for someone rather like General de Gaulle: a figure at the height of his power, who has, let us say, shown a genius for getting his country out of a tight spot, for running a system in trouble. What would such voters say? Well, they would of course say many different things. But the ones who were worried by the idea of autocratic genius might well say, 'The case against him is not personal; it's just that autocracy is inherently dangerous. Of course, we cannot predict with certainty that he will behave corruptly, it is just that he may, and because of that bare possibility it is our duty to stop him.' The seemingly factual character of formally indicative sentences like 'Autocracy is bad' resolves itself, in practice, into a cloud of (very serious) probabilities.

Assassination is, to be sure, somewhat more drastic than a transferred vote, but nevertheless Brutus's speech is both moving and impressive in its refusal to dress up a political rationale as something more watertight than it really is. It is curiously refreshing after reading the words of current politicians (who are under very great pressure to sound more certain than they can ever really be). The best place in Brutus's speech is the marvellously laconic

> So Caesar may.
> Then, lest he may, prevent.
> (II. i. 27–8)

The lines beginning 'And since the quarrel / Will bear no colour for the thing he is, / Fashion it thus' (II. i. 28–30) have also been misinterpreted. I used to think that this was an example of what may be called 'dissociated motivation', the kind of thing which we shall see later in Iago, a man who *decides* what he will believe, what he will be moved by. This puzzled me, because it meant that, according to the scheme which was beginning to form in my mind, Brutus would have to be classified as 'overevolved'.

The underevolved archaic man includes in his ego many things we consider external. The ordinarily evolved man includes within the ego such things as feelings and beliefs but excludes physical attributes, to a greater or lesser extent. According to this sequence the overevolved man might narrow the field of the ego still further, until it was able to watch, in arrogant isolation, the inept dance of emotions and appetites, now psychically objectified. But I was wrong. Although there is a faint pre-echo of Iago here, this sentence has a different context and a different logic.

Brutus is not, in fact, proposing to feign a belief and then to execute the fiction in real life. He is saying to himself 'It is no use trying to construct this case with reference to what I know of Caesar, now. Rather, put it this way. . . . ' To paraphrase thus is indeed to soften the worrying word 'fashion', which obstinately retains a suggestion of fiction (I have conceded a faint anticipation of Iago's *manner*). Nevertheless, the main tenor of the idiom is donnishly abstract rather than cynically self-manipulative. It is much closer to the philosopher's 'Let's try the argument this way . . . ' than to 'This shall be my motive.' If it is asked, 'Why, then, granting that the Iago-subaudition is only a subaudition, did Shakespeare allow it into the line?' the answer is, perhaps, because he wished to hint that the second state of mind was, in a sinister fashion, latent in the first; that the proper corruption of moral abstraction is diabolical cynicism. Brutus stands on the edge of a pit, but he has not yet fallen.

Moreover this psychic isolation of the reflective ego is not natural to Brutus as it is to Iago. It is really the product of a special moral effort, the

Stoic assertion of reason against disabling emotion. For the beginning of 'overevolved' dissociation of the ego from ordinary feeling is likewise latent, or present as a potential corruption, in Stoic philosophy. Aeneas, weeping yet successfully separating his reason from his love of Dido, is great and at the same time rather weird. The panic-stricken retreat into a private area of the mind as being alone governable by the rational will can lead, almost by its own inner impetus, to forms of scepticism which would have shocked the Stoics themselves. The person who is broken-hearted is given the dangerous consolation (dangerous, because it can in the long run erode the very notion of value) 'You yourself can decide what is good and what is bad.' Hamlet's 'There is nothing either good or bad, but thinking makes it so' (II. ii. 248) is pivotal. It reaches back into Stoicism and forward into abysses of modern scepticism. But the contraction of the ego is the principal point at issue, and it is important to remember that in Stoicism this contraction always takes place in a context of moral effort. There is therefore a real difference between Brutus's straining to bring to bear reason, and reason alone, on the one hand and Iago's unblinking survey of his own motives on the other. Nevertheless there is in *Julius Caesar* a real, though faint, analogue to Iago, and that is Mark Antony.

Consider the behaviour of Mark Antony, first, when he moves into the circle of the assassins as they stand round the body of the newly slain Caesar (III. i) and, second, in his great oration (III. ii). In III. i Antony moves, with great circumspection but also with extraordinary 'nerve' within sword's length of men who may at any moment turn on him. He is their greatest potential danger, but the potentiality (as with Caesar) is fraught with doubt. These are the reasonings of a Brutus and it is on them that Antony counts. The conscientiousness of Brutus is for him a weakness to be exploited. Antony knows just how much of his grief for Caesar it is safe to express. He shakes hands with the murderers and is left alone on the stage, to plot the ruin of Rome.

Notice, in passing, that my entire account of this scene has been written in bull-bloodedly Transparent language; I have been considering Shakespeare's Brutus and Antony, not indeed as direct portraits of their historical originals, but at least as possible human beings and I have not scrupled to make inferences and even, at times, to guess. Yet, in the closing sentence of the last paragraph, I wrote, not 'left alone in the Capitol', but 'left alone on the stage'. The logical slippage from the tenor to vehicle is entirely easy and creates no difficulties for the reader, because it mirrors a movement of the mind which is habitual to play-goers and play-readers.

We may further ask, is Antony sincere? The question, oddly enough, can be answered with slightly more confidence when the reference is to a fictional person (where the clues are finite) than with reference to a real-life person (where they are indefinite and in any case liable to subversion).

I think that Antony is sincere. He feels real grief for Caesar but is, so to speak, effortlessly separate from the grief even while he feels it. We therefore have something which is psychologically more disquieting than the ordinary machiavel, who pretends emotion while he coldly intrigues for power. Antony feels his emotions and then *rides* them, controls them, moderating their force as need arises.

Thus the great oration is at once artificial and an authentically passional performance. I would have the actor, if he can, go so far as to weep in the delivery of it ('his eyes are red as fire with weeping'—III. ii. 115) in order to give maximum effect to the conclusion of the oration, at which point Antony, his own emotion ebbing from its licensed height, watches the mob run screaming from him and says, like one who has administered a mass injection, 'Now let it work. Mischief, thou art afoot' (III. iii. 261). Naturally it is Brutus who is the man of the past, the doomed order of things, and Antony who is the man of the future. When Brutus patiently explained, with lucid logic, how he had killed his friend to save Rome from the rule of an individual, the crowd applauds him with the dreadful 'Let him be Caesar' (III. ii. 50). They do not understand the rigorous, tormented morality of his action and he, in his turn, does not understand the place in history to which he has come.

The Roman-ness, the un-English-ness, of all this is evident. Moreover, within that powerfully imagined Roman-ness we have, not only contrasts of individual with individual, but prior contrasts, operating in the region intermediate between individuals and the cultural remoteness of Rome. I mean a contrast between different degrees of psychic and political evolution within a Roman setting. Brutus, the Republican, addresses a populace which spontaneously embraces monarchy, thus exemplifying one of the paradoxes of liberalism identified by Sir Karl Popper (though Plato was there before him): what happens when a democracy decides in favour of tyranny?[12] Brutus, the aristocrat, his theoretic Stoicism borne on a foundation of shame-culture, on ancient heroic dignity, belongs to the Roman past. He can do the Stoic trick (rather like 'isolating' a muscle) of separating his reason from his passions but he cannot exploit his own motivating passions with the coolness of an Antony. With all his fondness for statuesque postures Brutus remains morally more spontaneous than Antony.

In IV. iii there is a notorious textual crux. Brutus and Cassius quarrel and are uneasily reconciled. Shakespeare presents the quarrel with great realism and elicits from his audience a high degree of sympathy with both figures. At IV. iii. 141 Cassius observes, wonderingly, 'I did not think you could have been so angry', and, a moment later, with a hint of a taunt so that we fear the quarrel may break out again, he adds,

Of your philosophy you make no use,
If you give place to accidental evils.
   (IV. iii. 143–4)

Brutus answers, bleakly, that Portia, his wife, is dead. Cassius is at once overwhelmed with contrition at his own coarse hostility. Brutus tells, shortly, the horrible story of Portia's suicide by swallowing fire and calls for wine, to 'bury all unkindness' (IV. iii. 152). Titinius and Messala then enter. Brutus welcomes them, volubly, and the talk is all of military movements and public events in Rome. Then the spate of talk dries up and the following dialogue takes place:

MESSALA
  Had you your letters from your wife, lord?
BRUTUS
  No, Messala.
MESSALA
  Nor nothing in your letters writ of her?
BRUTUS
  Nothing, Messala.
MESSALA
  That, methinks, is strange.
BRUTUS
  Why ask you? Hear you aught of her in yours?
MESSALA
  No, my lord.
BRUTUS
  Now as you are a Roman, tell me true.
MESSALA
  Then like a Roman bear the truth I tell:
  For certain she is dead, and by strange manner.
BRUTUS
  Why, farewell, Portia. We must die, Messala.
  With meditating that she must die once,
  I have the patience to endure it now.
MESSALA
  Even so great men great losses should endure.
CASSIUS
  I have as much of this in art as you,
  But yet my nature could not bear it so.
   (IV. iii. 179–93)

Brutus receives the news from Messala as if for the first time, although he has just confided to Cassius that he knows, and Cassius is still there, listening to every word. To make matters worse, Brutus's self-control is applauded as a Stoic feat and Brutus accepts the applause. And still Cassius is there, watching and listening.

The easiest way out of these difficulties is to suppose that Shakespeare wrote two alternative versions and that both have somehow survived, in incongruous juxtaposition, in the 1623 Folio text (the sole authority for this play). To take this course at one stroke removes both the difficulties and the tense excitement of the scene. Brents Stirling, in a article which may serve as a model of the proper marriage of literary criticism and textual scholarship,[13] argued for the retention of both versions. He observes that Brutus is in a state of nervous excitement after the quarrel with Cassius (notice his extreme irritation with the sententious poet who enters at IV. iii. 122). In this state, bordering on exhaustion, Brutus attempts to put Messala aside with his blankly mendacious 'Nothing' at line 182. But Messala will not be put off and Brutus is forced to question him. Thereupon *Messala* 'turns witless in the crisis' and answers 'No, my lord' at 184. Brutus tries to resolve the impossible situation with 'Now, as you are a Roman, tell me true.' Messala catches the manner, is freed from his petrified immobility by the familiar *style*, and from here on forces Brutus to play out the episode in the full Stoic manner. At its conclusion Brutus's head is bowed at the humiliating praise he has received from Messala.

Given this reading, the comment of Cassius is immediately luminous. He has watched his fellow commander, in a state of near-collapse, lie and then reassert, artificially, his command over himself and his subordinates. Brutus's 'Nothing' was pure nature. It is the kind of speech which in life is wholly probable and becomes 'impossible' only when challenged by the customary canons of art. Brutus then pulled himself back and this too was nature. From the recovered ground he framed his formal response to Messala and secured the required result. Cassius who has seen the 'nature' of Brutus humiliated in the lie also perceives in the very recovery of will a feat of natural endurance. His comment is almost ironic but is at the same time movingly generous and intelligent; he observes that he could just about match Brutus's rhetoric, but he could never be so strong and brave.

This is not to say that there are no rough edges in the text as we have it. There is formal evidence in the Folio of revision. This has been investigated by Brents Stirling in a second article.[14] The speech headings give '*Cassi*' until '*Enter* a *Poet*'. Then, in the lines which report the death of Portia we get *Cas*. At line 164, 'Portia, art thou gone?' (which may be a single-line insertion), we get '*Cass*'. The passage containing suspected additions has different prefix forms and the passages both before and after it have standard forms. Admittedly there is considerable variation of '*Cassi*' and '*Cas*' throughout the play and this must weaken the presumption of interpolation in so far as it is founded on speech headings. But the changes are so timed (in conjunction with the obvious oddity of the presentation) as to suggest some sort of process of revision, which has not been satisfactorily completed. What is not shown at all is that the revision was intended as a replacement of one version by another. It remains entirely possible that Shakespeare, revising, determined to show us a Brutus reacting twice to the same event and merely failed to complete the 'joinery'. Brutus's lie might then have been more carefully 'framed'. We need not infer that it would have been removed.

Thus, even when Brutus's Stoicism is most artificial, most plainly exerted by will, we sense not only what is exerted but the human will which exerts; we sense a person with an emotional life. That indeed is why the artificiality is so excruciating. In Antony it would scarcely be noticed.

Brutus is presented by Shakespeare as an interplay of nature and art; the art, to be sure, is Brutus's. If we step back and view the whole, both the art and the nature of Brutus are equally formed by the art of Shakespeare. Brutus's nature is Shakespeare's art. But in conveying something which the audience will receive as nature, Shakespeare must (and does) consult and defer to reality. Therefore among the many excellencies of *Julius Caesar* we may include a specific success in realism.

Coriolanus shows us an older Rome, a city which has just become something more than a strangely warlike country town. Pope wrote that Shakespeare not only noticed the difference between Romans and English people but also saw the difference between different stages of Roman development. In *Coriolanus* the populace is only a little less contemptible than the mob in *Julius Caesar*, but at least it is interested in its political rights. Rome is firmly and consciously republican. The day of the autocrat has not yet come. The play even exhibits some awareness of economic factors. The populace in *Coriolanus* is not a Marxian proletariat of first-order producers, nor is Coriolanus himself an economic parasite. The city lives by military conquest; conquest produces tribute and the citizens are sustained by a gratuitous dole. In warfare it appears that they have been of little use (though one itches to step outside the data of the play and dispute this). Coriolanus, because he is a great killer, is in this society a great provider.

Coriolanus is at one and same time a sort of Titan and a baby. Modern critical accounts of him perhaps stress the second too much at the expense of the first. We should not forget that if any of us were to meet him on a battle field the patronizing critical smile would be wiped away very quickly. As a warrior he is almost superhuman. But at the same time he is like a 2 year old in his tantrums, his stubbornness, his tendency to stamp or hide his face.

And then there is his pride. Here, as usual, Shakespeare refuses to give the sentimentalist an easy ride. It would be nice to think that Coriolanus's contempt for the people is unmixed folly. Shakespeare keeps the situation uncomfortable by insinuating on the one hand that Coriolanus's pride has something pathological in it and on the other hand that the people are in fact much as he describes them. Strange world, where only the egomaniac speaks the truth!

In *Julius Caesar* we saw a fundamental problem of democracy broached; what happens when the people choose tyranny? In *Coriolanus* we have another, still more fundamental problem, one so uncomfortable that people prefer to set it aside as 'ludicrously abstract': what happens when it can be predicted that the people, through vice or folly will choose corruptly? Is democracy right if the *demos* is bad? What does the good man do, placed in such a society? If you make liberty a terminal value of democracy (that is, if you believe that liberty is not only good because it promotes happiness but is also good in itself and moreover is the most important good of all) then you have no difficulty in answering this question. You will oppose Coriolanus. Perhaps older Americans will do this more confidently than other people. W.H. Auden wrote in an introduction to Henry James's *The American Scene*[15] that many Americans have given up *Romanitas*. *Romanitas*, for Auden, means making virtue prior to freedom. People who give up Romanitas are people who would rather do wrong freely than do right under compulsion. It is interesting in view of the applicability of this conception to Coriolanus that Auden chose to express his idea with a word which literally means 'Roman-ness'.

Of course the Rome shown by Shakespeare is not a democracy but a republic. Nevertheless, there are moments in both *Julius Caesar* and *Coriolanus* when the political wishes of the people make themselves felt. In the tribunician elections of *Coriolanus* one has an actual specimen of rudimentary democratic machinery.

In III. i Coriolanus is therefore in an odd position. He is standing for election and he despises the electors. Falsehood is beneath him. His open electoral programme is therefore to strip the people of the very rights they exercise in electing him. It is almost a logical paradox, and equally close to being a joke. For if the people elect him, by their shrewdness they disprove his theory. Coriolanus would then be like Groucho Marx, who resigned from a golf club because it proved itself—through electing him—insufficiently exclusive. At this stage in Shakespeare's play I suppose most of the spectators have begun to feel that Coriolanus is a little mad. Yet a strand of moral integrity persists in him. He had said at the beginning of the play that he believed the populace to be in truth so cowardly and stupid that they could not even pursue their own interest:

> Your affections are
> As a sick man's appetite, who desires most that
> Which would increase his evil.
> (I. i. 175–7)

By the beginning of Act III Coriolanus's contempt for the people has reached such a pitch that he can scarcely be expected even to think about their interests. But, if he did, he would maintain his course. He plainly believes that it would be to the advantage of the people if those rights which they exercise with so little intelligence were taken from them. And the strangely pitiless dramatist, who has not a grain of compassion for the hunger of the starving in this play, inserts not a line to show that Coriolanus is wrong.

Can Coriolanus ask the people to sign away their privileges by electing him? He might answer that a populace capable of self-knowledge could and should do so. But, as we saw, a populace capable of self-knowledge would be utterly unlike this populace. Self-knowledge would in *its* case disclose intelligence and, given this intelligence, it would actually be wrong to sign away political rights. Coriolanus really is in a logical prison. There is, seemingly, a fundamental discrepancy between his warrior nature and the very institutions of a civil polity.

This brings us to the central pathos of Coriolanus's nature and the central tension of the play. Coriolanus has been made, by his overwhelming mother, Volumnia, into an instrument of war. We know roughly how it was done from the episode in I. iii, where we are told how Coriolanus's son, little Marcius, a miniature replica of his father, chased 'a gilded butterfly', caught it and let it go over and over again until he fell in the chase and then seized the butterfly and '*mammocked*' it—that is, tore at it with his teeth (I. iii. 64). Volumnia greets the story with an indulgent, reminiscent smile: 'One on's father's moods.' Plainly, Coriolanus was rewarded with love for displays of aggression.

Notice how odd bits and pieces of *King Lear* are floating in this play. Shakespeare, who is full of recyclings, never merely repeats himself. In *King Lear* there are two especially powerful images. The first occurs in Gloucester's line:

> As flies to wanton boys are we to th' gods—
> They kill us for their sport.
> (IV. i. 37–8)

The second comes when Lear, restored to sanity after his ordeal in the storm, is reunited with Cordelia. He says to her,

> So we'll live,
> And pray, and sing, and tell old tales, and laugh
> At gilded butterflies.
> (V. iii. 11–13)

When he was writing *King Lear* Shakespeare had a vision compounded, one suspects, of memory and imagination. The memory was of cruel village boys tormenting insects. Imagination showed him gods who, while possessed of superhuman power, were morally identical with those remembered boys. In *Coriolanus*, which is about a hero-god who is himself like a violent child, the images naturally rose again in his mind—not only in the picture of little Marcius teasing and tearing the gilded butterfly but also later, when Coriolanus's army is described as coming on with no less confidence

> Than boys pursuing summer butterflies,
> Or butchers killing flies.
> (IV. vi. 94–6)

Volumnia, then, has forged Coriolanus as an instrument of war. But then she encounters a problem. She needs an instrument to achieve her political ends within the city and she has built her son in a way which does not serve her purpose. It is like trying to saw with a sword. At a word he will hack and kill, but he is set to shy away from the very idea of compromise or conciliation. Yet his mother's power over him remains the strongest force in his life. In III. ii Volumnia tries in vain to get Coriolanus to sue for office and only succeeds when she gives up rational persuasion and instead remarks—quite lightly—that she will be very pleased with him if he does it (III. ii. 109). At once he does what she wants.

I have said that Coriolanus's character is one of great pathos. The pathos lies in the fact that he has no inside. All he has was given him by his mother and confirmed in him in the physical stress of battle. What existentialists say is true of man in general is certainly true of Coriolanus in particular—namely, that in himself he is a kind of nothing and acquires what positive nature he possesses by adventitious role-adoption. It may be thought that in asserting this I go too far for sane historical scholarship—for everyone knows that in the sixteenth and seventeenth centuries men had a very strong and firm sense of the real nature of man, and his place in the great chain of being. But the Elizabethan world picture, as unified and frozen by scholars, is a retrospective historical myth. The existentialist idea that man's original nature lies in the negation of all essence is anticipated by Pico della Mirandola, in his *De hominis dignitate*. There the philosopher tells how God created the world, and framed it as a great ladder, blazing with light and colour, every rung loaded with being, all disposed in hierarchical splendour; and how God having completed his immense cosmos, paused, and then resolved to make something quite different. And so he made man, a creature with no given nature at all, and unleashed this little darkness into his glittering creation, a flickering total freedom among all the splendid certainties, and bade it *take* on any nature it chose, be it God, beast or devil.[16] The idea belongs clearly with that immensely influential body of thought known as Hermetism.[17] If one must look for a single cosmology appropriate to Shakespeare surely this fits better than the bland system expounded by E.M.W. Tillyard?[18] Certainly it was current in Shakespeare's time. John Donne wrote in a 'Letter to a Lord' (1624) that, 'to make myself believe that our life is something, I use in my thoughts to compare it to something; if it be like anything that is something'[19] and lyrically explored the idea of a constitutive negation in his 'Nocturnall upon St. Lucies Day'.[20] A similar way of speaking and thinking appears in Shakespeare's play, when Cominius says of Coriolanus,

> He was a kind of nothing, title-less,
> Till he had forg'd himself a name i' th' fire
> Of burning Rome.
>   (V. i. 13–15)

From being a kind of nothing he became—never a person, but rather a *thing*, insentient, an instrument, a machine. He is repeatedly spoken of in these terms. Cominius calls him 'a thing of blood' (II. ii. 107). Coriolanus himself, in strange exultation, cries out to his men, 'O, me alone! Make you a sword of me?' (I. vi. 76). Cominius later says of him,

> He leads them like a thing
> Made by some other deity than Nature.
>   (IV. vi. 91–2)

and Menenius calls him both 'engine' and 'thing' (V. iv. 20, 24). There is something very sad in the way this artfully brutalized piece of nothingness is at last brought to deny its own conditioning. In V. iii Coriolanus has returned to destroy Rome and his mother goes out to dissuade him, just once more, from his natural course. As he sees her coming he says, feeling himself weakening,

> I'll never
> Be such a gosling to obey instinct, but stand

> As if a man were author of himself
> And knew no other kin.
>   (V. iii. 34–7)

Here Coriolanus clutches at a Stoic attitude for the support it gives to the isolated self. Yet the speech expresses a wish, not an achievement. Here, surely, was one who existed as a mere relation before he existed substantially as himself; he is, timelessly, a son before he is a man.

Again I have written in a freely Transparent language, treating the character of Coriolanus as a study in possible psychology. To write and think in this way is to find oneself engaged in a dialogue with a text which proves richly responsive. A rigorously formal approach might easily prevent a reader or spectator from noticing the wholly remarkable sense Shakespeare displays of the possible formative tyranny of the parent. This alone is sufficiently astonishing in a pre-Freudian writer and yet it is certainly there, in the text. The curious and the historically sceptical can discover how Shakespeare found hints of his conception in Plutarch. But *Coriolanus* like *Julius Caesar* is at the same time a study of cultural change. This time, the conception we have labelled 'shame-culture' is a little closer than it was with Brutus.

There is no contradiction in saying both that Coriolanus exemplifies a particular cultural pattern and that his personality was formed for him by another individual, his mother. Volumnia made her son according to a still available cultural model, that of the warrior. Coriolanus is therefore an artificial, but therefore especially pure, specimen of the type. Certainly he has the entire courage, the big language and perhaps the unreadiness for marriage (think of Othello) which Shakespeare seems to associate with the kind. Moreover, Shakespeare, in setting forth the growing civic institutions of Rome as existing in tension with the warlike mode is working with almost the same subject matter as a modern cultural historian. A.W.H. Adkins, for example, in his *Merit and Responsibility*[21] traces the process by which what he calls 'the co-operative values' gradually came to replace the 'competitive values', as Greek society gradually settled into relatively stable city states. Terms like 'temperate' came to carry more ethical weight than terms like 'brave'. The level of historical abstraction we find in Adkins's book seems quintessentially modern. But Shakespeare picked up from Plutarch the fact that the early Romans made much of *virtus* in its etymological sense, 'manliness', 'virile heroism'. He chose to exhibit this virile courage in a civic context to which it is not suited. The audience can quite simply watch 'the co-operative virtues' gathering power in the forum. Shakespeare shows with great clarity, first, how useful Coriolanus is to Rome in time of war and, second, how much happier the city is without him once peace has been attained. The second observation is emphasized in IV. vi where the citizens greet each other courteously and Sicinius says,

> This is a happier and more comely time
> Than when these fellows ran about the streets
> Crying confusion.
>   (IV. vi. 27–9)

It is perhaps impossible to say with precision to what extent the shame-culture of Coriolanus has assumed the introverted form given to it by Stoicism. It might be said that the true shame-culture figure rejoices above all in glory, in reputation, and that Coriolanus's refusal to court the people shows in him the egoistic withdrawal of the Stoic. But we must remember that when Coriolanus goes among the people he is with men who to him are little better than slaves. Even Homer's Achilles or Ajax, the purest examples we have of archaic shame-culture, would balk at seeking the favour of such base people. Certainly there should be no suggestion in production that Coriolanus is here displaying the 'co-operative' virtue of modesty. Coriolanus wishes to hide his scars from the populace, not because he thinks them insignificant, but because he thinks them too glorious. He says,

> To brag unto them 'Thus I did, and thus!'
> Show them th'unaching scars which I should hide,
> As if I had received them for the hire
> Of their breath only!
>   (II. ii. 144–8)

The people correctly identify his reluctance as springing from aristocratic pride.

It is true that when we see Coriolanus amid his fellow warriors, flushed with victory in I. ix, he keeps up a certain social opposition to praise and it must be conceded that this alone places him in a post-shame-culture period. But his resistance is shallow compared with his violent revulsion in Rome. Indeed, it is little more than a half-embarrassed shrugging of the shoulders:

> I will go wash;
> And when my face is fair you shall perceive
> Whether I blush or no. Howbeit, I thank you.
>   (I. ix. 68–70)

The battle over, his energy drains from him and with aristocratic negligence he fails to recall the name of the poor man who sheltered him, the man for whom a little earlier he had pleaded with equally typical aristocratic magnanimity. Nietzsche, who is the father of all modern cultural historians of antiquity, would recognize at once both the largeness and the shallowness of Coriolanus's aristocratic spirit.

NOTES

1. But not uncritically. See his review of Stoll's *Art and Artifice in Shakespeare*, in *Scrutiny*, 3 (1934–5), pp. 85–9.

2. In *How Many Children had Lady Macbeth?*, Cambridge, 1933, p. 21, n. The observation does not appear in the version printed in Knights's *Explorations*, London, 1946.

3. All references to Shakespeare are to *William Shakespeare: The Complete Works*, ed. Peter Alexander, London, 1951.

4. *A Preface to Paradise Lost*, London, 1960, pp. 62–3.

5. *Eighteenth Century Essays on Shakespeare*, ed. D. Nichol Smith, 2nd edn, Oxford, 1963, p. 49.

6. J.B. Leishman, *Translating Horace*, Oxford, 1956, p. 28.

7. In *Seneca's Moral Essays*, ed. with an English translation by J.W. Basore, London, 1958, vol. ii, p. 348.

8. ibid., vol. ii, pp. 456, 458.

9. Berkeley, California, 1951.

10. See e.g. Ruth Benedict, *The Chrysanthemum and the Sword: Patterns in Japanese Culture*, Boston, 1946.

11. *Somnium Scipionis*, iii. 2, in *Ambrosii Theodosii Macrobii Commentarii in Somnium Scipionis*, ed. J. Willis, Leipzig, 1970, p. 157.

12. See *The Open Society and its Enemies*, 5th edn, London, 1966, vol. 1, p. 123, and *Conjectures and Refutations*, 4th edn, London, 1972, p. 351. Cf. Plato, *Republic*, 565C–D.

13. 'Brutus and the death of Portia', *Shakespeare Quarterly*, 10 (1959), pp. 211–17.

14. 'Julius Caesar in revision', *Shakespeare Quarterly*, 13 (1962), pp. 187–205.

15. Reprinted in *Horizon*, 15 (1947), pp. 77–90.

16. Pico della Mirandola, *De hominis dignitate, Heptaplus, De ente et uno*, ed. Eugenio Garin, Florence, 1942, pp. 104–6.

17. See e.g. Hermes Trismegistus, *Corpus Hermeticum*, ed. A.D. Nock, trans. A.-J. Festugière, Paris, 1960, vol. 2, pp. 301–2.

18. *The Elizabethan World Picture*, Harmondsworth, 1963.

19. 'Letter to a Lord' (possibly the Earl of Dorset, probably 1624), in Edmund Gosse, *Life and Letters of John Donne*, London, 1899, vol. 2, p. 208.

20. *The Poems of John Donne*, ed. H.J.C. Grierson, Oxford, 1912, vol. 1, p. 44.

21. Oxford, 1960.

E.A.J. HONIGMANN

The Uniqueness of King Lear:
Genre and Production Problems

Thirty years ago it was not a punishable offence to talk about 'Shakespearian tragedy'. Literary critics even dared to discuss 'Shakespeare's tragic period' and 'Shakespeare's tragic vision' in that golden age, that age of innocence, which has passed away like a dream. The fashionable thing now is that you analyse a single work—sorry, you deconstruct a text; you put it against a wall, frisk it, remove all its explosive devices, and ensure that it looks exactly like every other beaten-up text to which you have applied your theory.

We have travelled a long way since the appearance of the most perceptive of all Shakespeare critics, A. C. Bradley. Bradley has been accused of many crimes, almost always unfairly, but it is true that he sanctified the 'Shakespearian tragedy' approach in his well-known chapters on 'the substance of Shakespearian tragedy' and 'construction'. Those who clamour for due recognition of the single text, and therefore 'the death of the author', would be surprised by the many similarities in the substance and construction of Shakespeare's tragedies, as described by Bradley—similarities that point back to a not entirely unnecessary factor, the humble author. But, Bradley discovered, there is an important exception. One play does not really fit in with his account of the essential sameness of Shakespearian tragedy. That difficult old man, King Lear, refuses to play the game.

From *Myriad-minded Shakespeare: Essays on the Tragedies, Problem Comedies and Shakespeare the Man*, pp. 73–92, 239. © 1989, 1998 by E.A.J. Honigmann.

We all remember Bradley's problem. 'King Lear alone among these plays', he said, 'has a distinct double action.' More awkwardly, Lear himself cannot be the 'leading figure', since he does not 'initiate action' after Act I. It is impossible, Bradley thought,

> from the point of view of construction, to regard the hero as the leading figure. If we attempt to do so, we must either find the crisis in the First Act (for after it Lear's course is downward), and this is absurd; or else we must say that the usual movement is present but its direction is reversed, the hero's cause first sinking to the lowest point (in the Storm-scenes), and then rising again. But this also will not do. . . . The truth is, that after the First Act . . . Lear suffers but hardly initiates action at all; and the right way to look at the matter, *from the point of view of construction*, is to regard Goneril, Regan and Edmund as the leading characters.[1]

That is the sort of tangle you get into if, again, you commit yourself too enthusiastically to a theory, and it helps to explain why some recent critics have abandoned 'Shakespearian tragedy', and prefer to hack their way through less difficult territory, the single text.

I had better say clearly, at the start, that I am not opposed to a genre approach to Shakespeare—quite the contrary. The 'genre approach' remains valuable, even if we have been strangely careless in identifying genre. One could plead, in our excuse, that Heminge and Condell, in the First Folio, were content with rough and ready labels, *comedy, history, tragedy*, so our willingness to put up with them is historically justified. On the other hand, Shakespeare himself signals that the old genre-boundaries are breaking down, when Polonius announces 'the best actors in the world, either for tragedy, comedy, history, pastoral, pastoral-comical, historical-pastoral, tragical-historical, tragical-comical-historical-pastoral', and so on. A play first published as the 'true chronicle history of the life and death of King Lear and his three daughters' may seem, on reflection, to have some claim to be called a tragedy—but what kind of tragedy? I am going to argue that *King Lear* is fundamentally different from Shakespeare's other tragedies, and that, following this trail, we are led to a new understanding of the uniqueness of Shakespeare's masterpiece.

First, let us list some of the superficial differences. I have already referred to two—a fully developed double plot, and a tragic hero who suffers but scarcely initiates action after Act I. In addition *King Lear* includes a more prominent Fool (there is a clown in *Othello*, another in *Antony and Cleopatra*, two in *Hamlet*, and a Porter in *Macbeth*—but all restricted to one or two scenes). Physical disguise is much more prominently used, and involves 'disguised speech' (both Edgar and Kent). These two features, the Fool and disguise, are merely the two most obvious ones borrowed by this tragedy from comedy, a cross-fertilisation that several recent critics have dwelt upon.[2] To continue: the storm-scenes are much more protracted, and imaginatively potent, than in the other tragedies. Madness plays a much bigger part, as does stage-violence (the blinding of Gloucester); *King Lear* is the only mature tragedy to resemble *Titus Andronicus* in these two respects, hang-overs from the 'tragedy of blood'. Lear's age, as I have argued elsewhere, also sharply distinguishes him: being so much older than the other tragic heroes, his relationships with secondary characters are different. He never interests us as a husband or lover; he alone comes to life, emotionally speaking, through his children. Because of his aggressiveness, verbalised in his tendency to threaten and curse, and because of his madness and age, the audience responds to him at a certain distance; our 'over-view' of the play is therefore more distanced—an effect also achieved by the neat parallelism of the double plot.

I called them superficial differences, but I take it back. Any one of these factors—the Fool, disguise, the storm, madness, violence, double plot, overview—significantly affects the total impression. When it is revealed that they are all related, we become conscious of a qualitative difference in the play's very fabric, compared with Shakespeare's other tragedies.

How soon do we notice this in the theatre? The play visibly slows down after the opening scenes, instead of gathering momentum. This is partly disguised by Lear's rising passion, though not for long. It becomes obvious that Lear has nowhere to go, and no plans for the future.

> I will do such things—
> What they are yet I know not; but they shall be
> The terrors of the earth.
>   (II.4.279)

The hero is given no task to perform, as are Brutus, Hamlet, Macbeth; equally, the villains have no clearly defined intentions, such as Iago's—so the play points forward to no 'promised end', through the normal channels of expectation. True, Lear refers several times to the possibility of revenge, but again without clearly knowing what he wants—

> I will have such revenges on you both
> That all the world shall—I will do such things....
>   (278)

How, indeed, can one revenge oneself on one's own children?

> Is it not as this mouth should tear this hand ... ?
>   (III.4.15)

Later, Lear's fantasy suggests

> To have a thousand with red burning spits
> Come hizzing in upon 'em
>   (III.6.15)

and

> It were a delicate stratagem, to shoe
> A troop of horse with felt; I'll put't in proof,
> And when I have stol'n upon these son-in-laws,
> Then kill, kill, kill, kill, kill, kill!
>   (IV.6.185)

These, though, are the ravings of a madman, not options seriously proposed by the play; their very improbability underlines the fact that Lear's situation defeats him—that he cannot imagine an appropriate course of action. And this failure of the hero and of the villains to 'look forward', to fix the audience's attention on a task or plot, deprives the play itself of forward-looking suspense, a characteristic strength of the other tragedies.

Not content with a tragic hero marooned in purposelessness, Shakespeare daringly added Gloucester, a second father with nowhere to go. 'I have no way,' he says 'and therefore want no eyes' (IV.1.19). Two fathers cast adrift, with little or nothing to do: they appear to work loose from the plot and just 'hang around'. As Lady Bracknell almost said, 'to lose one father may be regarded as a misfortune, to lose two looks like carelessness'. But of course there is Edgar as well, a third drifter whose most positive forward-thinking can be summed up in the words 'Lurk, lurk' (III.6.115), meaning 'hang around, and hope for the best'. Not really the most exciting recipe, you may think, for a grand tragedy.

When Jan Kott wrote so interestingly about *King Lear* and Beckett's *Endgame* it was the drifting talk of the middle scenes that he had in mind, particularly Leafs meeting with Gloucester. Peter Brook's subsequent production of *Lear* pushed the whole play towards Beckett—too much so, since there is much more to *King Lear* than drifting talk. Nevertheless, Kott has identified another genre that we must keep in mind, one that specialises in characters who 'hang around' and talk rather than act. *Endgame*, however, is best seen as a sub-genre, part of a larger tradition that goes back to the

Greeks and is found in many later literatures—the drama of the man who wants to understand the universe. The hero tries to understand the injustice of the gods, man's inhumanity to man, and sometimes embarks on a journey leading to redemption, or self-knowledge. I am thinking of *Oedipus, Faust, Peer Gynt,* Beckett, and, particularly, of a pre-Shakespearian English variant, the morality-play concerned with man's moral education, such as *Magnificence* and *Everyman.*

In what I shall call 'the Oedipus-Everyman play' the hero is, characteristically, a sinner who becomes a thinker; in the course of the play he suffers rather than initiates action. (Goethe's Faust does not conform exactly; nor does *King Lear*—the greatest works of art inevitably burst the bonds of tradition.) Now, since the thrust of these plays is towards understanding, not action, we see that all the 'hanging around' in the middle scenes of *King Lear* is not due to carelessness after all; it is artfully contrived, to create opportunities for thinking, for intellectual discovery, the real business of the play.

> O, reason not the need! our basest beggars
> Are in the poorest thing superfluous.
> Allow not nature more than nature needs,
> Man's life is cheap as beast's.
>   (II.4.263)

Here, and in the many speeches about man and nature, and in all the 'mad scenes' (the mock trial, the speeches on female sexuality or the rascal beadle), Shakespeare could be said to 'slow down' the play, since the 'outer action' does not move forward; yet, as every theatre-goer instinctively feels, these speeches are not digressions but the very life-blood of the tragedy.

In *King Lear* this inner action competes with the outer one of domestic and political intrigue, and our attention is fixed more and more on mental events, Lear's state of mind and the 'visions' he sees and describes in those apocalyptic speeches—speeches that the other characters partly ignore, or dismiss as the ravings of a madman. It is all managed so naturally: for what do you do if you're a poor lost soul, rejected by the young and regarded as useless? You go around giving lectures—and those lectures, of course, are terribly exciting—to yourself—even if no one listens. Lear becomes a kind of lecturer, with urgent messages for the betterment of mankind, and he has to learn a discouraging lesson: a lecturer is a man who usually talks in someone else's sleep.

I have reached my first production-problem. It is a normal courtesy on-stage that when another actor addresses you, you pretend to listen; if your company's leading actor addresses you, you listen. *King Lear,* however, is different. After Lear has abdicated people pay less attention to him, a point immediately visualised in Act I scene 4, when the steward Oswald, crossing the stage, does not answer him properly. 'You, you, sirrah, where's my daughter?' In a hurry, Oswald slips past him, saying 'So please you—', and disappears, enraging the King. As Lear's rage gradually takes possession of him, others regard him less and less—rage, after all, is one way of demanding attention, and the king's rage mounts partly because he senses that others fail to listen. The producer's problem is that while the theatre-audience finds everything Lear says fascinating, the *dramatis personae* or 'stage-audience' in a sense lose interest in him. First Goneril and Regan treat his complaints as dotage, only half-attending to him; later, in the storm-scenes, his faithful attendants are anxious about his well-being without always heeding his rambling words. More and more, Lear turns into a man talking to himself. The common stage practice that the other actors 'freeze' attentively during Lear's great speeches is therefore, in my view, a mistake; indeed, it is arguable that those speeches will affect us more powerfully if in some cases—not all—the other characters pointedly busy themselves with other things (whispering privately, eating a sandwich) so that Lear's most passionate words fall on indifferent ears.

* * *

I want to pursue these introductory thoughts by looking more closely at some of the special features of *King Lear*. And, first, the storm-scenes. Now you may think that there is nothing very special about the storm in *King Lear*, except that it does not know where to stop. Are there not storms in *Julius Caesar* and *Othello*, thunder and lightning in *Macbeth*, not to mention *Pericles*, *The Winter's Tale*, *The Tempest*? You may say that dear old William simply enjoyed a good rumble. One might reply, more seriously, that no two things that look alike in Shakespeare are undifferentiated; the storm in *King Lear* differs in many important ways from those in other plays and, given some attention, leads to the very heart of this tragedy. It is not just that it continues through so many scenes, but that it seems to be intimately connected with Lear's mental and emotional states, the 'inner action'.

How and when does the storm begin? As Lear's 'rage' gathers within him it *suggests* a storm to his imagination:

> You nimble lightnings, dart your blinding flames
> Into her scornful eyes.
>   (II.4.163)

The first clear sign of a storm in the text comes more than a hundred lines later, when Cornwall says 'Let us withdraw; 'twill be a storm' (II.4.286);

editors normally insert a stage direction, '*Storm and tempest*', at about this point—misleadingly, I think, since "twill be a storm' only implies preliminary winds. Sometimes, though, producers call for preliminary noises somewhat earlier, making the storm gather momentum more gradually, and this can have a bearing on interpretation. For, if preliminary winds are audible before Lear addresses the 'nimble lightnings', the image comes to him quite naturally, triggered off by what he hears; on the other hand, if Lear's white-hot imagination thinks of 'nimble lightnings', and he then appeals to the gods—

> O heavens,
> If you do love old men, if your sweet sway
> Allow obedience, if you yourselves are old,
> Make it your cause; send down, and take my part!
> (II.4.188)

—and *then*, shortly after, the first rumblings are heard, something quite different is intimated; namely, that the storm is somehow connected with Lear's condition, or even comes in answer to his appeal. Notice that there are at least two possibilities; when the gods respond too unmistakably, as if answering on the telephone, the effect is not the same (there is a good example of this in *The Revenger's Tragedy*, V.3). Shakespeare, never committing his play to the view that the gods actually exist and hear our prayers, manages to suggest that, just possibly, the outer storm is *willed* by King Lear, is, so to say, an extension of his rage, an impression that is reinforced when Lear himself speaks in the same breath of 'this contentious storm' and 'this tempest in my mind' (III.4.6ff.), as if the two are connected.

I feel that it can be no accident that the storm is pretty well coextensive with Lear's madness—or rather, let us say, with his enraged madness. He is in *high rage* when the *high winds* begin to ruffle (II.4.295); later we hear of his *ungovern'd rage* (IV.4.18), and finally that his *great rage* is killed (IV.7.78). If, instead of talking of Lear's madness, we think of his madness as a great *rage*, as Shakespeare encourages us to do, we shall begin to understand the significance of the outer storm:

> Blow, winds, and crack your cheeks; *rage*, blow. . . .
> (III.2.1)

But, of course, when Shakespeare's imagination fastens on to a good multi-purpose symbol, there is no end to the different uses he may find for it. The storm in *King Lear* is connected with another highly original technique in the play, the way human beings talk past one another, as if insulated from one another—as if they cannot hear properly. I have already mentioned that other characters do not always listen to the king, when he loses his grip on things; the emphasis upon 'not hearing properly' is, however, much more pervasive. Cordelia seems unable to hear what her father tries to say to her in the 'love-test'; she shuts him out, mentally, very much as her sisters later shut the gates on him physically; Lear cannot hear what she and Kent say to him, and fails to hear the danger, the 'glib and oily art' (I.1.223), in Goneril and Regan's words. When the Fool appears, and Lear literally does not listen to him, his attention switching on and off, the play's concern with 'not hearing properly' is unmistakable; the climax comes in the encounters of Lear, the Fool and Poor Tom (III.4 and 6), where each of the three seems to speak from inside a private world. 'What, has his daughters brought him to this pass?'; 'Take heed o' th' foul fiend!' 'Prithee, nuncle, tell me whether a madman be a gentleman or a yeoman?' They all talk to themselves. During these scenes, the central storm-scenes, the speakers are further insulated from each other by the sheer noise of wind and thunder; each of them struggles, almost drowns, in a chaos of sound. A related technique is Shakespeare's use of disguise (a special feature of this tragedy, as I have already said): Kent and Edgar, disguised, may not utter their true feelings, cannot make themselves heard (hence the special use of asides in *King Lear*). The blinded Gloucester, groping on his own or clinging to Poor Tom, also exists in a self-enclosed world, and reinforces the play's emphasis upon individuals locked away from others. Not hearing and not seeing therefore have a similar function in *King Lear*.

Among other things, the storm-scenes press home the view that every man is an island. After the storm is over this view persists for a while, until Lear and Cordelia are reunited. When Lear and Gloucester meet in Act IV scene 6, each is still locked away in a private world, but the play prepares for the Lear–Cordelia scene by focusing on man's struggle to reach out to others. Having been totally self-absorbed, in his blindness, Gloucester now tries to 'get through' to Lear:

> I know that voice. . . .
> The trick of that voice I do well remember.
> Is't not the king? . . .
> O, let me kiss that hand!
>   (IV.6.95)

But Lear is almost unreachable, wrapped away in visions. And those visions, significantly, also dwell on man's inability to 'get through' to others.

When I do stare, see how the subject quakes....
Down from the waist they are centaurs....
Thou rascal beadle, hold thy bloody hand.
(108)

These visions are still generated by Lear's *great rage*, which began before the 'outer storm' and continues vibrating after it.

By the next scene (IV.7) the outer and the inner storm have passed away, and the king for the first time opens himself to human contact, for the first time genuinely *hears*. It is a gradual process, artfully prolonged by Shakespeare because it is the climactic 'recognition-scene', one of a series in which Lear grapples with the same problem, truly identifying other people—

So young and so untender?
(I.1.105, to Cordelia)

Your name, fair gentlewoman?
(I.4.235, to Goneril)

I'll talk a word with this same learned Theban
(III.4.153, of Poor Tom)

Ha! Goneril, with a white beard!
(IV.6.96, to Gloucester)

In these earlier attempts to identify others we are conscious of grotesque, almost wilful, misunderstanding—a habit that has not left him when he wakes from his sleep and identifies Cordelia as an angel ('Thou art a soul in bliss'—IV.7.46). But Lear's imperious need to impose false identities upon others, to make others conform to *his* view of the world, melts away in Cordelia's presence. Please observe that the scene requires several tensely expectant silences (and how much more effective they are after the earlier storm-scenes!), electrically charged silences during which we see the king reaching out to 'get through' to Cordelia, reaching out to understand the here and now. Superficially this 'recognition-scene' presents a father identifying his daughter; in addition, though, we sense that everything in the play climaxes here, as the old man struggles to identify and understand—Cordelia, love, forgiveness, the moral nature of the universe.

Methinks I should *know* you, and *know* this man;
Yet I am doubtful; for I am mainly ignorant

What place this is; and all the skill I have
Remembers not these garments; nor I *know* not
Where I did lodge last night. Do not laugh at me;
For, as I am a man, I *think* this lady
To be my child, Cordelia.
CORDELIA.
And so I am, I am!
LEAR.
Be your tears wet? Yes, faith. I pray, weep not;
If you have poison for me I will drink it.
(IV.7.64)

This is the most intimate human contact in the play, traditionally brought to its flash-point as the father touches his daughter's cheek, to make sure of her tears. The touch, first introduced by Garrick, is as implication-packed as Michelangelo's God the Father transmitting life to Adam—and yet I have seen this traditional stage-business improved. The actor of King Lear touched Cordelia's tears, and then, scarcely knowing what he was doing, put his finger to his mouth to taste their saltiness, another wonderfully suggestive moment. The tasting, it was later discovered, had been thought of before, by Henry Irving, but was not what the actor had been told to do in rehearsal: it came to him, instinctively, during performance, surprising him as much as the audience, and was felt to belong there, to be right. Why? Well, it reinforces Lear's wondering incredulity, his need to make absolutely certain that he is not dreaming (he sees, touches and tastes the tears); it gives a further hint of something dimly visible in Lear's faltering helplessness, that the old man becomes Cordelia's child (children suck their fingers); also, the tasting, a physical mingle, the finger between the lips, hints at sexual overtones, and adds to the mystery of the intimate contact here.

The storm, therefore, has an extraordinary number of interlocking functions, and, in addition, prepares for the 'resonant' silences of the Lear–Cordelia scene, where, again, so much is said *without words*. The 'outer' storm seems to emerge from Lear's 'inner' storm—or, perhaps, to be the response of sympathetic gods. It insulates Lear from human contact (others cannot hear him, he has to shout); indeed, from all contact (the thunder and the gods seem not to hear). It symbolises the chaos of the moral universe that Lear tries to understand. And of course it is a threatening physical presence, a major character in the play's central scenes—and, accordingly, its 'voice' must be as carefully controlled as that of any human character. How often, though, do producers 'block in' off-stage noises as meticulously as stage-movement, or the intonations of the human voice?

The storm in *King Lear* needs to be scored like music, with split-second timing for every thunder-clap, the storm-noise swallowing up only those spoken words that are of secondary importance. 'Rumble thy bellyful. Spit, fire; spout, rain' Lear cries to the elements (III.2.14), probably just after a rumbling thunder-blast—which, however, must not drown Lear's own poetry. Shakespeare therefore inserted the Fool's speech ('O nuncle, court holy water in a dry house is better than this rain-water ...'). The Fool's high-pitched voice can pierce through the sound of thunder more easily than the Lear-actor's baritone; and if we miss some of the Fool's wisdom it does not matter so much. I am not suggesting that every reference to thunder or wind synchronises exactly with what the audience hears, but only that it must sometimes be so, intimating a mysterious connection, not a cause-and-effect relationship; and, consequently, that every single sound-effect must be perfectly timed.

Having argued that the orchestration of the storm is so important, I had better confess that we do not know precisely how it was done. Modern producers, so much cleverer than the 'Elizabethans', may use recordings or electronic devices; not so long ago they would have called for the 'thunder-sheet', a sheet of metal that generates a prodigious noise, the sort of gadget every lecturer needs to wake up a drowsy audience. Who invented this delicate musical instrument, and when? The infallible *Oxford English Dictionary* tells us—very little. It does not record 'thunder-sheet', but mentions that in the late sixteenth century 'sheet' was used quasi-adjectivally, meaning 'rolled out in a sheet; especially of metals' (sb. 13). Perhaps then, just as Haydn's clock-symphony was inspired by the metronome, and the Pastoral Symphony by the cuckoo-clock, we owe the magnificent bravura of *King Lear* to the humble, newly invented thunder-sheet? But, as Dr Johnson said, of such idle fancies enough! Our only clear-cut evidence as to storms in Shakespeare's theatre occurs in the Prologue to *Every Man in his Humour:*

> Nor nimble squib is seen, to make afeard
> The gentlewomen; nor roll'd bullet heard
> To say, it thunders; nor tempestuous drum
> Rumbles, to tell you when the storm doth come.

Bullets (that is, cannon-balls) rolled in metal containers, explosive devices, kettle-drums (and probably other percussion instruments) were all available for stage-storms. The drums would be played by professional musicians; and other sound-effects, I believe, would be executed with equal precision. Professional actors who could perfectly imitate a cock-crow, as in *Hamlet*, will have known how to apply split-second timing to the storm in *King Lear*.

* * *

Recent critics have rightly emphasised the 'resonances' in *King Lear*—the play's meaningful repetitions and suggestiveness. Such resonances can be found in the other tragedies, but not as an end in themselves, displacing the outer action. In *King Lear* they often demand our chief attention, whereas in the other tragedies they support a story; and in this respect *King Lear* resembles the Last Plays, where symbolism and mythic resonances also compete with the 'story interest'. The storm in *King Lear*, indeed, has more in common with Prospero's tempest, which expresses his fury against those who have wronged him, than with any storm in the tragedies—for both Prospero's tempest and the storm in *King Lear* 'resonate' with implications that point beyond mere story.

Such comparisons are helpful because they can reveal what is unique in a play. 'Honour' and 'honourable' in *Julius Caesar* resemble the repeated 'honest' in *Othello*; once we identify a similarity, we quickly perceive how uniquely each word functions. Lear's waking up to the sound of music resembles a scene in *Pericles*, where Marina sings to her father, and he returns to life; in *Pericles*, however, the dramatic effect is thinner, the resonances being less potent. Let us look again at this climactic scene in *King Lear*, and try to understand the demands the play makes upon us, over and above its 'story interest'. Why is Lear's awakening so different from that of Pericles, despite the superficial similarities?

I have already suggested one reason for the special magic of Lear's slow awakening: the scene counterpoints the frantic bustle and noise of the storm-scenes. Another is that here for the first time the old king, who could not make others listen to him, has the total attention of Cordelia, who hangs breathlessly on his every word—so that every word becomes precious, a jewel tremulously offered to an angel.

> You do me wrong to take me out o'th' grave.
> Thou art a soul in bliss; but I am bound
> Upon a wheel of fire. . . .
>   (IV.7.45)

'You do me wrong' had been Lear's refrain to all three daughters, to the gods, the storm, the world; now this 'resonating' thought swims to the surface again. The effect depends partly on our awareness that, while Lear's tone has changed, deep down he remains the man he was.

> I know you do not love me; for your sisters
> Have, as I do remember, done me wrong:

You have some cause, they have not.
    (73)

He remains the man he was, for 'I know you do not love me' makes the same pathetic appeal as the love-test—'say you love me!'

Lear's madness gives Shakespeare many opportunities for meaningful repetition, particularly in Lear's fixed ideas. Repetition being so important where Lear's own thoughts and actions are concerned, we see that Shakespeare's decision to echo the main plot in the sub-plot could not have been taken lightly—for it makes 'resonance' a life-principle of the play. Two fathers and their children, nature, ingratitude, patience, blindness in the main plot and sub-plot: it is almost too obvious. And most readers see that Shakespeare connects the two plots at the outset: 'Nothing, my lord.—Nothing!—Nothing.—Nothing will come of nothing. Speak again' (I.1.86). 'Nothing, my lord.—... The quality of nothing hath not such need to hide itself.... Come, if it be nothing, I shall not need spectacles' (I.2.31). Not everyone realises, though, that the mysterious connection established here between the two plots resembles others that follow, such as the undefined connection between Lear and the storm.

The interconnections of the two plots are infinitely suggestive—let me give another example from Lear's reunion with Cordelia. Lear at first thinks that he wakes up in the other world, and only gradually accepts that he is still alive. In the previous scene Gloucester steels himself for death, leaps, as he thinks, from Dover cliff, and also has to be painfully persuaded by his own child that he is still alive. Both men, to adapt Keats's phrase, 'die into life'; as they cross-question their child and learn what has happened, each finds himself in the same predicament, in the same kind of 'recognition-scene'. Gloucester and Lear both have to 'recognise themselves'—that is the whole point of the Oedipus-Everyman play, understanding oneself being the most difficult part of 'understanding the universe'. We should be reminded, as Lear grapples with the problem and kneels to Cordelia, of his earlier mock-kneeling to Goneril—

'Dear daughter, I confess that I am old;
Age is unnecessary; on my knees I beg
That you'll vouchsafe me raiment, bed, and food.'
    (II.4.152)

But when Lear kneels to Cordelia, theatre-goers should perhaps be reminded of another 'resonance', Gloucester's kneeling to Edgar.

Here is another production-problem. *Should* Gloucester kneel to Edgar? After his 'death-leap' Gloucester does not stand on his feet until twenty-five lines of dialogue have passed (Shakespeare takes some trouble to pin-point the exact moment when he rises, in Edgar's speech. 'Give me your arm. / Up—so. How is't? Feel you your legs? You stand.') Should Gloucester simply lie there, like a dying animal, for twenty-five lines? I believe that it would be natural for Gloucester to struggle first of all into a kneeling position, before he stands up, and that Edgar hovers breathlessly above him, exactly anticipating Lear and Cordelia in the next scene—a tableau that makes its point in an instant: the father kneels, the son stands.

Producers, I have to admit, do not always allow Lear to kneel to Cordelia, perhaps because she does not want him to—but can Cordelia know what he so strangely intends, until he is actually on his knees? It seems to me psychologically right that the king, who had refused to kneel to Goneril, now kneels before Cordelia, and symbolically right that, just as Gloucester is taught by Edgar, Lear learns to 'know himself' mothered by his child.

> CORDELIA.
> No, sir, you must not kneel.
> LEAR.
> Pray, do not mock me:
> I am a very foolish fond old man,
> Fourscore and upward, not an hour more nor less;
> And, to deal plainly,
> I fear I am not in my perfect mind.
> (IV.7.59)[3]

The resonances in *King Lear* add to the play's suggestive uncertainties in plot and theme echoes that are deliberately left undefined. It is a characteristic Shakespearian touch that we are not told why the king kneels. Could it be that he simply imitates Cordelia, who has just knelt for his blessing? Or that he wants to ask for her pardon? If the latter, he only says so in his exit-line, almost an afterthought. 'Pray you now, forget and forgive; I am old and foolish.' Between his awakening and his kneel, he seems disoriented—and exactly how much he understands is not clear. Because we are uncertain about his mental state, the effect is all the more wonderful when at last he does understand.

> Pray, do not mock me:
> I am a very foolish fond old man.

It may be that this *understanding* brings him to his knees—the sacramental moment when he finally recognises Cordelia and, in the same instant, the immensity of all that he has done.

I have emphasised the difficulties we have in following Lear's mental processes (they begin before his madness, in the love-test scene, and continue to the very end of the play); and similar difficulties are multiplied by the 'resonances' of the two plots, and by other repetitions that manifestly demand our attention, pulling us away from the 'outer story'. Another trick of the play with a similar effect is its habit of bringing the story close to folk-tale, myth, parable or emblem, without ever superimposing this other image exactly upon the play's realism (as happens when Hamlet meditates with Yorick's skull in his hand, that familiar emblem of the melancholy man). In *King Lear* we are frequently reminded of emblems and the like, but the 'story' and this other image come uneasily together, so that we cannot be sure of our bearings. Producers who strongly suggest, at the beginning, that *King Lear* is to be the story of Cinderella and her two ugly sisters deprive the play of some of its magic, for it works at least as well when Goneril and Regan are glitteringly beautiful; and perhaps the 'other image' here should remind us, though not too obviously, of the judgement of Paris, and of the three goddesses who bid for his favour. At the other end of the play, when Lear cradles the dead Cordelia in his arms, Shakespeare creates a tableau very like a *pietà*, even though he stops short of identifying Cordelia as a 'Christ figure'. An emblem recommending *patience* in the *storms* and *tempests* of life also has its relevance, as has one that claims that 'the wealth of the tyrant is the poverty of his subjects', which reminds me of Lear's prayer for 'Poor naked wretches' (III.4.28ff.). Shakespeare's poetry, however, transcends all such two-dimensional emblems.

The critic who has done more than anyone else to explain the resonances of *King Lear*, Maynard Mack, has not I think gone far enough in writing of the play's distinctive 'combination of parable and parable situations with acute realism'.[4] As I have tried to argue, *King Lear* pulls away from 'acute realism' at many points, and for this and other reasons differs so profoundly from *Hamlet*, *Othello* and *Macbeth*. When Gloucester bids farewell to Edgar and casts himself down, as he thinks, from Dover cliff, producers who are unwilling to disengage from realism meet their nemesis. How far, they wonder, should Gloucester fall to make the leap 'realistic' and convincing? Should the blind man inch to the edge of an overhang, and fall down two or three feet into a conveniently placed sand-pit? Marvin Rosenberg rightly rejects 'an actual fall from some height', and also another 'realistic' expedient. 'Theatre Edgars', he tells us, 'have sometimes circled to catch Gloster as he falls, to make clear to audiences that the scenery described is wholly illusory.'[5] Gloucester's leap is, surely, as decisive a moment in the play as is the statue that stirs and breathes at the end of *The Winter's Tale*; when Gloucester so improbably thumps down on the stage, like a sack of coal, an instantaneous physical impact, and Edgar persuades him that he fell like 'gossamer, feathers, air', we are at the farthest possible remove from acute realism, and can only explain what we see as a wonder, exactly as Shakespeare asks us to understand the awakening of Pericles, and the return to life of the statue in *The Winter's Tale*. Gloucester and Lear think themselves dead, and then are miraculously reborn.

The 'rebirth' of Gloucester and Lear creates two more production-problems that are related. Those who know the story *expect* Gloucester to rise and Lear to wake up cured; Shakespeare, however, asks us to be prepared for other possibilities. Gloucester's leap, though not in fact from Dover cliff, may still destroy him with shock, as Edgar acknowledges—

> I know not how conceit may rob The treasury of life. . . .
>   (IV.6.42)

When Edgar asks 'Alive or dead?' the answer should not be a foregone conclusion. Similarly, there are several warnings that Lear maybe permanently deranged (III.6.97ff.; IV.4.11ff.) if 'repose' is withheld; he continues to wander without repose, and at the end of Act IV scene 6 we are told, with seeming finality, 'The King is mad.' Lear's coma-like sleep, his slow awakening and initial confusion, all point forward to the possibility that he may not be cured after all, despite the doctor's hopeful reassurances. Shakespeare wants us to believe that Gloucester may be dead after his leap, and that Lear may be incurably mad—because the magic of their 'rebirth' is so important to the play.

And of course their rebirth is intimately connected with Lear's last entry—'*Enter Lear, with Cordelia dead in his arms.*' So we read it in just about every modern text, although the Quarto and Folio stage-direction, '*Enter Lear, with Cordelia in his arms*', by no means assures us that she is dead; on the contrary, it leaves open the possibility of another return to life—a miracle we long for with Lear, just as in *The Winter's Tale* we identify with Leontes' yearning that the statue should move, and live. This possibility has been prepared for by the 'rebirth' of Gloucester and Lear in Act IV, and by the repentance of Edmund, another miraculous 'rebirth':

> I pant for life. Some good I mean to do,
> Despite of mine own nature.
>   (V.3.242)

These 'resonances' suggest that in the world of *King Lear* miracles are possible, and that Cordelia may after all be saved in time. Yet in all the productions that I have seen one felt that Albany, Kent and Edgar had enjoyed the doubtful privilege of learning their parts from a modern text; they accepted that Lear enters with Cordelia *'dead in his arms'*, and displayed little interest in what they took to be a corpse.

Let us examine the credentials of this stage-direction, which so crucially influences our reading of Shakespeare's most powerful tragic ending. The word 'dead' was first inserted by Nicholas Rowe in 1709 (i.e. *'Enter Lear, with Cordelia* dead *in his arms'*); and Rowe could not have followed a stage-tradition here, since Tate's adaptation was the only version of the play acted in the theatre from 1681, and in Tate's version Cordelia did not die. In 1681 Rowe was only seven years old—so his stage-direction, *'Cordelia* dead *in his arms'*, can only be a guess, and, like some of Rowe's other editorial decisions, may be a bad guess. It has no textual authority whatsoever.

Could it be that when one actor carries on another 'in his arms' the second one must be presumed dead? Certainly not. In *Titus Andronicus* Aaron enters *'with his child in his arms'* (V.I.19), and the child is alive. A stage-direction in *Cymbeline* (IV. 2.196) is even more revealing: *'Enter Aruiragus, with Imogen dead, bearing her in his Armes'* (Folio). Imogen only seems to be dead at this point, and Cordelia, who is not described as dead in the Quarto or Folio, may equally be alive when Lear carries her on *'in his arms'*. Since the familiar stage-direction, *'with Cordelia dead in his arms'*, has absolutely no authority, let us consider the alternative. I do not wish to propose that Shakespeare merely copied the master-stroke from his previous tragedy, *Othello*, where Desdemona, seemingly dead, revives, speaks a few broken words, and then really dies. Shakespeare never repeated himself so obviously, and Cordelia is not asked to 'do a Desdemona'. If Cordelia returns to consciousness and then dies, as I would suggest, the final twist of the knife is that she is unable to speak. (Lear found her 'hanging'; perhaps her neck is broken.) She opens her eyes; now it is the father who hangs breathlessly over his child. She wants to speak, but the words do not come; father and daughter are locked together in a look—again, so much has to be said *without words*; again, as Lear gazes into his dying daughter's eyes, the mystery of the universe, the need to *understand*.

Could it be done in the theatre? An eye-witness of a production of *Othello*, in 1610, wrote in Latin that 'Desdemona, killed by her husband, although she always acted her part excellently, moved us still more in her death; when lying in her bed she invoked the pity of the spectators merely by her facial expression.'[6] The boy-actor's speaking look, just before death, could evidently hold the audience spell-bound; and that audience, of course, was more familiar than we are with public executions and would know that criminals were frequently taken down from the gallows alive—were hung, drawn and quartered alive—and therefore would not assume automatically that Cordelia must be dead when Lear enters *'with Cordelia in his arms'*.

This, then, is a very different way of explaining the tragic ending. It has exactly the same authority as Rowe's guess that Cordelia is already dead—neither more, nor less—but in my opinion it has some intrinsic advantages. It recapitulates the father's and daughter's earlier attempts to 'get through' to one another, and repeats the tragic message that we are all 'locked away' within ourselves. It could be seen as the climax of this 'Oedipus-Everyman play', the tragic hero's last opportunity to understand, a 'resonance' that sums up all that has gone before. Indeed, the interpretation of *King Lear* that I have proposed, emphasising the mystery of the storm, the mysterious interconnections of the two plots, and a tragic hero who exists not to 'initiate action' but to understand, leads quite naturally to this ending—a silent communion, appropriate in a play that reaches beyond words for so many of its finest effects.

And how relevant are these speculations to the production of *King Lear* that we all look forward to this evening? I hope that I have convinced you that it is our duty to look beyond the story. *King Lear* differs so markedly from the other tragedies because Shakespeare is here less concerned with an exciting 'outer action' than with intellectual and emotional insight: and of course not only the tragic hero but also the audience is asked to understand, and to wrestle with mysteries. I realise that a lecturer cannot hope to convince his listeners in every detail—but, if some seemingly dead Cordelias in this audience would now miraculously open their eyes, I would find that very encouraging.[7]

NOTES

1. Bradley, *Shakespearean Tragedy*, p. 53.

2. For example Susan Snyder, *The Comic Matrix of Shakespeare's Tragedies* (1977).

3. I assume that Cordelia rises when Lear kneels, and tries to help him to his feet.

4. Maynard Mack, *King Lear in our Time* (1966) p. 56.

5. Marvin Rosenberg, *The Masks of King Lear* (1972) pp. 264–5.

6. See G. Tillotson, *Essays in Criticism and Research* (Cambridge, 1942) pp. 41–5.

7. In this chapter I am indebted to T. W. Craik's discussion of the 'entry of Lear carrying Cordelia's inert body' in 'I know when one is dead . . . ' (British Academy Shakespeare Lecture, 1979, in the Academy's *Proceedings*, vol. lxv).

ARTHUR KIRSCH

"For He Was Great of Heart"

In his account of a performance of *Macbeth* at the Globe in 1611, the Elizabethan astrologer and playgoer Simon Forman focused on the action, its high moments as well as its subtle causations. But what he seems to have remembered most vividly (he gives it his longest description) is Macbeth's reaction to Banquo's ghost in the banquet scene. In treating this moment in the play, he comments not only upon the event and its place in the evolving action, but upon Macbeth's state of mind. He writes that when Macbeth "sawe the goste of banco, which fronted him so," he "fell into a great passion of fear and fury."[1] The phrase speaks clearly enough across the centuries—as indicative a stage direction for the actor now as it would have been then—and it discriminates the emotional keynote of Macbeth's whole characterization: not just its particularity, its peculiar conjunction of hesitancy and rashness, dread and anger, but equally important its magnitude, what Forman calls its greatness.

Forman's term at the same time has specifically Elizabethan connotations. For the majority of Renaissance moral philosophers, as for earlier Christian and classical writers, the passions, "the passions of the mind" as they were called, comprehended the whole spectrum of human emotions, including the realm of the imagination. The concupiscible "power" of the soul, which moves it to "follow that which the Soule thinketh to be good for it,

---

From *The Passions of Shakespeare's Tragic Heroes*, pp. 1–20, 147–48. © 1990 by the Rector and Visitors of the University of Virginia.

or to flie that which it takes to be evill," was considered to spawn three pairs of contrary passions—love and hatred, desire and aversion, joy and sadness.[2] The irascible power of the soul, which tries to overcome impediments to the operation of the concupiscible power was also considered to generate three groups of passions—hope and despair, fear and daring, and anger, whose contrary was not a passion of the "sensitive" part of the soul, but belonged rather to what Prospero, when he resolves in *The Tempest* to forgive his enemies, calls the "nobler reason" (5.1.26).[3]

In this ancient schema, the passions did not usually emerge as subjects of approval. Human passions, and especially the kind of inordinate passion Forman seems to note with wonder in Macbeth, were considered perturbations in the Renaissance, ultimately expressions of "the infected root of originall sinne," the imperfection in man's nature that both caused the Fall and constituted his state forever after it.[4] Pierre de La Primaudaye's *The French Academie*, an extensive and well-known treatise of moral psychology first translated into English in 1586, offers a typical homiletic elucidation of these assumptions:

> THE PHILOSOPHERS teach us by their writings; and experience doth better shew it unto us, that to covet and desire is proper to the soule, and that from thence all the affections and desires of men proceede, which draw them hither and thither diversly, that they may attaine to that thing, which they thinke is able to leade them to the enjoying of some good, whereby they may live a contented and happie life. Which felicitie, the most part of men, through a false opinion, or ignorance rather of that which is good, and by following the inclination of their corrupted nature, do seeke and labor to find in humane and earthlie things, as in riches, glorie, honor, and pleasure. But forasmuch as the enjoying of these things doth not bring with it sufficient cause of contentation, they perceive themselves alwaies deprived of the end of their desires, and are constrained to wander all their life time beyond all bounds and measure, according to the rashnes and inconstancie of their lusts. And although they rejoice for a little while at everie new change, yet presently they loath the selfesame thing, which not long before they earnestly desired. Their owne estate alwaies seemeth unto them to be woorst, and everie present condition of life, to be burdensome. From one estate they seeke after another.[5]

La Primaudaye's assumptions are traditionally Christian and moralistic, and his ensuing accounts of the various passions, like those of many of his contemporaries, are often conventional. But if the observations are not originally his, they are not therefore uninteresting or unobservant. Most of what he and his contemporaries have to say about human nature and behavior is true, and their anatomies, if not always valuations, of human emotions inform the unsurpassed psychological sophistication of a writer like Montaigne, upon whom some of the later French moral commentators themselves drew.[6] They also inform the representation of human feeling and behavior in Shakespearian drama.

The biblical sense of the mutability and vanity, as well as force, of human passion, of which La Primaudaye speaks, for example, is endemic and deep in Shakespeare's plays. In the come dies, from the earlier romantic comedies, through the problem plays to the final romances, the attitude toward passion is cautionary, and the goal of the action tends to be the achievement of temperance. In *The Merchant of Venice*, for example, Portia actually schools her passion for Bassanio as he prepares to choose the lead casket:

> How all the other passions fleet to air,
> As doubtful thoughts, and rash-embraced despair,
> And shudd'ring fear, and green-eyed jealousy.
> O love, be moderate! Allay thy ecstasy.
> In measure rain thy joy; scant this excess.
> I feel too much thy blessing: make it less,
> For fear I surfeit.
>   (3.2.108–14)

Claudio expresses a similar attitude, in a harsher key, in an astringent speech in *Measure for Measure*:

> As surfeit is the father of much fast,
> So every scope, by the immoderate use,
> Turns to restraint. Our natures do pursue,
> Like rats that raven down their proper bane,
> A thirsty evil; and when we drink, we die.
>   (1.2.118–22)

He is referring to sexual passion, the play's particular preoccupation, but the lines have a resonance that subsumes the entire tragicomic texture of the problem comedy. The same motif of temperance informs the emotional, if not spiritual, movement of the last plays, where potentially tragic passions, though often enacted, are comically depleted or tempered. The murderous lust that lies behind Posthumus's jealousy in *Cymbeline*, for example, is purged by being acted out and displaced onto his farcically grotesque double, Cloten.[7] In *The Tempest* a portion of Prospero's anger is acted out in the imaginary ordeals of the court party and the physical punishment of Stephano, Trinculo, and Caliban, but not the whole of it, and the sea change that he and other characters "suffer" (1.2.404) is more difficult and complex. Prospero says to Ariel, who has been moved by the distress of Prospero's kinsmen:

> Hast thou, which art but air, a touch, a feeling
> Of their afflictions, and shall not myself,
> One of their kind, that relish all as sharply
> Passion as they, be kindlier mov'd than thou art?
> Though with their high wrongs I am struck to th' quick,
> Yet with my nobler reason 'gainst my fury
> Do I take part. The rarer action is
> In virtue than in vengeance.
> (5.1.21–28)

A large measure of the Renaissance psychology of the passions lies behind Prospero's resolution of his anger and desire for revenge, and as the source of these lines in Montaigne's essay "Of Cruelty" unequivocally confirms[8] his action is rare not because he transcends his fury and forgives his enemies out of goodness, which is an attribute of God, but because his human virtue enables him to work through and temper his passion. The incipient passion that marks Prospero's characterization for most of the play—his continuously "beating mind," his irascibility not only with Caliban but with Ferdinand and Ariel and even Miranda—authenticates this achievement of temperance and forgiveness rather than questions or devalues it.

Similar attitudes toward temperance and the passions are expressed in the tragedies. When Romeo, as he anticipates his marriage with Juliet, tells the Friar:

> But come what sorrow can,
> It cannot countervail the exchange of joy
> That one short minute gives me in her sight.
> Do thou but close our hands with holy words,
> Then love-devouring death do what he dare—
> It is enough I may but call her mine;

the Friar answers:

These violent delights have violent ends,
And in their triumph die like fire and powder,
Which as they kiss consume. The sweetest honey
Is loathsome in his own deliciousness,
And in the taste confounds the appetite.
Therefore love moderately. Long love doth so.
Too swift arrives as tardy as too slow.
    (2.5.3–15)

At the center of *Hamlet*, in language that resembles the Friar's, the Player King says:

What to ourselves in passion we propose,
The passion ending, doth the purpose lose.
The violence of either grief or joy
Their own enactures with themselves destroy.
    (3.2.185–88)

Hamlet himself explicitly endorses these ideas. He tells Horatio that he has chosen him as a friend, because

                thou hast been
As one in suffering all that suffers nothing,
A man that Fortune's buffets and rewards
Hath ta'en with equal thanks; and blest are those
Whose blood and judgment are so well commingled
That they are not a pipe for Fortune's finger
To sound what stop she please. Give me that man
That is not passion's slave, and I will wear him
In my heart's core, ay, in my heart of heart,
As I do thee.
    (3.2.63–72)

These sentiments, however, have a much different perspective in Shakespeare's tragedies than they do in his comedies and romances. The Friar may be correct, and Horatio may be a Renaissance model as well as Hamlet's, but neither can be mistaken for a tragic hero. In the "intensification of the life they share with others," as A. C. Bradley observed, it is precisely intemperance, the "marked one-sidedness," the identification of "the whole being" with one passion, that most characterizes the heroes in Shakespeare's tragedies.[9] The blaze of erotic passion, initially perhaps partly funny but eventually almost intrusively grave, is what defines Romeo and Juliet as moving tragic figures, and the vulnerability to passion and suffering is what distinguishes Hamlet as a tragic hero and compels our own deepest imaginative sympathies. As A. O. Rossiter remarked in an excellent and neglected essay, "Shakespeare's conception of tragedy plainly and constantly concerns the man who is 'passion's slave'."[10] All the heroes of Shakespeare's tragedies—and especially those of the four titanic plays *Hamlet, Othello, Macbeth,* and *King Lear*—suffer to the heart's core and suffer everything in suffering all. "Suffering," as Rossiter says, "beyond solace, beyond any moral palliation, and suffering because of a human greatness which is great because great in passion: that, above everything else, is central to Shakespeare's tragic conception."[11]

The heart was generally considered to be the seat of the passions in the Renaissance, and the passionate movement of the heart is at the center of all four of the great tragedies. Hamlet, for example, is probably most often admired for his intellectual energy, for the copiousness and eloquence of his thoughts. But we have to remember, as Hamlet is always compelled to remember, that behind these thoughts, and usually their occasion, is a continuous and tremendous experience of pain and suffering. As he himself tells us, it is his heart that he unpacks with words; it is against what he calls the "heartache" (3.1.64) of human existence that he protests in his most famous soliloquy (and this is the first use of the term in that sense the *OED* records); and it is the heart's core, the heart of heart, of which he is always conscious. Hamlet's "noble heart" is what the temperate Horatio first pays tribute to at the moment of his death (5.2.312), and in an almost literal sense the "heart of [his] mystery" (3.2.353–54) is what we ourselves are most interested in.

Othello also, and obviously, is permeated by the language of the heart. Brabantio dies of his "bruised heart" (1.3.218); Emilia says her heart is "full" (5.2.182) just before her own death, when she turns against Iago; and Iago himself, interestingly, talks repeatedly of the heart he hides. Desdemona is presented from first to last in the play as a woman of steadfast and loving heart: "My heart's subdued / Even to the very quality of my lord" (1.3.250–51). Othello himself, finally, is always defined by his heart, in his rage and eventual despair, as well as in his love. He draws from Desdemona the "prayer of earnest heart" to tell the story that initiates their courtship (1.3.151); at the apogee of their reunion on the shores of Cyprus, he says, "And this, (*they kiss*), and this, the greatest discords be / That e'er our hearts shall make" (2.1.199–200); and it is because he has so completely, as he says, "garnered up my heart" (4.2.59) in Desdemona that his collapse is intelligible as well as appalling. He says during that collapse that his "heart is turned to stone" (4.1.178–79), but though that may be his wish it is never his achievement, which is what gives stature to him even in his savagery. When he commits suicide, Cassio's epitaph is proper: "This did I fear, but thought he had no weapon, / For he was great of heart" (5.2.370–71).

Macbeth, as we have seen, is especially remembered by Forman for his "great passion" and passions of the heart (and their cauterization) mark the whole course of his tragic career, as well as of Lady Macbeth's. At first apparently immune to feelings, by the time of the sleepwalking scene Lady Macbeth's heart has become "sorely charged" by them: "I would not have such a heart in my bosom," her attendant says, "for the dignity of the whole body" (5.1.51–53). Macbeth's tragedy begins when his "seated heart knock[s] at [his] ribs" (1.3.135). The famous literal knocking at the gates after the murder of Duncan is in part a reverberation of that state of emotion, and Macbeth's tragic career is punctuated by references to the heart. When he resolves to murder Macduff's family, he says, "The very firstlings of my heart shall be / The firstlings of my hand" (4.1.163–64), a statement, as we shall see, that has particular and extraordinary force in the play, and at the end he tells Seyton, what is once again literalized in the state of Scotland, that he is "sick at heart" (5.3.21). Scotland's recovery from that sickness is significantly heralded by Macduff's feeling for the loss of his family, a feeling that Malcolm successfully, if also callowly, urges Macduff to convert to rage: "Let grief / Convert to anger: blunt not the heart, enrage it" (4.3.230–31).

Finally, the word *heart* itself resonates in *King Lear*, describing the extremes of the play's characterizations, from the "honest-hearted" Kent (1.4.19) to the "marble-hearted" ingratitude and "hard-hearts" of Goneril and Regan (1.4.237; 3.6.36).[12] "Heart" is the metonym for Lear himself in the storm—"poor old heart, he holp the heavens to rain" (3.7.60)—and it is the primary register of Lear's experience. He rejects Cordelia because she cannot heave her "heart" into her "mouth" (1.1.92) and he pronounces her banishment as the divorce of her heart from his own: "So be my grave my peace as here I give / Her father's heart from her" (1.1.125–26), an uncanny line that predicates his eventual reunion with her in death. The heart is physically palpable to Lear. He says he is "struck ... upon the very heart" by Goneril's "tongue" (2.2.333–34), and the same tactile sense of the heart emerges in the synapse between physical and emotional pain that prompts the first movement of fellow feeling in him:

> My wits begin to turn.
> (*To Fool*) Come on, my boy. How dost, my boy? Art cold?
> I am cold myself. . . .
> Poor fool and knave, I have one part in my heart
> That's sorry yet for thee.
>   (3.2.67–69, 72–73)

As Lear moves toward madness, he recognizes that his rage against Cordelia drew from his "heart all love" and "wrenched" his "frame of nature / From the fixed place" (1.4.247–48); he then repeatedly identifies his incipient madness with his heart: "O, how this mother swells up toward my heart! / *Histerica passio* down, thou climbing sorrow" (2.2.231–32); "O me, my heart! My rising heart! But down" (2.2.292); "But this heart shall break into a hundred thousand flaws / Or ere I'll weep" (2.2.458–59). The breaking of the heart "into a hundred thousand flaws" defines the point toward which most references to the heart in *Lear* eventually move, and as we shall see, it suggests the extremity of pain and suffering that is the play's peculiar concern, most particularly in its depiction of Lear's relation to the faithful and loving daughter whose very name is the heart.

Richard Burbage, the premier actor of Shakespeare's company, was praised in a contemporary elegy for his capacity to become the characters he played, and the elegist singled out his sympathetic portrayals of "kind Leer," the "greved Moor," and the "sadd lover" Hamlet.[13] These descriptions, like many others in theatrical criticism of the time, suggest the essential propriety of sympathizing, if not identifying, with the passions and suffering of Shakespeare's heroes. As A. C. Bradley wrote, "We might not object to the statement that Lear deserved to suffer for his folly, selfishness and tyranny, but to assert that he deserved to suffer what he did suffer is to do violence to any healthy moral sense." "Our everyday legal and moral notions" "of justice and desert" are "in *all* cases, even those of Richard III and of Macbeth and Lady Macbeth, untrue to our imaginative experience. When we are immersed in a tragedy, we feel towards dispositions, actions, and persons such emotions as attraction and repulsion, pity, wonder, fear, horror, perhaps hatred; but we do not *judge*." "We watch what is," Bradley continued, "seeing that so it happened, and must have happened, feeling that it is piteous, dreadful, awful, mysterious, but neither passing sentence on the agents, nor asking whether the behaviour of the ultimate power towards them is just. And, therefore, the use of such language in attempts to render our imaginative experience in terms of the understanding is, to say the least, full of danger."[14]

Since Renaissance moral (as opposed to theatrical) commentators on the passions do habitually use such language and do habitually judge, Bradley's remarks suggest the need to separate their analyses of passion and suffering from their homiletic judgments of them. Lily B. Campbell's important early study, *Shakespeare's Tragic Heroes: Slaves of Passion* suffers from the failure to make this distinction.[15] In his comedies as well as his tragedies Shakespeare's representation of human experience is always multivalent. The same Friar who chastises the excess of Romeo's passion for Juliet remarks that

The earth, that's nature's mother, is her tomb.
What is her burying grave, that is her womb,
And from her womb children of divers kind
We sucking on her natural bosom find,
Many for many virtues excellent,
None but for some, and yet all different.
O mickle is the powerful grace that lies
In plants, herbs, stones, and their true qualities,
For naught so vile that on the earth doth live
But to the earth some special good doth give;
Nor aught so good but, strained from that fair use,
Revolts from true birth, stumbling on abuse.
Virtue itself turns vice being misapplied,
And vice sometime's by action dignified.
　　(2.2.9–22)

Perhaps no other Renaissance writer, with the exception of Montaigne, expresses so catholic an understanding of human behavior, and in approaching his tragedies it is better to err on the side of Bradley's biases than those of the Renaissance moralists.

It is best of all, however, to try to achieve a balance. As William Empson pointed out, the distinction of Elizabethan drama, and Shakespeare's preeminently, is its combination of sympathy and judgment, engagement and detachment."[16] The differing emotions that Bradley says we feel toward the hero are a result of a constant interplay of empathy and judgment in our responses to him, and the disengaging paradoxes of the Friar's statement rest, of course, upon a foundation of normative moral expectations. Though passions can indeed be said to "spin the plot" of Shakespearean tragedy, as the Victorians thought, Shakespeare does not sentimentalize the passions, still less glamorize them. There is a pervasive counterpoint of irony in all of Shakespeare's representations of his tragic heroes, which the morally clinical Renaissance anatomies of the passions simply make explicit. This irony is in a large sense "comic" but it only exacerbates the passions of the heroes. For Shakespeare's heroes not only are obviously subject to the evanescence of human passion, but they also consciously protest against it, and that consciousness and ultimately unavailing protest constitute a substantial part of their suffering. One can reasonably imagine that Hamlet himself, for example, may have written the Player King's lines, but in any case their truth is a continuous torment to him (as well as, interestingly, to the Ghost, who is clearly more disturbed by the inconstancy of Gertrude than by the usurpation of his crown). Hamlet's

exclamation "frailty, thy name is woman" (1.2.146) is a specific indictment
of his mother's hasty remarriage, but it is at the same time an outcry against
the mutability and decay of human affection of which her action is only an
example, a condition of life that he cannot bring himself to accept until very
near the end of the play and of his own life. And the experience of such decay,
as we shall see, informs his relations to Ophelia and Rosencrantz and Guildenstern as well.

Othello too protests against the limits and impermanence of affections,
and his protest is no less powerful because it is based on a partially self-cre-
ated delusion. It is in fact more powerful and more painful because Desdemona's love, like that of the heroines in the romances, offers the promise of
the transcendence of the mutability of passion that tragedy usually does not
provide or provides only in death. The sources of Othello's decomposition are
manifold, but not the least important is the boundlessness of his love. His
claim that he loved Desdemona "too well" (5.2.353) may be partly self-justifi-
cation, but it is also true, and it accounts for why the thought of her mutability becomes so destructive. There are, no doubt, other and more sensible ways
of dealing with a wife whom one thinks is unfaithful, but Othello's, though
horrifying, is proper to his tragedy and a function of his heroism. Othello says
of Desdemona,

> Perdition catch my soul
> But I do love thee! And when I love thee not,
> Chaos is come again.
> (3.3.92–94)

Such chaos does come in no small measure because of the vicissitudes of
Othello's own emotional life, but it comes also, as we shall see, because such
vicissitudes, a condition of adult existence, are those which, in his idealism
and absoluteness, he tries to transcend.

The same is true of Macbeth, though with a different inflection. Both he
and Lady Macbeth directly endure the emptiness of passion, "where," as Lady
Macbeth remarks, "our desire is got without content" (3.2.7), and that motif, a
favorite of the homilists, is enacted over and over again in *Macbeth*, including
in the Porter's speech about drink, which "provokes the desire but . . . takes
away the performance" (2.3.26–29). But the experience of the insatiability
of desire is exponentially acute in Macbeth, as we shall see, because it is the
very gap between the consciousness of desire and its achievement, again a
condition of human existence, against which Macbeth sets himself and which
makes him actually wish for death. "Better be with the dead," he says soon
after killing Duncan and becoming king,

Whom we to gain our peace have sent to peace,
Than on the torture of the mind to lie
In restless ecstasy.
    (3.2.21–24)

The lines are an epigraph to his whole tragic career.

The suffering caused by the consciousness of the mutability of passion, finally, is everywhere evident in *Lear*. It virtually defines all those who are good in the play, and it is the substance of the experience of Lear and Gloucester, both of whom suffer the betrayal of their children but are most tormented by the consciousness of the mutability and limits of their own affections. Gloucester is literally blinded by the appetite that created Edmond, but his heart is said to burst at his death, "twixt two extremes of passion, joy and grief" (5.3.190) in his reunion with Edgar, the son whom he loves and whom he denied. Lear, similarly is enraged by the ingratitude of Goneril and Regan, by the question that echoes through the play: "Is there any cause in nature that makes these hard-hearts?" (3.6.35–36); but he is actually driven mad, as the Fool makes searingly clear, by his consciousness of his denial of his own love for Cordelia, and his reunion with her in death is coordinate with the breaking of his heart as well.

Lear's agony especially crystallizes the peculiarly tragic power of the representation of the passions in all the tragedies, because behind the suffering consciousness of all Shakespeare's tragic heroes is a protest against the reality of which the frailty and decay of human passion is itself an image, the reality of human mortality. As Northrop Frye has said, "The basis of the tragic vision is being in time" in which "death is, not an incident in life, not even the inevitable end of life, but the essential event that gives shape and form to life." This ironic apprehension, he argues, is complemented by "a counter-movement of being that we call heroic, a capacity for action or passion, for doing or suffering, which is above ordinary human experience." He concludes that "in tragedy the ironic vision survives the heroic one, but the heroic vision is the one we remember, and the tragedy is for its sake."[17]

Frye's conception has a particular cogency in understanding the representation of suffering and of the passions in Shakespeare. The passions of the mind were often explicitly associated with man's mortality in Elizabethan thinking, and in Shakespeare the display of passion, which is often simultaneously heroic and ironic, is always ultimately informed by the apprehension of the immanence of death. It is explicit in Romeo's dialogue with the Friar, in his presentiment of "love-devouring death," and in the answering puns on dying and sexual consummation that emerge in the Friar's homily. That these commonplace Elizabethan puns on "die" are literalized in the action of the play hardly needs demonstration. The Prologue invites us to watch "the fearful passage of" Romeo and Juliet's "death-marked love," and there is a clear intimation that the love is "death-marked" in the sense not only that it is foredoomed, but also that death may be its cognate state, if not its goal. This perspective is supported by the lovers' repeated premonitions of disaster, by the many references associating the marriage bed with the grave, and of course by the enactment of the final scene, the last of the love scenes, in the tomb, the "triumphant grave," the "feasting presence," Romeo says, made "full of light" by Juliet's beauty (5.3.83, 86). Both Romeo and Juliet commingle images of their passion and death, Romeo suggesting that death itself has become Juliet's lover and Juliet treating the dagger with which she stabs herself as an erotic object. Both lovers die with a kiss.

 Othello, which to some extent internalizes the external circumstances of *Romeo and Juliet* into the soul of the hero, also mingles images of love and death. Othello says to Desdemona, when he is first reunited with her in Cyprus,

> If it were now to die
> 'Twere now to be most happy, for I fear
> My soul hath her content so absolute
> That not another comfort like to this
> Succeeds in unknown fate.
>   (2.1.190–94)

The speech is highly reminiscent of Romeo's lines to the Friar linking the "exchange of joy" with death, and at this point in the play it is less a reflection of Othello's own psychology, one of his alleged insufficiencies, than it is a reflection, in his characterization, of the mortal undertow of passion that is common to all the tragedies. As in *Romeo and Juliet*, but even more literally, the marriage bed in *Othello* becomes the bride's funeral bier; and like the lovers in the earlier play, Othello himself dies "upon a kiss" (5.2.369). Othello's love, like Romeo's (though far more complexly), is always "death-marked," as he himself suggests when he stands over her body at the end of the play: "Here is my journey's end, here is my butt, / And very sea-mark of my utmost sail" (5.2.274–75).

 The inherent association of passion and death in *Macbeth*, though perhaps less obvious, is equally significant. It is possible to forget in reading, though hardly in performance, that the play is awash in blood, and of course Macbeth's "great passion of fear and fury" is itself continuously murderous. But there is another and more important sense in which passion and death are associated in the play, for as I have already suggested and shall later argue in detail, it is the very uncertainty and insatiability of passion in human life that Macbeth cannot tolerate and against which he tries to act. This is what gives such intricacy to his characterization. The usual critical question about *Macbeth* is how we can sympathize with a hero who is so barbaric. The more interesting question, it seems to me, is how Shakespeare can maintain our sympathy for a hero who is deliberating draining himself of emotion. Part of the answer, which Renaissance conceptions of passion can help make intelligible, is that in Macbeth we watch a man whose conscious wish is to accelerate the natural self-consumption of passion, to find "peace" with the dead. We watch a suicide.

In *Hamlet* and *King Lear*, finally, death is itself the manifest and most important subject of passion. With an egotism—the Renaissance would have called it presumption—that marks all the tragic heroes, Hamlet says: "The time is out of joint. O cursed spite, / That ever I was born to set it right!" (1.5.189–90). This is the injunction of the Ghost and of the revenge play genre itself, but insofar as it is a reflection of Hamlet's character, it is also a protest against death, and not only that of his father. As I have already suggested, it is the mortality of which his mother's remarriage is an instance as well as a result that most animates him, as from the first, it is his own mortality and limits that he must come to accept, as he does finally and perspicuously in the last act when he accepts the "special providence in the fall of a sparrow" (5.2.165–66). Hamlet's passion, as we shall see, is grief, its anger as well as its sorrow.

King Lear, a play that is primarily concerned with two very old and dying men, is even more deeply, if sometimes less obviously, informed by a protest against death. Lear's rage, his prevailing passion, is ostensibly against the mutability of affection that he sees in his daughters and in himself, but at root, as I shall try to show, it is a passionate denial of what his abdication nominally acknowledges, his own impending death. Edgar tells Gloucester,

> Men must endure
> Their going hence even as their coming hither.
> Ripeness is all.
>   (5.2.9–11)

Both Gloucester and Lear do in fact exhaustively "endure" the truth of this homily, as Edgar himself realizes, when he says in the closing lines that we should

> Speak what we feel, not what we ought to say.
> The oldest hath borne most. We that are young

Shall never see so much, nor live so long.
(5.3.300–302)

In Ecclesiastes, upon which I think Shakespeare drew deeply in *King Lear,* the Preacher, whose focus is also upon the transitoriness of human bonds and the immanence of death in human life, remarks that "he that encreaseth knowledge encreaseth sorrow" (1:18).[18] It is this peculiarly passionate "knowledge" that is the substance of Shakespearian tragedy and the subject of this book.

In the chapters that follow, I draw upon Freud, as well as Renaissance and earlier Christian texts, in interpreting the passions and suffering of Hamlet, Othello, Macbeth, and Lear. Justifications of the use of such ideas do not usually disarm critics who are hostile to them (they often only provide ammunition), and the interpretations must finally speak for themselves. But I do not wish to write only for initiates of Freudian or Christian criticism—I am not myself committed to either as an ideology—and some preliminary explanation of my critical approach may be helpful. To begin with, Shakespeare's heroes are often regressively childlike, which is what can make their passions at once awesome and ironic, if not grotesque, and Freud's explorations of the origins of adult behavior in early childhood are peculiarly suited to help explain the dramatic power as well as psychological integrity of this combination. Moreover, Freud's range is far greater than is usually recognized. In addition to the subject of sexuality, with which he tends to be too reductively identified, he writes with enduring insights about human growth, about many adult as well as childish emotions and ways of thinking, about the feeling of being in love, about grief, about the way human beings try to deny their mortality, about the very processes of human passions and suffering. The Bible too reflects upon such experiences, and Shakespeare of course represents them. To the extent that he and the Bible and Freud are true to these experiences, they have insights in common that can be explored, legitimately and interestingly. Moreover, as I shall suggest in a moment, the allegorical detritus of Shakespearian (and biblical) representations of character makes them more, rather than less, susceptible to a modern understanding of depth psychology.

I also assume that however considerable the cultural differences between Shakespeare's age and ours may be, there are also, and have to be, significant similarities in order for us to understand anything about earlier times and texts. In his admirable book *A New Mimesis,* A. D. Nuttall remarks that Shakespeare himself anticipates the results of many "seemingly modern tools of thought, such as the concepts of cultural history," and that "the easiest way—no, the *only* way—to account for this is to say that Shakespeare was looking very hard at the same world (400 years younger, but still the same world) that we are looking at now."[19] It seems to me, in addition, that culture, in any case, does not entirely determine the fundamental passions of an individual human life; that individuals in the Renaissance had particular as well as representative emotional lives that we can understand; and finally, that the revelation of such emotional life is at the heart of Shakespeare's great tragedies and of their continuing power to move us. These propositions all go against the grain of much recent modern criticism, and I shall return to them in the concluding chapter of this book. I hope, however, that they will be most validated for the reader as I practice them, in my interpretations of the plays.

At the same time, I want to make clear that I sympathize with such contentions as Nuttall's that the use of what he calls Freud's "images" in literary criticism is often more "ornamental" than "corroborative," since these images "seem seldom to function in a genuinely heuristic manner." I think there is also some truth to his assertion that in the depiction of human behavior "Freud is the allegorist, Shakespeare the psychologist."[20] It is certainly evident that psychoanalytic (as well as theological) interpretations of Shakespeare are often, if not habitually, reductive, doctrinaire, and remote both in tone and substance from the kind of experience Shakespeare gives us. But unlike Nuttall, I think these problems can be modulated as long as a critic does not displace an interest in Shakespeare's text with an interest in Freudian or Christian thought (which seems to me to be the most endemic failing of both theological and psychoanalytic critics) and as long as he or she looks on the text, as Jean Starobinski suggests, with a "gaze of knowledge that is also the gaze of love," rather than the gaze of Actaeon upon Diana, the gaze of "sacrilegious indiscretion" and of "aggression."[21] Freudian and Christian ideas do not have to be applied clinically, in a diagnostic, if not predatory, hunt for pathology. They can instead be used to enhance our understanding of the experiences which the plays both represent and elicit from us. The Bible is not simply a long homily, and Freud was from the first interested in explaining normal human behavior as well as emotional illness. Freudian and Christian ideas are far more humane and illuminating than the uses to which literary critics have usually put them, and they can help explain why his plays continue to be so alive and to reach so wide an audience of spectators and readers.

There is historical warrant for such an approach. Christian images, of course, pervaded Shakespeare's culture, and throughout his career he obviously thought in terms of them. If those images are themselves frequently allegorical, then we should consider the extent to which the allegories are incorporated into the living texture of Shakespeare's creations. The medieval drama that was his inheritance provided a model for just such a creative transmutation of Christian allegory into theatrical life. The morality play especially, though by definition a homiletic presentation of the moral struggle between personified virtues and vices for the soul of man, is also at the same time an intrapsychic drama, a depiction in concrete images of an action *within* the soul of the play's protagonist. The moralities present a mental landscape that is, at least incipiently, as psychological as it is moral. As I have suggested elsewhere,[22] the unique staging of such a play as *The Castle of Perseverance*, for example, is itself interesting. The image presented in the drawing that has come down to us—of Mankind's castle, with his bed under it, surrounded by the scaffolds of God, the World, the Flesh, Belial, and Covetousness—literalizes the scaffolding of a human life and reflects the same allegorical impulse, if not essentially the same mental topography, that is to be found in Freud's diagrams depicting the composition of the human psyche. In any event, the action of the play evokes such a topography with great scope as well as richness of concrete detail. We witness the panorama of Mankind's spiritual progress from birth to death and judgment, and in the course of that progress we are introduced to virtually all, to borrow Dr. Johnson's praise of Shakespeare, "those general passions and principles by which all minds are agitated, and the whole system of life is continued in motion."[23] The cast of characters alone presents us with a conspectus of elemental human experience: Belial, and with him Pride, Wrath, and Envy; Flesh, and with him Gluttony, Lechery, and Sloth, Covetousness, Backbiter; Shrift, Penitence; Meekness, Patience, Charity, Temperance, Chastity, Business, and Generosity; Death, the Soul (after Mankind's death); Mercy, Truth, Righteousness, and Peace; the Father sitting on his throne.

Mankind himself, Humanum Genus, and with him the Good Angel and the Bad Angel, does not interact with all the characters, but he is nonetheless ultimately inseparable from almost everything that happens in the play. Most of the action is not only about him, it constitutes him. He exists as a separate character, with all the definition and vitality an actor could give him, but he is also, if not finally, made up of the primitive impulses and energies of the forces that are represented in the characters surrounding him. The play as a whole thus composes as well as decomposes his "personality." The characters, the set, and the action are visualizations of the processes of his experience.

Such allegorizations of human experience accustomed medieval audiences to a way of understanding the primitive components and dynamics of human behavior, that Freud, in a sense, had to recover through psychoanalytic excavation. This understanding is shown to a significant degree in Renaissance moral psychologies of the passions, and persists as well, without necessarily entailing moral judgments, in Elizabethan drama, both in the psychomachic structure of the characterization of the hero and in the remnants of popular parts of the psychomachia, especially the Vice. The joining of Freudian and

Renaissance ideas in interpreting Shakespeare's portrayal of the emotional and spiritual life of his tragic heroes, therefore, makes historical as well as critical sense.

Notes

1. Simon Forman, *The Booke of Plaies and Notes therof per Formans for Common Pollicie*, quoted in the introduction to the New Arden ed. of *Macbeth*, ed. Kenneth Muir (London: Methuen, 1977), pp. xiii–xiv. For an interesting discussion of Forman's accounts of Shakespeare performances, see Don LePan, *The Cognitive Revolution in Western Culture* (London: Macmillan, 1989), pp. 280–302.

2. Pierre Charron, Of *Wisedome*, trans. Samson Lennard (London: ca. 1606; facsim. ed., New York: Da Capo Press, 1971), sig. F4. Transcriptions of sixteenth- and seventeenth-century texts in this study, whether from early or modern editions, follow modern practice with *i, j, v*, and long *s*.

3. All references to Shakespeare are to *The Complete Works*, ed. Stanley Wells and Gary Taylor (New York: Oxford Univ. Press, 1986).

4. Thomas Wright, *The Passions of the Minde in Generall* (London, 1604; facsim. ed., Urbana: Univ. of Illinois Press, 1971), sig. Bv. The introduction to this edition, by Thomas O. Sloan, gives a cogent summary of Renaissance views of the passions.

5. Pierre de La Primaudaye, *The French Academie* (London, 1586), sig. A2.

6. Much commentary in Charron's *Of Wisedome*, for example, is paraphrased from Montaigne, without attribution.

7. For a further discussion of Posthumus's relation to Cloten, see Arthur Kirsch, *Shakespeare and the Experience of Love* (Cambridge: Cambridge Univ. Press, 1981), pp. 153–61.

8. See Eleanor Prosser, "Shakespeare, Montaigne, and the 'Rarer Action,'" *Shakespeare Studies* 1 (1965): 261–64.

9. A. C. Bradley, *Shakespearean Tragedy* (London: Macmillan, 1905), p. 20.

10. A. P. Rossiter, *Angel with Horns* (New York: Theatre Arts Books, 1961), p. 263.

11. Ibid., p. 264.

12. All references to *King Lear* in this book are to *The Tragedy of King Lear: The Folio Text* in the Oxford *Complete Works*.

13. Quoted in E. K. Chambers, *The Elizabethan Stage*, 4 vols. (Oxford: Clarendon Press, 1961), 2: 309.

14. Bradley, *Shakespearean Tragedy*, pp. 32–33.

15. Lily B. Campbell, *Shakespeare's Tragic Heroes: Slaves of Passion* (Cambridge: Cambridge Univ. Press, 1930).

16. William Empson, *Some Versions of Pastoral* (New York: New Directions, 1960), chap. 2, "Double Plots."

17. Northrop Frye, *Fools of Time* (Toronto: Univ. of Toronto Press, 1967), pp. 3,4–5,6.

18. All references to the Bible are to *The Geneva Bible*, a facsimile ed. of the 1560 translation (Madison: Univ. of Wisconsin Press, 1969).

19. A. D. Nuttall, *A New Mimesis: Shakespeare and the Representation of Reality* (London: Methuen, 1983), pp. 166–67.

20. Ibid., pp. 28, 177.

21. Jean Starobinski, "Psychoanalysis and Literary Understanding," *The Living Eye*, trans. Arthur Goldhammer (Cambridge: Harvard Univ. Press, 1989), pp. 146–47.

22. See Kirsch, *Shakespeare and the Experience of Love*, pp. 3–8, for a fuller discussion of the bearing of mysteries as well as the moralities upon the use of Freudian and Christian ideas in interpreting Shakespeare's plays.

23. Samuel Johnson, *Johnson on Shakespeare*, ed. Arthur Sherbo, vols. 7 and 8 of *The Yale Edition of the Works of Samuel Johnson* (New Haven: Yale Univ. Press, 1968), 7:62.

NICHOLAS GRENE

Antony and Cleopatra

*A*ntony and Cleopatra is a play in two minds, as no other of the tragedies is, least of all *Macbeth*, written immediately before it, quite possibly in the same year 1606.[1] 'In *Macbeth* we are never in any doubt of our moral bearings. *Antony and Cleopatra*, on the other hand, embodies different and apparently irreconcilable evaluations of the central experience.'[2] It is a striking change from the spiritually polarised world of one play to the problematic moral relativism of the other: 'as we pass from *Macbeth* to *Antony and Cleopatra* we see the problem of evil suddenly lose urgency for Shakespeare'.[3] Yet this alteration need not be seen as unique, a single 'sudden' loss of urgency of the issue of good and evil, a stage beyond the tragic concerns of *Macbeth* and *King Lear*, *Othello* and *Hamlet*.

The disappearance of metaphysical absolutes from *Macbeth* to *Antony and Cleopatra* is only the final instance of the recurrent pattern of alternation between one imaginative milieu and its complementary other through the tragedies, the pattern this book has been designed to explore. The self-consciously determined Roman ethos of *Julius Caesar* is comparably distinct from the haunted universe of *Hamlet*; the ironising perspectives of *Troilus and Cressida* are equally contrasted with *Othello*'s vision of love and its damning denial. *Timon*, like *Antony and Cleopatra* derived from Plutarch, is without the order of transcendent values which is the shaping need of the characters

From *Shakespeare's Tragic Imagination*, pp. 223–248, 297–98. © 1992 by Nicholas Grene.

of *King Lear*. Thus the difference of mode between *Antony and Cleopatra* and *Macbeth* is not anomalous and problematic, but representative of the dialectic doubleness of Shakespeare's tragic imagination.

* * *

In *Othello*, Shakespeare risked opening the play with a maliciously distorted vision of its hero from his most prejudiced enemy. Iago's bias, however, soon became apparent as bias. By contrast, in the opening lines of *Antony and Cleopatra*, Philo's negative view of Antony is positively reinforced by his almost immediate entrance. For once in Shakespeare there appears to be a specified parallel between verbal and visual image. Philo has been conjuring up for Demetrius a picture of the deplorable metamorphosis of their general—

> His captain's heart,
> Which in the scuffles of great fights hath burst
> The buckles on his breast, reneges all temper,
> And is become the bellows and the fan
> To cool a gipsy's lust

—when on cue 'Flourish. Enter Antony, Cleopatra, her Ladies, the Train, with Eunuchs fanning her' (I.i.6–10). 'Look where they come!', exclaims Philo, at the spectacle so perfectly confirming his judgement. Leaving aside the question of how Shakespeare's eunuchs would have been recognisable as eunuchs in the theatre, the effect of the stage direction is deliberately to associate Antony, the metaphoric 'fan to cool a gipsy's lust', and the castrated attendants who appear literally fanning the queen.[4] Here visibly before us, as Philo suggests, is the great warrior emasculated, unmanned by his 'dotage'.

The scene that follows does indeed reveal an Antony completely in thrall to Cleopatra. One of her strategies in the display of her dominance is to taunt him with a lack of manliness. She urges him with elaborate sarcasm to give due deference to the messengers from Rome:

> Nay, hear them, Antony.
> Fulvia perchance is angry; or who knows
> If the scarce-bearded Caesar have not sent
> His pow'rful mandate to you: 'Do this or this;
> Take in that kingdom and enfranchise that;
> Perform't, or else we damn thee'.
>   I.i.19–24

Antony is guyed as the hen-pecked husband of Fulvia, the terrified subordinate of the boy Caesar, the two constantly interlinked:

> You must not stay here longer; your dismission
> Is come from Caesar; therefore hear it, Antony.
> Where's Fulvia's process? Caesar's I would say? Both?
> Call in the messengers. As I am Egypt's Queen,
> Thou blushest, Antony, and that blood of thine
> Is Caesar's homager. Else so thy cheek pays shame
> When shrill-tongu'd Fulvia scolds.
>   I.i.26–32

Different as the tone may be, the attitude adopted by Cleopatra here is akin to Lady Macbeth's in the crucial scene where she persuades Macbeth back towards murder. Both women use the spectre of unmanliness to goad their partners into being the men they want them to be. Lady Macbeth threatens her husband that he will 'live a coward in [his] own esteem' and in hers. Cleopatra challenges Antony to prove that he is not the hey-you of Octavius, the uxorious spouse of the scold Fulvia. In both scenes what we actually see is the man dominated by the woman for whom the image of manhood is only an instrument of domination.

The idea of sexual roles reversed recurs frequently in *Antony and Cleopatra* and often with a heavy load of disapproval. With pursed lips Octavius complains to Lepidus of Antony's carry-on in Alexandria:

> he fishes, drinks, and wastes
> The lamps of night in revel; is not more manlike
> Than Cleopatra, nor the queen of Ptolemy
> More womanly than he
>   I.iv.4–7

From the Egyptian side, what is perceptibly the same behaviour is the stuff of Cleopatra's reminiscences:

> That time? O times!
> I laugh'd him out of patience; and that night
> I laugh'd him into patience; and next morn,
> Ere the ninth hour, I drunk him to his bed,
> Then put my tires and mantles on him, whilst
> I wore his sword Philippian.
>   II.v.18–23

The image of role-swapping has been related to the story of Hercules enslaved to Omphale, which Plutarch uses as an exemplum of Antony's weakness: 'as we see in painted tables, where Omphale secretlie stealeth away Hercules clubbe, and tooke his Lyons skinne from him. Even so Cleopatra oftentimes unarmed Antonius' (Bullough, V, 319).[5] The violent indecorum of the comatose Antony pranked up in the robes of Cleopatra, the Queen wearing the weapon of the hero of Philippi, reinforces the idea of manhood travestied and womanised.

A Jacobean audience might well have shared Roman censoriousness of the transsexual antics of Antony and Cleopatra. Yet the play lacks the full sense of transgression attached to the overstepping of sexual roles in *Macbeth*. Lady Macbeth appeals to the forces of darkness to be unsexed—not to become manlike, but to become inhuman. When Macbeth dares do more than may become a man, he is none. Antony and Cleopatra, on the other hand, are never more human than when they give themselves up entirely to their pleasures and one another. They behave outrageously, disgracefully, indecorously. They offend against all sorts of principles and ideals: of manliness and womanliness, of responsibility and duty, of honesty and truth. But none of these offences provoke the judgement that they are wicked or sinful. The delinquencies of Antony and Cleopatra are without that perverse will to evil of the Macbeths.

Philo's opening vision of Antony, the warrior besotted by an unworthy love, 'the triple pillar of the world transform'd into a strumpet's fool', is confirmed by much that we see from the first appearance of the protagonists on. But it is also challenged from the beginning by an alternative vision, voiced in Antony's lyrical speech:

> Let Rome in Tiber melt, and the wide arch
> Of the rang'd empire fall! Here is my space.
> Kingdoms are clay; our dungy earth alike
> Feeds beast as man. The nobleness of life
> Is to do thus [*embracing*], when such a mutual pair
> And such a twain can do't, in which I bind,
> On pain of punishment, the world to weet
> We stand up peerless.
>   I.i.33–40

The strategy here is to take on and turn inside out the conventional values by which love is judged and found wanting. 'What is a man', asked Hamlet, 'If his chief good and market of his time Be but to sleep and feed? A beast, no more!' Hamlet's was the orthodox view: man's 'godlike reason' differentiated him from the animals. Sexuality was normally thought of as one of the appetitive forces which, in overruling reason, reduced man to the bestial. Antony inverts this, proclaiming that it is in the lovers' embrace that humans transcend the dependency on 'dungy earth' which they share with their fellow animals. 'The nobleness of life is to do thus'—the phrase is a flamboyant gesture against all that nobility means to Philo and his like, manly resolution, self-discipline, self-sacrifice. Antony glorifies the erotic in the language of a heroism antithetical to it.

The provocative paradoxes here are those of Donne in 'The Sun Rising'. Antony, like Donne's lover, posits an erotocentric world, grandly dismissive of the mere realities of empire or solar system. 'She is all states, and all princes,' 'I. Nothing else is.' 'Here is my space. Kingdoms are clay.' But the lyric poem, unlike the drama, is inhabited only by the voice and viewpoint of the lover. When he sends the sun contemptuously about his workaday business—'Go tell court-huntsmen, that the King will ride'[6]—there are no court huntsmen or kings there to remind us of their importance. If the poem's rhetoric implies a consciousness of its own outrageousness, it nonetheless invites us to share without reservation in the bravado of love. Antony's hyperboles, on the other hand, are declaimed to a public audience some of whom will be visibly scandalised. 'Let Rome in Tiber melt' is a poetic figure markedly altered by the presence of such very solid and unmelting representatives of Rome as Philo and Demetrius. In other words, Antony must make good the solipsism of his love-poetry within the contrarieties of an observed dramatic scene. There is no easy assenting to 'the nobleness of life is to do thus'. Rather the play puts before us as an open question the issue of what constitutes the nobleness of life, suspending absolute criteria of judgement by which that question might be decided.

* * *

The lack of assured moral standards in viewing the central characters is compounded by the play's lack of political principles. *Antony and Cleopatra* is centrally concerned with power, no less a question than the control of the whole of the known world. The word 'world' sounds and resounds throughout, aggrandising the triumvirs, amplifying the sense of all that is at stake in the struggle between Antony and Octavius. Given the scale of this power struggle, there is a remarkable absence in the play of anything which could be called a body politic. Paul Cantor has commented that the 'world of *Antony and Cleopatra* is essentially cityless'.[7] It is also almost peopleless. Though the stage is filled with the leaders, their soldiers, henchmen and attendants, there is never the impression of a society dependent for its welfare on the

actions of its rulers. Certainly the triumvirs never show the slightest awareness of the public responsibilities of their office. Their aims 'are as personal
as if they were captains of banditti'.[8]

Because *Antony and Cleopatra* is without an idea of political legitimacy,
its metaphors for the rulers are seen to be that only—metaphors more or less
apt. The image of Antony as 'triple pillar of the world' is potent only insofar
as it measures the scale of loss in his transformation into strumpet's fool.
The irony in Pompey's tone bites as he acclaims the triumvirs as 'the senators
alone of this great world, Chief factors for the gods' (II.vi.9–10); three men
by themselves make up a whole senate, become business managers for the
deities. Poor Lepidus, never more than a shaky pillar at best, is downed by the
drink on Pompey's galley and carried off, a pathetic 'third part of the world'
(II.vii.89). With Lepidus deposed, it is Enobarbus who provides the grimly
vivid image for the situation remaining:

> Then, world, thou hast a pair of chaps—no more;
> And throw between them all the food thou hast,
> They'll grind the one the other.
>   III.v.13–15

Kingdoms, countries, peoples are only grist to the predatory jaws of Antony
and Octavius.

We are remote here from the monarch-centred community of *Macbeth*
where the body of the king is the sacred body of the state, the 'Lord's anointed
temple' sacrilegiously broken open by murder. Lady Macbeth wondered, in the
haunted bewilderment of her sleep-walking state, 'who would have thought
the old man to have had so much blood in him?' Blood, the principle of life in
the doctrine of the humours, dried up as a man grew old; so, for instance, the
aged Menenius is threatened by the sentry in the hostile Volscian camp: 'go,
lest I let forth your half pint of blood' (*Coriolanus*, V.ii.53–4). But Duncan is
more than just an old man, an almost used up life: he bleeds for all Scotland.
No figure of authority in *Antony and Cleopatra* can be vested with this sort
of significance born of the symbolic identity of king and country. Indeed
authority in its fullest sense hardly exists in the play, as power is unsupported
by any sanctioning system relating ruler to ruled.

The political atmosphere of *Antony and Cleopatra*, concerned with the
period of the triumvirate preceding the establishment of the Empire, was
perhaps bound to be very different from that of the medieval Scotland of
Macbeth, but it is noticeably distinct from its Plutarchan predecessor *Julius
Caesar* also. Though often treated as a sequel, *Antony and Cleopatra* is imaginatively discontinuous to *Julius Caesar*, not only in the characterisation of

(Mark) Antony but in the changed political ethos. Around the figure of Sextus Pompey, as M. W. MacCallum so acutely remarked, there is 'a certain afterglow of free republican sentiment'.[9] It is Pompey who is given the only detailed recollection of the events of the earlier play:

> What was't
> That mov'd pale Cassius to conspire? and what
> Made the all-honour'd honest Roman, Brutus,
> With the arm'd rest, courtiers of beauteous freedom,
> To drench the Capitol, but that they would
> Have one man but a man?
>   II.vi.14–19

Pompey's stance here, however, is ironised and undercut by the *realpolitik* which surrounds it, and in which he joins. After the barest show of idealist defiance in this scene, he discloses that he had come to the meeting with the triumvirs prepared in advance to accept their wholly expedient deal. The inconsistent shreds of principle adhering to Pompey are merely impeding weaknesses in a catch-as-catch-can power-game. It is only a queasy conscience which causes him to turn down the pirate Menas's offer of world domination by cutting the triumvirs' throats. Hence the weight of Menas's verdict on him:

> For this,
> I'll never follow thy pall'd fortunes more.
> Who seeks, and will not take when once 'tis offer'd,
> Will never find it more.
>   II.vii.80–3

Exit Pompey—we never see him after this scene. Elsewhere in the play, the events dramatised in *Julius Caesar* are never recalled with any of the ideological colouring they had then. Philippi is remembered as a great personal triumph for Antony—hence the significance of his 'sword Philippian' donned by Cleopatra at the height of their drunken play-acting. After his death at Philippi Brutus was celebrated by Mark Antony as 'the noblest Roman of them all'. To this latter-day Antony he is recalled as 'the mad Brutus' whom he boasts he 'ended', along with the 'lean and wrinkled Cassius', while Octavius 'kept his sword e'en like a dancer' (Ill. xi. 35–8). The battle between the libertarian conspirators and the avengers of Caesar is reduced to an occasion of individual heroics, and the issue on which they fought is forgotten.

* * *

Shakespeare seems to flatten out deliberately the historical background of
Antony and Cleopatra, to deny its politics any sort of principled significance.
The effect at times appears to be close to the satiric iconoclasm of *Troilus
and Cressida*. However, it is often difficult to be sure how puncturing the
irony is intended to be, as much of the action is so closely derived from
the unironical Plutarch narrative. To take one minor instance, Octavius
justifies his deposition of Lepidus from the triumvirate on the grounds
that 'he was grown too cruel' and 'his high authority abus'd' (III.vi.32–3).
Given Shakespeare's characterisation of Lepidus as the feeblest of peace-
makers, it seems tempting to assume that this is intended to be evidence
of the grossness of Octavius' hypocrisy. Lepidus too cruel? A likely story!
But this, along with much of the rest of the scene, is taken over *literatim*
from Plutarch, where there is no particular sense of the improbability
of the charge against Lepidus. Octavius has come in for a good deal of
critical abuse as the bloodless politician who defeats Antony by his cold-
hearted single-mindedness—'the most repellent Roman of them all'.[10] A
subtler judgement is that of John Danby who sees Octavius as the last of
Shakespeare's Machiavels, from whom the dramatist has 'refined away all
the accidentals ... the diabolism, the rhetoric, the elaborate hypocrisy,
the perverse glamour'.[11] It may be, though, that Octavius is only incidentally so characterised, that his function in the play is to act as the neutral
instrument of Antony's defeat, an antithetical foil in his tenacity, his clear
purposefulness and his 'Roman' asceticism. If he cannot be taken to represent the positive ideals of Romanness associated with a Brutus, he is not
necessarily designed to be condemned for lacking them.

Enobarbus, who was almost entirely Shakespeare's creation from the
merest hints in Plutarch, is crucially important in defining the perspective
of unillusioned scepticism which the play encourages towards its action.
From his very first appearance his key-note is one of sardonic reductiv-
ism, as he snorts in reaction to the Soothsayer's fortune-telling, 'Mine, and
most of our fortunes, tonight, shall be—drunk to bed' (I.ii.42–3). He has
the conventional sharp cynicism of the bluff soldier, and cuts through the
delicate diplomacy of the triumvirs' negotiations over a united front against
Pompey:

> if you borrow one another's love for the instant, you may, when you
> hear no more words of Pompey, return it again. You shall have time
> to wrangle in when you have nothing else to do.
>
> II.ii.106–10

With his sour wit he here plots the course of what is to follow, the temporary patched-up truce between Antony and Octavius, followed by the renewal of the conflict as soon as the threat of Pompey is removed. He is hushed by Antony: 'Thou art a soldier only. Speak no more'; to which he retorts, 'That truth should be silent I had almost forgot' (II.ii.111–12).

This is a line like the Fool's in *King Lear*—'Truth's a dog must to kennel'—and Enobarbus is, like the Fool, a truth-teller in the play. What sort of truth-teller is he, and what sort of truths does he tell? He has the role of satirical commentator of a Thersites, without Thersites' pathological need for nay-saying. He can be responsive to the glamour of Cleopatra and to the grandeur of Antony, a responsiveness which makes his detached perspective very different from the satiric tones of Thersites. Among the many figures who surround the protagonists with framing commentary, he alone carries choric weight. His loyalty to Antony, his (limited) sympathy with Cleopatra win him credit and credibility with an audience.

For this very reason, the point at which his loyalty and sympathy give out is significant. After the disgrace of Actium and the increasing outrageousness of Antony's behaviour, Enobarbus reasonably begins to wonder how long it makes sense to go on following him.

> Mine honesty and I begin to square.
> The loyalty well held to fools does make
> Our faith mere folly.
> III.xiii.41–3

This is forceful worldly wisdom in the rationally observed world of the play. Returning to Lear's Fool provides a point of contrast. For when he mock-salutes Kent as fool for 'taking one's part that's out of favour', it is an ironic praise of folly reinforcing the absolute value of fidelity, which comes out of hiding in his later song:

> I will tarry; the fool will stay
> And let the wise man fly.
> The knave turns fool that runs away;
> The fool no knave, perdy.
> II.iv.80–3

Such a higher order of truth which can invert worldly standards of folly and wisdom is unavailable to Enobarbus.

* * *

There is, all the same, a consideration which holds Enobarbus back, at least temporarily, from the desertion which reason requires.

> Yet he that can endure
> To follow with allegiance a fall'n lord
> Does conquer him that did his master conquer,
> And earns a place i th' story.
> III.xiii.43–6

This is the best that the world of *Antony and Cleopatra* can offer, 'a place i th' story'. All the characters in Shakespeare's classically derived tragedies inhabit stories which are more or less laid down for them. They live up to or fall short of reputations which are pre-established. Julius Caesar plays the part of the Olympian Caesar, 'constant as the northern star' until the knives of the conspirators cut him short. Brutus and Cassius enact a bloody drama to be repeated down the ages, though in a spirit they little foresee. Troilus and Cressida swear themselves into the stereotypes they are to become. Even the less well-known Timon lives out the afterlife of his own legend as idealist turned misanthrope. But in *Antony and Cleopatra* there is a special scrutiny of the story of the protagonists and the roles they play in it. History itself hardly gives them their significant meaning. Though the play is built round the contrasting image systems of Rome and Egypt, it is not in any real sense a conflict between the values of East and West. No compelling political necessity drives towards the victory of Octavius which is expected as mere inevitability. Instead the focus is almost entirely on Antony and Cleopatra's capacity to imagine identities for themselves, to create and sustain their parts in the story in the face of the ironies and disbelief which surround them.[12]

A myth of Antony haunts the play which is partly, but only partly, the myth of his past. Philo, in the opening lines, conjures up the superhuman warrior of former battles, 'like plated Mars' himself. The deplorable metamorphosis of that hero into the 'strumpet's fool', Philo yet tries to excuse as a temporary lapse:

> sometimes when he is not Antony,
> He comes too short of that great property
> Which still should go with Antony.
> I.i.56–9

Antony, it seems, is something other than the person he happens to be: he is, or ought to be, the 'great property' which belongs to his name. Enobarbus uses the same figure when Lepidus urges him to 'entreat your captain to soft and gentle speech' in the negotiations with Octavius:

> I shall entreat him
> To answer like himself. If Caesar move him
> Let Antony look over Caesar's head
> And speak as loud as Mars.
>   II.ii.3–6

Once again the ideal Antony is Mars-like, out-topping the puny Octavius; but once again also, it is an Antony used as Antony's own super-ego.

This heroic warrior-image casts a huge shadow in the play. Its reality, though, is called in question by the Antony we actually see in action, or more often in inaction, who only intermittently if at all resembles his alleged self. He excuses his Egyptian lethargy to Octavius as a time 'when poisoned hours had bound me up From mine own knowledge' (II.ii.94–5); the return visit to Rome represents a vigorous shaking of himself awake. But within stage minutes of his good resolutions to his newly married wife Octavia—'I have not kept my square; but that to come Shall all be done by th' rule' (II.iii.6–7)—the Roman rule-book is once again abandoned:

> I will to Egypt;
> And though I make this marriage for my peace,
> I' th' East my pleasure lies.
>   II.iii.39–41

The imperial magnificence of Antony depends largely on his heroic warrior-ship. This is ironically called in question not only by his Egyptian backslidings, but by the damaging little scene of Ventidius in Parthia. Though the substance of this scene is derived from Plutarch, its very extraneousness to the action draws attention to it, making the effect more pointed. Ventidius who has triumphed over the Parthians—something, according to Plutarch, no other Roman general ever did—refrains from pushing home his victory for fear of arousing Antony's jealousy. Instead the good lieutenant will, in his dispatches to Antony,

> humbly signify what in his name,
> That magical name of war, we have effected.
>   III.i.30–1

'His name . . . *we* have effected': the disjunction of pronouns helps to expose satirically the totemic idea of Antony 'the greatest soldier of the world'.

In the later parts of the play, there are glimpses of something like the reported Antony of old. They are, though, only glimpses, and in being something like actually show their unlikeness. After Actium, Antony oscillates between a shame-struck, paralysed defeatism, and bursts of blustering rodomontade. In one of the latter veins, he sends his personal challenge to Octavius to 'answer me declin'd, sword against sword, Ourselves alone' (III. xiii.27–8). Enobarbus' aside underscores the absurdity of the gesture:

> Yes, like enough high-battled Caesar will
> Unstate his happiness, and be stag'd to th' show
> Against a sworder!
>   III.xiii.29–31

No-one doubts that Antony is the stronger soldier, but the imperial power is not a heavyweight boxing championship. Octavius' contemptuous reply to the challenge strips Antony of all his titles: 'Let the old ruffian know I have many other ways to die' (IV.i.4–5). 'I am Antony yet', he shouts as he calls up what remaining attendants he has to whip the messenger of Octavius. This, though, is no Senecan proclamation of continuing integrity, *'Medea super est'*; it is a hollow attempt to reassure himself as 'authority melts' from him. Antony is granted a kind of warrior's grandeur as he prepares for the last fight in Alexandria, a grandeur we have hardly seen anywhere else in the play. He dignifies himself and the joy of battle he evokes to Cleopatra:

>   O love,
> That thou couldst see my wars to-day, and knew'st
> The royal occupation! Thou shouldst see
> A workman in't.
>   IV.iv.15–18

This last arming, however, and the glory that briefly plays about him as he comes home at the end of the day in triumph, is only a prelude to the final despair:

> Unarm, Eros; the long day's task is done,
> And we must sleep.
>   IV.xiv.35–6

* * *

As far as the heroic Roman warrior Antony is concerned, it might seem that, after a temporary return to energetic resolution in Act II, the action of the play is one long slide down to defeat. Yet the identity of the character is complicated by the partly antithetical, partly overlapping, image of Cleopatra's Antony. For just as Antony challenges the Roman ideal of the 'nobleness of life' in the opening scene, he posits a self not betrayed but sustained by his love. Cleopatra has pretended to disbelieve his absolute assurances of devotion; still, she says

> I'll seem the fool I am not. Antony
> Will be himself.
> ANTONY
> But stirr'd by Cleopatra.
> I.i.42–3

What Antony affirms here is that his true self, which Cleopatra professes to think is dishonest, is only true and only itself as she inspires it. This interdependence of self recurs through the play, as each feels bound to live up to the imagined majesty of the other. 'Since my lord Is Antony again, I will be Cleopatra' (III.xiii.186–7), the Queen declares after the reconciliation following the quarrel over her suspiciously kind reception of Octavius' messenger. Cleopatra has relatively little difficulty being herself, that highly volatile self whose very essence seems to be its shape-shifting. The identity of Antony, on the other hand, which is dependent on Cleopatra for validation, remains unstable; he can never be assuredly himself against the assault of doubt about her truth.

Ernest Schanzer says of Antony that 'instead of being "with himself at war", like Brutus, or Macbeth, or Othello, he is like a chronic deserter, forever changing sides in the struggle, and this emotional pattern mirrors and underlines the structural pattern of the entire play'.[13] Even if Brutus' internal conflict is limited to the period before he decides to murder Caesar, Schanzer's statement helps to illuminate an essential difference between the tragedy of Antony and that of Othello, Macbeth or, he might have added, Lear and Hamlet. In all four tragedies, there is an implosion of identity of the central figure bound up with a profound dislocation of the worlds in which they exist. The madness of Hamlet and of Lear, the frenzied anguish of Othello and Macbeth, originate in a fragmentation of the self which mirrors, precipitates, amplifies out into, the convulsions of their dramatic environment. With Antony, by contrast, there is a constant movement between alternative selves, a fluctuating to and fro of belief and disbelief in the potential identities available. Rome and Egypt are states of mind which he can occupy by turns. Antony's world is not destroyed by his self-division nor he by its; rather both hero and context are the constructs of imagination liable to arbitrary dissolution and reconstruction.

'Dissolution' is a key word. The importance of ideas of melting in the play, the commonness of the vocabulary of liquefaction including unique coinages such as 'discandy', have often been pointed out.[14] The omnipresence of such images makes Antony's meditation on defeat especially significant.

ANTONY
Eros, thou yet behold'st me?
EROS
Ay, noble lord.
ANTONY
Sometimes we see a cloud that's dragonish;
A vapour sometime like a bear or lion,
A tower'd citadel, a pendent rock,
A forked mountain, or blue promontory
With trees upon't that nod unto the world
And mock our eyes with air. Thou hast seen these signs;
They are black vesper's pageants.
EROS
Ay, my lord.
ANTONY
That which is now a horse, even with a thought
The rack dislimns, and makes it indistinct,
As water is in water.
EROS
It does, my lord.
ANTONY
My good knave Eros, now thy captain is
Even such a body. Here I am Antony;
Yet cannot hold this visible shape, my knave.
        IV.xiv.1–14

Antony's mood of bewildered self-alienation is figured in the very movement of this passage. Sharing the intimacy of Antony's personal attendant Eros, we can only give tentative gestures of assent to the speech which so slowly reveals its direction. There seems at first a complete disjunction between the opening question 'thou yet behold'st me?' and the extended evocation of the cloud-world that follows. Perhaps, with the suggestiveness of 'signs' and 'black vesper's pageants', it may appear momentarily that it is with omens of coming death that Antony is preoccupied. At last the straying consciousness settles back on the person which, in straying away, it has emptied out of substance. Eros's 'captain', a word of armoured definiteness, has become a thing as 'indistinct, As water is in water'. It is Cleopatra who has left Antony thus dematerialised, the Queen 'whose heart I thought I had, for she had mine'. Her imagined betrayal denies Antony reality and makes of the world itself no more than an illusory cloud-drift.

Contrast the Macbeth of 'To-morrow, and to-morrow, and to-morrow'. In Macbeth's speech, there is a horror, an indignation at life's meaninglessness, absent from Antony's cloudscape. Antony yields himself up to a dissolving world in which his own separate identity is dissolved, whereas for Macbeth individual consciousness continues as the unending finality of despair. 'I gin to be aweary of the sun', says Macbeth, 'And wish th' estate o' th' world were now undone'. For him there is no escaping the 'estate o' th' world': he must arm for his last fight, an empty effigy of the heroic warrior he once was, whose violent death in battle will renew the kingdom. Antony, unarmed, slips protractedly down towards a death dependent for its significance, as his life was, on the imagination of Cleopatra.

* * *

'I dreamt there was an Emperor Antony', says Cleopatra after his death. The word 'dream' accepts the imaginative, possibly fictive, element in the conception, while the very grandeur of the phrase 'an Emperor Antony' and the extraordinary cosmic vision of him which follows, defiantly proclaim their own reality. Cleopatra throughout the play is both the source and the object of a hyperbolic imagination which lives always with the actualities it attempts to transcend. The mock catechism of her very first exchanges with Antony sets the pace:

CLEOPATRA
  If it be love indeed, tell me how much.
ANTONY
  There's beggary in the love that can be reckon'd.
CLEOPATRA
  I'll set a bourn how far to be belov'd.
ANTONY
  Then must thou needs find out new heaven, new earth.
    I.i.14–17

The pretence of establishing limits is only a stimulant to urge love on beyond itself into the infinite. Her constant changes of mood and changes of role, part natural, part tactical, are a means of resisting definition. She takes on and lives out the expected images of herself, but by setting one against another constantly challenges them.

Cleopatra is both queen and whore: Enobarbus' famous tribute to her in the description of her first meeting with Antony at Cydnus is an appreciation of both. The set-piece evocation of the scene—'The barge she sat on like a burnish'd throne Burn'd on the water'—represents the erotic raised to the power of majesty. At the same time, there is a coarse and reductive voyeurism in the Roman Agrippa's reaction:

> Royal wench!
> She made great Caesar lay his sword to bed.
> He plough'd her, and she cropp'd.
>   II.ii.230–2

Even Enobarbus' final judgement, often quoted as the supreme accolade to Cleopatra's eternal attractiveness, is also a tribute to the superwhore:

> Age cannot wither her, nor custom stale
> Her infinite variety. Other women cloy
> The appetites they feed, but she makes hungry
> Where most she satisfies; for vilest things
> Become themselves in her, that the holy priests
> Bless her when she is riggish.
>   II.ii.239–44

Here, and recurrently through the play, Cleopatra's sexuality is imagined in terms of consumption. 'He will to his Egyptian dish again' (II.vi.121) Enobarbus says of Antony when in less lyrical mood. Even more disgustedly reductive is Antony's own repudiation of Cleopatra in the scene with Octavius' messenger:

> I found you as a morsel cold upon
> Dead Caesar's trencher. Nay you were a fragment
> Of Cneius Pompey's, besides what hotter hours,
> Unregist'red in vulgar fame, you have
> Luxuriously pick'd out
>   III.xiii.116–20

This is close to the mood of *Troilus and Cressida*—Troilus' revulsion at the 'fragments, scraps, the bits, and greasy relics' of Cressida's 'o'er-eaten faith'. The words of Troilus, though, reflect a once-and-for-all disillusionment reducing idealised love to a nauseating physicality. Antony's abusiveness is one end of an emotional spectrum which will take him back to devoted faith within the scene. What is more, Cleopatra can see herself as edible sex-object without any sense of degradation:

> Broad-fronted Caesar,
> When thou wast here above the ground, I was
> A morsel for a monarch; and great Pompey
> Would stand and make his eyes grow in my brow;
> There would he anchor his aspect and die
> With looking on his life.
>   I.v.29–34

So far from regarding her sexual past with shame, she proclaims with pride the vitality which has survived the great conquerors she has conquered. This list of lovers is headed by the sun-god himself, as she transmutes her age and her complexion into the most daring image of all. 'Think on me', she enjoins the absent Antony,

> That am with Phoebus' amorous pinches black,
> And wrinkled deep in time.
>   I.v.27–9

The grotesque is outfaced here in an exultant sexuality extended on to a cosmic scale.

Cleopatra can take such risks and bring them off because she is queen as well as whore. If the idea of Antony is amplified by his position as triumvir, 'triple pillar of the world', Cleopatra has an answering magnificence as monarch of Egypt. She can prepare for death as for an enthronement, making her suicide an act 'fitting for a princess Descended of so many royal kings' (V.ii.324–5). Stricken after Antony's death, she sets aside the titles, 'Royal Egypt, Empress!', with which Iras tries to recall her to herself:

> No more but e'en a woman, and commanded
> By such poor passion as the maid that milks
> And does the meanest chares.
>   IV.xv.73–5

Even when she affirms the ordinariness of her humanity, it is with the grace of magnanimity only possible in the great. She is named as Egypt in the formal synecdoche of king for kingdom: 'I made these wars for Egypt'

says Antony; 'I am dying, Egypt, dying'. All that is strange, exotic, luxuri-
ous in the imagination of Egypt, as well as what from a Roman viewpoint
is sinister and decadent, all this inheres in Cleopatra. She is her country,
though not as its mystical centre for good or ill of the monarchical system
as conceived in *Hamlet* or *Macbeth*. There is even less sense of Egypt as a
body politic than there is of Rome. Rather, there is a constant identification
of Cleopatra with things Egyptian, the Nile with its fertilising fluidity, its
serpents and its crocodiles, a world of spontaneous generation.

* * *

The grandeur of Antony and Cleopatra is central to the play's imaginative
expansiveness. The protagonists are not only monarchs, imperial rulers; in
their own imagination and that of those around them, they are enlarged
to the dimensions of gods or demigods. The exceptionally high number
of legendary and mythological allusions in the play has often been noted.
Cleopatra is associated with the goddesses Isis and Venus, Antony with
Hercules and Mars; the two of them as lovers are analogues of Dido and
Aeneas.[15] Yet throughout they remain the images of a purely human imagination straining towards transcendence. When Antony is imagined 'like
plated Mars', or Cleopatra 'o'erpicturing that Venus where we see the fancy
outwork nature', these are larger than life projections of heroic strength and
beauty. The amplitude lent by images of pagan gods and heroes has very
little of its potential allegorical significance—War versus Love—and even
less of the resonance of the numinous. In *Antony and Cleopatra*, 'the "divine"
manifests itself—if at all—only in the forms and processes of nature'.[16]

   No gods govern the world of *Antony and Cleopatra*, it is not felt to move
by the action of forces beyond itself. In the second scene the tragic fates of the
attendants of Cleopatra are laid down in the prophecies of the Soothsayer. He
is given a sombre dignity in his modest indication of his limited powers:

   In nature's infinite book of secrecy
   A little I can read.
      I.ii.9–10

That blank verse dignity, however, is almost overwhelmed by the atmosphere of heedless prose which surrounds it. The solemnity of the seer, shaping a tragic course ahead, is subverted by the frivolous jokes of Charmian
and Iras. 'You shall outlive the lady whom you serve', he tells Charmian.
'O, excellent!', she exclaims, 'I love long life better than figs' (I.ii.30–1).
The prophecy will be ironically fulfilled in the last scene when Charmian

dies minutes after Cleopatra; figs, with their sexual innuendo here, are to become the vehicle for death, which Charmian will finally prefer to a long life outliving her mistress. Iras and Charmian are cast by the Soothsayer for the high tragic parts they will eventually play in attendance on Cleopatra's suicide, even though in this scene they appear the dramatic stuff of comedy, irresponsible, lubricious, silly. The mixed tone brings out in how comic a world the tragedy of *Antony and Cleopatra* must make its way.

In the second scene where the Soothsayer appears, to warn Antony of the dangers of Octavius to him, though the effect is fully serious, the sense of the supernatural is again limited. Antony asks the Soothsayer 'Whose fortunes shall rise higher, Caesar's or mine?':

> Caesar's.
> Therefore, O Antony, stay not by his side.
> Thy daemon, that thy spirit which keeps thee, is
> Noble, courageous, high, unmatchable,
> Where Caesar's is not; but near him thy angel
> Becomes a fear, as being o'erpow'r'd.
>   II.iv.17–23

The ascendancy of Octavius over Antony is short of a full fatality; it is a localised operation of luck or fortune. It was this idea from Plutarch which Shakespeare had in mind when he gave Macbeth the lines about Banquo:

> under him
> My Genius is rebuk'd, as it is said
> Mark Antony's was by Caesar.
>   III.i.54–6

But Banquo's superiority, and Macbeth's awareness of it, involved a true 'royalty of nature' feared by a usurper. No such co-ordinates of good and evil, no such concept of ultimate destiny, define Antony's lucklessness against Octavius.

The victory of Octavius over Antony is inevitable, not only as a known historical fact, the event which finally initiated the principate but, in the influential vision of Virgil's *Aeneid*, the Providential goal to which all Roman history had been working. To this sort of inevitability *Antony and Cleopatra* bears little witness. The defeat of Antony is accomplished by a slow and eddying drift of fortune rather than by any driven forces of necessity. Even such a key event as the decision to fight by sea at Actium, against all advice, is given as an oddly blank and unmotivated resolution on Antony's part. He is not persuaded to it by Cleopatra, though she approves the decision and there is a strong feeling that it represents a commitment to the Egyptian element of water rather than the Roman firmness of land. There remains a pitch-and-toss arbitrariness in the strategic move which is to determine the control of the whole world. The succession of large numbers of very brief scenes which make up Acts III and IV contributes to the impression of a desultory rather than directed movement to the action. No defeat seems quite definitive beyond the possibility of a recovery of fortunes; the erratic ebbing and flowing of Antony and Cleopatra's confidence in themselves overlays any clear pattern of catastrophe.

One scene only grants a visionary dimension to Antony's coming doom. Shakespeare makes of an omen recorded in Plutarch the lovely IV.iii in which the soldiers, posted on sentry duty the night before battle, hear 'music of the hautboys under the stage'.

> 2 SOLDIER
> Peace, what noise?
> 3 SOLDIER
> List, list!
> 2 SOLDIER
> Hark!
> 3 SOLDIER
> Music i' th' air.
> 4 SOLDIER
> Under the earth.
> 5 SOLDIER
> It signs well, does it not?
> 4 SOLDIER
> No.
> 3 SOLDIER
> Peace, I say!
> What should this mean?
> 2 SOLDIER
> 'Tis the god Hercules, whom Antony lov'd,
> Now leaves him.
> IV.iii.12–17

It is moment of mystery unparalleled elsewhere in the play, a mystery enhanced by the bewildered awe the music provokes in the sentries, and the strange certainty with which the Second Soldier stills their speculation as to its meaning. It is, however, a curiously unominous omen, in its beauty closer to the spirit of the bewitching unearthly music of *The Tempest* than to the signs which presage the death of Julius Caesar, much less those before the assassination of Duncan. It is noticeable that it does not provoke panic or desertion among the soldiers. In fact, such is the dislocation of omen from event that what follows immediately after is not the defeat of Antony but his last unexpected victory.

When Antony is finally defeated and his death announced to Octavius, it is experienced as anticlimax in its very lack of the signs which should have attended it:

> The breaking of so great a thing should make
> A greater crack. The round world
> Should have shook lions into civil streets,
> And citizens to their dens. The death of Antony
> Is not a single doom: in the name lay
> A moiety of the world.
>   V.i.14–19

In *Antony and Cleopatra* the age of miracles is past; no lion appears on the city streets as it did the night before the Ides of March. Though in his name 'lay a moiety of the world', Antony's death brings none of that universal cataclysm entailed by a monarch's 'cease of majesty'.

Cleopatra nonetheless contrives to make of Antony's death a moment of transcendent significance:

> O wither'd is the garland of the war,
> The soldier's pole is fall'n! Young boys and girls
> Are level now with men. The odds is gone,
> And there is nothing left remarkable
> Beneath the visiting moon.
>   IV.xv.64–8

Arnold Stein perceptively remarks that this 'is made of the same stuff, and partly of the same language, as Macbeth's lament for the death of Duncan. But that is a different scene, and language always imagines its reality in a scene.'[17] Macbeth's words, for all their surface hypocrisy, tell a truth supported by the play's whole experience: 'renown and grace *is* dead', their source in Duncan killed by Macbeth. With Cleopatra, rather, we can see 'language imagining its reality in a scene', a scene which she creates and dominates.

Cleopatra's re-imagination of Antony's greatness after his death she acknowledges as fictive. Her marvellous rhapsodic elegy of the fifth act is conceived in a reverie from which Dolabella tries vainly (and comically) to recall her to reality.

His legs bestrid the ocean; his rear'd arm
Crested the world. His voice was propertied
As all the tuned spheres, and that to friends;
But when he meant to quail and shake the orb,
He was as rattling thunder. For his bounty,
There was no winter in't; an autumn 'twas
That grew the more by reaping. His delights
Were dolphin-like: they shoved his back above
The elements they liv'd in. In his livery
Walk'd crowns and crownets; realms and islands were
As plates dropp'd from his pocket.
     V.ii.82–92

This bears some resemblance to the Antony of the play: the Colossus-like image of the 'triple pillar of the world', the 'mine of bounty' whose magnanimous generosity broke the tough-minded Enobarbus' heart, the exuberant sensuality of the lover with his 'dolphin-like' delights. Yet clearly no such person ever existed except as the utmost limit of hyperbole. Dolabella cannot well give any other reply than he does to Cleopatra's question:

CLEOPATRA
  Think you there was or might be such a man
  As this I dreamt of?
DOLABELLA
  Gentle madam, no.
     V.ii.93–4

Cleopatra's vehement repudiation of this deferential common sense is followed by a much more hypothetical argument of conditionals and subjunctives:

You lie, up to the hearing of the gods.
But if there be nor ever were one such,
It's past the size of dreaming. Nature wants stuff
To vie strange forms with fancy; yet t' imagine
An Antony were nature's piece 'gainst fancy,
Condemning shadows quite.
     V.ii.95–100

It is almost as if, like Descartes justifying the existence of God in the *Meditations*, Cleopatra is claiming reality for her idea of Antony by virtue of her very capacity to conceive of something so far beyond the scale of anything merely imagined.

It is in such a mood of exaltation that she can go further and imagine an afterlife and a celestial reunion with Antony in it. Antony himself, when he contemplated suicide believing Cleopatra dead, had conjured up an Elysian future for them:

> Where souls do couch on flowers, we'll hand in hand,
> And with our sprightly port make the ghosts gaze.
> Dido and her Aeneas shall want troops,
> And all the haunts be ours.
>   IV.xiv.51–4

As many commentators have pointed out, this is a strangely distorted view of the classical Elysium, not least in making Dido and Aeneas very unVirgilian reunited lovers. Where all the other inhabitants of the underworld are disembodied ghosts, ethereal souls couching on flowers, Antony and Cleopatra with their 'sprightly port' seem more substantial than mere sprites. It is an equally physical, equally tangible, world beyond death to which Cleopatra looks forward, as she imagines Iras, who dies before her, getting a head start in the race to reunion:

> If she first meet the curled Antony,
> He'll make demand of her, and spend that kiss
> Which is my heaven to have.
>   V.ii.299–301

The imagination of the protagonists' afterlife is exceptional among the tragedies. On the whole, 'Shakespeare is ... totally unconcerned with extrapolating the lives of his creatures beyond the stage and into a future estate of blessedness or damnation'.[18] In the case of *Antony and Cleopatra* the afterlife is so obviously imagined that there is no question of a theological judgement on blessedness or damnation. Janet Adelman usefully contrasts Othello's lines to the dead Desdemona, 'When we shall meet at compt, That look of thine will hurl my soul from heaven'.

> This is no mere poetic assertion of the impossible ... it is a statement about the highest reality which is terrifying precisely in its literalness. But in *Antony and Cleopatra*, there is no context which demands that we believe in the literal possibility of the afterlife.[19]

What we witness at Cleopatra's suicide is a pure histrionicism which defies disbelief and succeeds in imposing upon an audience a dream of apotheosis.

* * *

Antony and Cleopatra, with its lack of absolutes of faith or feeling, seems in some ways a strikingly modern play. A Hollywood-like glamour plays about the protagonists, their grandeur being no less grand for its artificial amplification or the awareness of its rackety meretriciousness. The tragedy does not attack the fraudulence of human pretensions to the heroic as polemically as *Troilus and Cressida*. Instead heroism is dramatised as the collaborative creation of the human imagination, in its potential for authentic greatness, in its vulnerability to doubt, in its measure of inherent factitiousness. It is a completely secular world from which, according to John Danby, Shakespeare has 'deliberately excise[d] the Christian core of his thought'.[20] That is to make the assumption that the core of Shakespeare's thought is Christian, whereas the aim of this book has been to show alternative non-Christian perspectives as integral to his tragic imagination. But *Antony and Cleopatra* does suspend the vision of a transcendent scheme of things which might give significance to the tragic action. The action must work itself out amid the relativising human evaluations of love and glory.

The play, with its close fidelity to Plutarch, is Antony grounded in history. The battle of Actium, the defeat of and Cleopatra, were the crucial events in establishing the principate, the Roman Empire of the following 400 years. 'The time of universal peace is near', promises Octavius as Antony's defeat is in sight.

> Prove this a prosp'rous day, the three-nook'd world
> Shall bear the olive freely.
>   IV.vi.5–7

These words would have had an extra dimension of significance for a Christian Renaissance audience because it was during the reign of Augustus that Christ was to be born, initiating the true 'time of universal peace'.[21] Yet this historical dimension to *Antony and Cleopatra* is never given the prominence we might expect. Octavius' words, for example, quoted above, come almost incidentally in a brief transition passage, in a scene where the main dramatic focus is on the unhappy renegade Enobarbus, looking back towards his deserted master Antony. As so often in the play, Octavius is the dramatically inert lay figure who supplies a fabric of historical narrative against which the protagonists are defined. His victory is not registered as an epochal moment in the history of the world, in the establishment of the Roman Empire or the coming inauguration of the Christian era. These are concepts notionally available but not dramatically realised in Shakespeare's play.

The secular historicity of the action of *Antony and Cleopatra* is felt only in relative contrast to the mythic mode of *Macbeth*. The restoration of Malcolm and the beheading of the tyrant Macbeth are experienced within a rhythmic cycle of the perpetual war of good and evil in the world. Octavius wins, Antony and Cleopatra lose, in something much more like mere historical continuum. In such a context, however, the story of the lovers is dramatised, personalised, to the point where it seems no more significantly historical than that of Romeo and Juliet. Antony and Cleopatra are what they make themselves rather than what history made them, or at least they play out with their own wilfulness the parts in which history has cast them. From this autogenesis of the heroic in *Antony and Cleopatra*, Shakespeare was to turn in *Coriolanus* to the figure of the hero in a far more determined world, a determinism of the historical, the political and the psychological.

NOTES

1. The most recent Shakespeare chronology, by the Oxford editors, assigns both plays to 1606. See Wells and Taylor *et al.*, *Textual Companion*, pp. 127–8.

2. L.C. Knights, *Some Shakespearean Themes* (London, 1959), p. 144.

3. Farnham, *Shakespeare's Tragic Frontier*, p. 203.

4. The stage direction is likely to be authorial, given that it appears in the Folio text, generally taken to derive from Shakespeare's own manuscript.

5. The analogy is made by Maurice Charney, *Shakespeare's Roman Plays* (Cambridge, Mass., 1961), p. 130. For commentary on this passage see also Janet Adelman, *The Common Liar: an Essay on Antony and Cleopatra* (New Haven and London, 1973), p. 91.

6. Quotations are from John Donne, *The Complete English Poems*, ed. A.J. Smith (Harmondsworth, 1971).

7. Paul Cantor, *Shakespeare's Rome: Republic and Empire* (Ithaca, NY, 1976), p. 205.

8. A.C. Bradley, Oxford *Lectures on Poetry* (London, 2nd edn, 1909, repr. 1959), p. 291.

9. M.W. MacCallum, *Shakespeare's Roman Plays* (London, 1910), p. 374.

10. Julian Markels, *The Pillar of the World* (Ohio, 1968), p. 43.

11. John F. Danby, *Poets on Fortune's Hill* (London, 1952), p. 144.

12. See David Grene, *The Actor in History: a Study in Shakespearean Stage Poetry* (University Park, Pa, and London, 1988), pp. 13–35.

13. Schanzer, *Problem Plays of Shakespeare*, p. 145.

14. See, among many others, Charney, *Shakespeare's Roman Plays*, p. 140.

15. See Janet Adelman, *The Common Liar*, Chapter 2, 'The Common Liar: Tradition as Source in *Antony and Cleopatra*' for a skilful analysis of the multiple

interpretive possibilities, both positive and negative, which these mythological figures afforded to a Renaissance audience.

16. S.L. Goldberg, 'A Tragedy of the Imagination: a Reading of *Antony and Cleopatra*', *Melbourne Critical Review* 4 (1961), 43.

17. Arnold Stein, 'The Image of Antony: Tragic and Lyric Imagination', *Kenyon Review* 21 (1959), 600.

18. Roland Mushat Frye, *Shakespeare and Christian Doctrine*, p. 51.

19. Adelman, *The Common Liar*, p. 166.

20. Danby, *Poets on Fortune's Hill*, p. 149.

21. See Andrew Fichter, '*Antony and Cleopatra*: The Time of Universal Peace', *Shakespeare Survey* 33 (1980), 99–111.

MAYNARD MACK

"The Readiness Is All":
Hamlet

1

Great plays, we know, each present us with something that can be called a world. A world like our own in being made of people, actions, situations, thoughts, feelings, and much more, but unlike our own in being perfectly, or almost perfectly, significant and coherent. In a play's world, each part implies the other parts, and each lives, means, with the life and meaning of the rest.

This is the reason, as we also know, why the worlds of great plays so greatly differ. Othello in Hamlet's position, we sometimes say, would have no problem; what we are really saying is that Othello in Hamlet's position would not exist. The conception we have of Othello is a function of the characters who help define him, Desdemona, honest Iago, Cassio, and the rest; of his history of travel and war; of a great storm that divides his ship from Cassio's, and a handkerchief; of a quiet night in Venice broken by cries about an old black ram; of a quiet night in Cyprus broken by sword-play; of a quiet bedroom where a woman goes to bed in her wedding sheets and a man comes in with a light to put out the light; and above all, of a language, a language with many voices in it, gentle, rasping, querulous, or foul, but all counterpointing the one great voice:

Keep up your bright swords, for the dew will rust them.
(1.2.59)

From *Everybody's Shakespeare: Reflections Chiefly on the Tragedies*, pp. 107–27, 267. © 1993 by Maynard Mack.

> O thou weed
> Who art so lovely fair and smell'st so sweet
> That the sense aches at thee....
> (4.2.67)

> Yet I'll not shed her blood
> Nor scar that whiter skin of hers than snow,
> And smooth as monumental alabaster.
> (5.2.3)

Without this particular world of voices, persons, events, the world that both expresses and contains him, Othello is unimaginable. And so, I think, are Brutus, Antony, King Lear, Macbeth—and Hamlet. We come back then to Hamlet's world, of all the tragic worlds that Shakespeare made, easily the most various and brilliant, the most elusive. It is with no thought of doing justice to it that I single out three of its attributes for comment. I know well that no one is likely to accept another's reading of *Hamlet*, that anyone who tries to throw light on one part of the play usually throws the rest into deeper shadow, and that what I have to say leaves out many problems—to mention only one, the knotty problem of the text. All I would say in defense of the materials I have chosen is that they seem to me interesting, close to the root of the matter even if we continue to differ about what the root of the matter is, and explanatory, in a modest way, of this play's peculiar hold on everyone's imagination, its almost mythic status, one might say, as a paradigm of the process of "growing up."

2

The first attribute that impresses us, I think, is the play's mysteriousness. We often hear it said, perhaps with truth, that every great work of art has a mystery at the heart; but the mystery of *Hamlet* is something else. We feel its presence in the numberless explanations that have been brought forward for Hamlet's delay, his madness, his ghost, his treatment of Polonius, or Ophelia, or his mother; and in the controversies that still go on about whether the play is "undoubtedly a failure" (T. S. Eliot's phrase) or one of the greatest artistic triumphs; whether, if it is a triumph, it belongs to the highest order of tragedy; whether, if it is such a tragedy, its hero is to be taken as a man of exquisite moral sensibility (Bradley's view) or an egomaniac (Madariaga's view).

Doubtless there have been more of these controversies and explanations than the play requires; for in Hamlet, to paraphrase a remark of Falstaff's quoted earlier, we have a character who is not only mad in himself but a cause that madness can seize on the rest of us. Still, the very existence of so many theories and counter-theories, many of them formulated by sober heads, gives food for thought. *Hamlet* seems to lie closer to the illogical logic of life than Shakespeare's other tragedies. And while the causes of this situation may be sought by saying that Shakespeare revised the play so often that eventually the motivations were smudged over, or that the original old play has been here or there imperfectly digested, or that the problems of Hamlet lay so close to Shakespeare's heart that he could not quite distance them in the formal terms of art, we have still as critics to deal with effects, not causes. As others have noted, the play's very lack of a rigorous type of causal logic seems to be a part of its point.

Moreover, the matter goes deeper than this. Hamlet's world is preeminently in the interrogative mood. It reverberates with questions, anguished, meditative, alarmed. There are questions that in this play, to an extent I think unparalleled in any other, mark the phases and even the nuances of the action, helping to establish its peculiar baffled tone. There are other questions whose interrogations, innocent at first glance, are subsequently seen to have reached beyond their contexts and to point toward some pervasive inscrutability in Hamlet's world as a whole. Such is that tense series of challenges with which the tragedy begins: Bernardo's of Francisco, "Who's there?" Francisco's of Horatio and Marcellus, "Who is there?" Horatio's of the ghost, "What art thou . . . ?"

And then there are the famous questions. In them the interrogations seem to point not only beyond the context but beyond the play, out of Hamlet's predicaments into everyone's: "What a piece of work is a man! . . . And yet to me what is this quintessence of dust?" (2.2.300). "To be, or not to be— that is the question" (3.1.56). "Get thee to a nunnery. Why wouldst thou be a breeder of sinners?" (3.1.121). "I am very proud, revengeful, ambitious, with more offenses at my beck than I have thoughts to put them in, imagination to give them shape, or time to act them in. What should such fellows as I do crawling between earth and heaven?" (3.1.124). "Dost thou think Alexander looked o' this fashion i' th' earth? . . . And smelt so?" (5.1.185).

Further, Hamlet's world is a world of riddles. The hero's own language is often riddling, as the critics have pointed out. When he puns, his puns have receding depths in them, like the one which constitutes his first speech: "A little more than kin, and less than kind!" (1.2.65). His utterances in madness, even if wild and whirling, are simultaneously, as Polonius discovers, pregnant: "Do you know me, my lord?" "Excellent well. You are a fishmonger" (2.2.173). Even the madness itself is riddling: How much is real? How much is feigned? What does it mean?

Sane or mad, Hamlet's mind plays restlessly about his world, turning up one riddle upon another. The riddle of character, for example, and how it is that in a man whose virtues else are "pure as grace," some vicious mole of nature, some "dram of evil," can "all the noble substance [oft adulter]" (1.4.36). Or the riddle of the player's art, and how a man can so project himself into a fiction, a dream of passion, that he can weep for Hecuba (2.2.535). Or the riddle of action: how we may think too little—"What to ourselves in passion we propose," says the player-king. "The passion ending, doth the purpose lose" (3.2.186); and again, how we may think too much: "Thus conscience does make cowards of us all, And thus the native hue of resolution Is sicklied o'er with the pale cast of thought" (3.1.83).

There are also more immediate riddles. His mother—how could she "on this fair mountain leave to feed, And batten on this moor" (3.4.67)? The ghost—which may be a devil, for "the devil hath power T' assume a pleasing shape" (2.2.585). Ophelia—what does her behavior to him mean? Surprising her in her closet, he falls to such perusal of her face as he would draw it (2.1.90). Even the king at his prayers is a riddle. Will a revenge that takes him in the purging of his soul be vengeance, or hire and salary (3.3.79)? As for himself, Hamlet realizes, he is the greatest riddle of all—a mystery, he warns Rosencrantz and Guildenstern, from which he will not have the heart plucked out. He cannot tell why he has of late lost all his mirth, forgone all custom of exercises. Still less can he tell why he delays: "I do not know Why yet I live to say, 'This thing's to do,' Sith I have cause, and will, and strength, and means To do 't" (4.4.43).

Thus the mysteriousness of Hamlet's world is of a piece. It is not simply a matter of missing motivations, to be expunged if only we could find the perfect clue. It is built in. It is evidently an important part of what the play wishes to say to us. And it is certainly an element that the play thrusts upon us from the opening word. Everyone, I think, recalls the mysteriousness of that first scene. The cold middle of the night on the castle platform, the muffled sentries, the uneasy atmosphere of apprehension, the challenges leaping out of the dark, the questions that follow the challenges, feeling out the darkness, searching for identities, for relations, for assurance. "Bernardo?" "Have you had quiet guard?" "Who hath relieved you?" "What, is Horatio there?" "What, has this thing appeared again tonight?" "Looks 'a not like the king?" "How now, Horatio! ... Is not this something more than fantasy? What think you on 't?" "Is it not like the King?" "Why this same strict and most observant watch ... ?" "Shall I strike at it with my partisan?" "Do you consent we shall acquaint [young Hamlet] with it?"

We need not be surprised that critics and playgoers alike have been tempted to see in this an evocation not simply of Hamlet's world but of their own. Human beings in their aspect of bafflement, moving in darkness on a rampart between two worlds, unable to reject, or quite accept, the one that, when they face it, "to-shakes" their dispositions with thoughts beyond the reaches of their souls—comforting themselves with hints and guesses. We hear these hints and guesses whispering through the darkness as the several watchers speak. "At least, the whisper goes so" (1.1.80), says one. "I think it be no other but e'en so," says another. "I have heard" that on the crowing of the cock "Th' extravagant and erring spirit hies To his confine," says a third. "Some say" at Christmas time "This bird of dawning" sings all night, "And then, they say, no spirit dare stir abroad." "So have I heard," says the first, "and do in part believe it." However we choose to take the scene, it is clear that it creates a world where uncertainties are of the essence.

3

Meantime, such is Shakespeare's economy, a second attribute of Hamlet's world has been put before us. This is the problematic nature of reality and the relation of reality to appearance. The play begins with an appearance, an "apparition," to use Marcellus's term—the ghost. And the ghost is somehow real, indeed the vehicle of realities. Through its revelation, the glittering surface of Claudius's court is pierced, and Hamlet comes to know, and we do, that the king is not only hateful to him but the murderer of his father, that his mother is guilty of adultery as well as incest. Yet there is a dilemma in the revelation. For possibly the apparition is an apparition, a devil who has assumed his father's shape.

This dilemma, once established, recurs on every hand. From the court's point of view, there is Hamlet's madness. Polonius investigates and gets some strange advice about his daughter: "Conception is a blessing, but as your daughter may conceive, friend, look to 't" (2.2.184). Rosencrantz and Guildenstern investigate and get the strange confidence that "Man delights not me—nor woman neither" (2.2.305). Ophelia is "loosed" to Hamlet (Polonius's vulgar word), while Polonius and the king hide behind the arras; and what they hear is a strange indictment of human nature, and a riddling threat: "Those that are married already—all but one—shall live" (3.1.147).

On the other hand, from Hamlet's point of view, there is Ophelia. Kneeling here at her prayers, she seems the image of innocence and devotion. Yet she is of the sex for whom he has already found the name Frailty, and she is also, as he seems either madly or sanely to divine, a decoy in a trick. The famous cry—"Get thee to a nunnery"—shows the anguish of his uncertainty. If Ophelia is what she seems, this dirty-minded world of murder, incest, lust, adultery, is no place for her. Were she "as chaste as ice, as pure as snow" (3.1.136), she could not escape its calumny. And if she is not what she seems, then a nunnery in its other sense of brothel is relevant to her. In the scene that follows he treats her as if she were indeed an inmate of a brothel.

Likewise, from Hamlet's point of view, there is the enigma of the king. If the ghost is *only* an appearance, then possibly the king's appearance is reality. He must try it further. By means of a second and different kind of "apparition," the play within the play, he does so. But then, immediately after, he stumbles on the king at prayer (3.3). This appearance has a relish of salvation in it. If the king dies now, his soul may yet be saved. Yet actually, as we know, the king's efforts to come to terms with heaven have been unavailing; his words fly up, his thoughts remain below. If Hamlet means the conventional revenger's reasons that he gives for sparing Claudius, it was the perfect moment not to spare him—when the sinner was acknowledging his guilt, yet unrepentant. The perfect moment, but it was hidden, like so much else in the play, behind an arras.

There are two arrases in his mother's room (3.4). Hamlet thrusts his sword through one of them. Now at last he has got to the heart of the evil, or so he thinks. But now it is the wrong man; now he himself is a murderer. The other arras he stabs through with his words—like daggers, says the queen. He makes her shrink under the contrast he points between her present husband and his father. But as the play now stands (matters are somewhat clearer in the bad Quarto), it is hard to be sure how far the queen grasps the fact that her second husband is the murderer of her first. And it is hard to say what may be signified by her inability to see the ghost, who now for the last time appears. In one sense at least, the ghost is the supreme reality, representative of the hidden ultimate power, in Bradley's terms—witnessing from beyond the grave against this hollow world. Yet the man who is capable of seeing through to this reality, the queen thinks is mad. "To whom do you speak this?" she cries to her son. "Do you see nothing there?" (3.4.132) he asks, incredulous. And she replies: "Nothing at all; yet all that is I see." Here certainly we have the imperturbable self-confidence of the worldly world, its layers on layers of habituation, so that when the reality is before its very eyes it cannot detect is presence.

Like mystery, this problem of reality is central to the play and written deep into its idiom. Shakespeare's favorite terms in *Hamlet* are words of ordinary usage that pose the question of appearances in a fundamental form. "Apparition" I have already mentioned. Another term is "seems." When we say, as Ophelia says of Hamlet leaving her closet, "He seemed to find his way without his eyes" (2.1.98), we mean one thing. When we say, as Hamlet says to his mother in the first court-scene, "Seems, Madam! . . . I know not 'seems'" (1.2.76), we mean another. And when we say, as Hamlet says to Horatio before the play within the play, "And after, we will both our judgments join In censure of his seeming" (3.2.83), we mean both at once. The ambiguities of "seem" coil and uncoil throughout this play, and over against them is set the idea of "seeing." So Hamlet challenges the king in his triumphant letter announcing his return to Denmark: "To-morrow shall I beg leave to see your kingly eyes" (4.7.44). Yet "seeing" itself can be ambiguous, as we recognize from Hamlet's uncertainty about the ghost; or from that statement of his mother's already quoted: "Nothing at all; yet all that is I see."

Another term of like importance is "assume." What we assume may be what we are not: "The devil hath power T'assume a pleasing shape" (2.2.585). But it may be what we are: "If it assume my noble father's person, I'll speak to it" (1.2.244). And it may be what we are not yet, but would become; thus Hamlet advises his mother, "Assume a virtue, if you have it not." The perplexity in the word points to a real perplexity in Hamlet's and our own experience. We assume our habits—and habits are like costumes, as the word implies: "My father, in his habit as he lived!" (3.4.136). Yet these habits become ourselves in time: "That monster custom, who all sense doth eat, Of habits devil, is angel yet in this, That to the use of actions fair and good He likewise gives a frock or livery That aptly is put on" (3.4.162).

Two other terms I wish to instance are "put on" and "shape." The shape of something is the form under which we are accustomed to apprehend it: "Do you see yonder cloud that's almost in shape of a camel?" But a shape may also be a disguise—even, in Shakespeare's time, an actor's costume or an actor's role. This is the meaning when the king says to Laertes as they lay the plot against Hamlet's life: "Weigh what convenience both of time and means May fit us to our shape" (4.7.148). "Put on" supplies an analogous ambiguity. Shakespeare's mind seems to worry this phrase in the play much as Hamlet's mind worries the problem of acting in a world of surfaces, or the king's mind worries the meaning of Hamlet's transformation. Hamlet has put an antic disposition on, that the king knows. But what does "put on" mean? A mask, or a frock or livery—our "habit"? The king is left guessing, and so are we.

4

What is found in the play's key terms is also found in its imagery. Miss Spurgeon has called attention to a pattern of disease images in *Hamlet*, to which I shall return. But the play has other patterns equally striking. One of these, as my earlier quotations hint, is based on clothes. In the world of surfaces to which Shakespeare exposes us in Hamlet, clothes are naturally a factor of importance. "The apparel oft proclaims the man," Polonius assures Laertes, cataloguing maxims in the young man's ear as he is about to leave for Paris (1.3.72). Oft, but not always. And so he sends his man Reynaldo to look into Laertes's life there—even, if need be, to put a false dress of accusation upon his son ("What forgeries you please"), the better by indirections to find directions out (2.1.66). On the same grounds, he takes Hamlet's vows to Ophelia as false apparel. They are bawds, he tells her—or if we do not like Theobald's emendation, they are bonds—in masquerade, "Not of that dye which their investments show, But mere implorators of unholy suits" (1.3.128).

This breach between the outer and the inner stirs no special emotion in Polonius, because he is always either behind an arras or prying into one, but it shakes Hamlet to the core. Here so recently was his mother in her widow's weeds, the tears still flushing in her gallèd eyes; yet now within a month, a little month, before even her funeral shoes are old, she has married with his uncle. Her mourning was all clothes. Not so his own, he bitterly replies, when she asks him to cast his "nighted color off." "'Tis not alone my inky cloak, good mother"—and not alone, he adds, the sighs, the tears, the dejected havior of the visage—"That can denote me truly."

> These indeed seem,
> For they are actions that a man might play,
> But I have that within which passeth show—
> These but the trappings and the suits of woe.

What we must not overlook here is Hamlet's visible attire, giving the verbal imagery a theatrical extension. Hamlet's apparel now is his inky cloak, mark of his grief for his father, mark also of his character as a man of melancholy, mark possibly too of his being one in whom appearance and reality are attuned. Later, in madness, with his mind disordered, he will wear his costume in a corresponding disarray, the disarray that Ophelia describes so vividly to Polonius and that producers of the play rarely give sufficient heed to: "Lord Hamlet with his doublet all unbraced, No hat upon his head, his stockings fouled, Ungartered, and down-gyvèd to his ankle" (2.1.78). Here the only question will be, as with the madness itself, how much is studied, how much is real. Still later, by a third costume, the simple traveler's garb in which we find him new come from shipboard, Shakespeare will show us that we have a third aspect of the man.

A second pattern of imagery springs from terms of painting: the paints, the colorings, the varnishes that may either conceal, or, as the painter's art, reveal. Art in Claudius conceals. "The harlot's cheek," he tells us in his one aside, "beautied with plast'ring art, Is not more ugly to the thing that helps it Than is my deed to my most painted word" (3.1.50). Art in Ophelia, loosed to Hamlet in the episode already noticed to which this speech of the king's is prelude, is more complex. She looks so beautiful—"the celestial, and my soul's idol, the most beautified Ophelia," Hamlet has called her in his love letter (2.2.109). But now, what does beautified mean? Perfected with all the innocent beauties of a lovely woman? Or "beautified" like the harlot's cheek? "I have heard of your paintings too, well enough. God hath given you one face, and you make yourselves another" (3.1.142).

Yet art, differently used, may serve the truth. By using an "image" (his own word) of a murder done in Vienna, Hamlet cuts through to the king's guilt; holds "as 'twere, the mirror up to nature," shows "virtue her own feature, scorn her own image, and the very age and body of the time"—which is out of joint—"his form and pressure" (3.2.20). Something similar he does again in his mother's bedroom, painting for her in words "the rank sweat of an enseamèd bed," making her recoil in horror from his "counterfeit present-ment of two brothers," and holding, if we may trust a stage tradition, his father's picture beside his uncle's. Here again the verbal imagery is realized visually on the stage.

The most pervasive of Shakespeare's image patterns in this play, however, is the pattern evolved around the three words, show, act, play. "Show" seems to be Shakespeare's unifying image in *Hamlet*. Through it he pulls together and exhibits in a single focus much of the diverse material in his play. The ideas of seeming, assuming, and putting on; the images of clothing, painting, mir-roring; the episode of the dumb show and the play within the play; the char-acters of Polonius, Laertes, Ophelia, Claudius, Gertrude, Rosencrantz and Guildenstern, Hamlet himself—all these at one time or another, and usually more than once, are drawn into the range of implications flung around the play by "show."

"Act," on the other hand, I take to be the play's radical metaphor. It distills the various perplexities about the character of reality into a residual perplexity about the character of an act. What, this play asks again and again, is an act? What is its relation to the inner act, the intent? "If I drown myself wittingly," says the clown in the graveyard, "it argues an act, and an act hath three branches—it is to act, to do, and to perform" (5.1.9). Or again, the play asks, how does action relate to passion, that "lapsed in time and passion" I can let "go by Th' important acting of your dread command" (3.4.108); and to thought, which can so sickly o'er the native hue of resolution that "enterprises of great pitch and moment With this regard their currents turn awry, And lose the name of action" (3.1.86); and to words, which are not acts, and so we dare not be content to unpack our hearts with them, and yet are acts of a sort, for we may speak daggers though we use none. Or still again, how does an act (a deed) relate to an act (a pretense)? For an action may be nothing but pretense. So Polonius readying Ophelia for the interview with Hamlet, with "pious action," as he phrases it, "sugar[s] o'er The devil himself" (3.1.48). Or it may not be a pretense, yet not what it appears. So Hamlet spares the king, finding him in an act that has some "relish of salvation in 't." Or it may be a pretense that is also the first foothold of a new reality, as when we assume a virtue though we have it not. Or it may be a pretense that is actually a mirroring of reality, like the play within the play, or the tragedy of Hamlet.

To this network of implications, the third term, "play," adds an additional dimension. "Play" is a more precise word, in Elizabethan parlance at least, for all the elements in *Hamlet* that pertain to the art of the theatre; and it extends their field of reference till we see that every major personage in the tragedy is a player in some sense, and every major episode a play. The court plays, Hamlet plays, the players play, Rosencrantz and Guildenstern try to play on Hamlet, though they cannot play on his recorders—here we have an extension to a musical sense. And the final duel, by a further extension, becomes itself a play, in which everyone but Claudius and Laertes plays his role in ignorance: "The queen desires you to use some gentle entertainment to Laertes before you fall to play" (5.2.195). "I . . . will this brother's wager frankly play." "Give him the cup."—"I'll play this bout first."

The full extension of this theme is best evidenced in the play within the play itself. Here, in the bodily presence of these traveling players, bringing with them the latest playhouse gossip out of London, we have suddenly a situation that tends to dissolve the normal barriers between the fictive and the real. For here on the stage before us is a play of false appearances in which an actor called the player-king is playing. But there is also on the stage, Claudius, another player-king, who is a spectator of this player. And there is on the stage, besides, a prince who is a spectator of both these player-kings and who plays with great intensity a player's role himself. And around these kings and that prince is a group of courtly spectators—Gertrude, Rosencrantz, Guildenstern, Polonius, and the rest—and they, as we have come to know, are players too. And lastly there are ourselves, an audience watching all these audiences who are also players. Where, it may suddenly occur to us to ask, does the playing end? Which are the guilty creatures sitting at a play? When is an act not an "act"?

5

The mysteriousness of Hamlet's world, while it pervades the tragedy, finds its point of greatest dramatic concentration in the first act, and its symbol in the first scene. The problems of appearance and reality also pervade the play as a whole, but come to a climax in Acts 2 and 3, and possibly their best symbol is the play-within-the-play. Our third attribute, though again it is one that crops out everywhere, reaches its full development in Acts 4 and 5. It is not easy to find an appropriate name for this attribute, but perhaps "mortality" will serve, if we remember to mean by mortality the heartache and the thousand natural shocks that flesh is heir to, not simply death.

The powerful sense of mortality in *Hamlet* is conveyed to us, I think, in three ways. First, there is the play's emphasis on human weakness, the instability of human purpose, the subjection of humanity to fortune—all that we might call the aspect of failure in human nature. Hamlet opens this theme in Act I, when he describes how from that single blemish, perhaps not even the victim's fault, a man's whole character may take corruption. Claudius dwells on it again, to an extent that goes far beyond the needs of the occasion, while engaged in seducing Laertes to step behind the arras of a seemer's world and dispose of Hamlet by a trick. Time qualifies everything, Claudius says, including love, including purpose. As for love—it has a "plurisy" in it and dies of its own too much. As for purpose—"That we would do, We should do when we would, for this 'would' changes, And hath abatements and delays as many As there are tongues, are hands, are accidents, And then this 'should' is like a spendthrift sigh, That hurts by easing" (4.7.116). The player-king, in his long speeches to his queen in the play within the play, sets the matter in a still darker light. She means these protestations of undying love, he knows, but our purposes depend on our memory, and our memory fades fast. Or else, he suggests, we propose something to ourselves in a condition of strong feeling, but then the feeling goes, and with it the resolve. Or else our fortunes change, he adds, and with these our loves: "The great man down, you mark his favorite flies" (3.2.180). The subjection of human aims to fortune is a reiterated theme in *Hamlet*, as earlier in *Julius Caesar* and subsequently in *Lear*. Fortune is the harlot goddess in whose secret parts men like Rosencrantz and Guildenstern live and thrive; the strumpet who threw down Troy and Hecuba and Priam; the outrageous foe whose slings and arrows a man of principle must suffer or seek release in suicide. Horatio suffers them with composure: he is one of the blessed few "Whose blood and judgment are so well commeddled That they are not a pipe for Fortune's finger To sound what stop she please" (3.2.66). For Hamlet the task is of a greater difficulty.

Next, and intimately related to this matter of infirmity, is the emphasis on infection—the ulcer, the hidden abscess, "th' imposthume of much wealth and peace That inward breaks, and shows no cause without Why the man dies" (4.4.27). Miss Spurgeon, who was the first to call attention to this aspect of the play, has well remarked that so far as Shakespeare's pictorial imagination is concerned, the problem in *Hamlet* is not a problem of the will and reason, "of a mind too philosophical or a nature temperamentally unfitted to act quickly," or even a problem of the individual at all. Rather, it is a condition—"a condition for which the individual himself is apparently not responsible, any more than the sick man is to blame for the infection which strikes and devours him, but which, nevertheless, in its course and development, impartially and relentlessly, annihilates him and others, innocent and guilty alike."[60] "That," she adds, "is the tragedy of *Hamlet*, as it is perhaps the chief tragic mystery of life." This is a perceptive comment, for it reminds us that Hamlet's situation is mainly not of his own manufacture, as are the situations of Shakespeare's other tragic heroes. He has inherited it; he is "born to set it right."

We must not, however, neglect to add to this what another student of Shakespeare's imagery has noticed—that the infection in Denmark is presented alternatively as poison. Here, of course, responsibility is implied, for the poisoner of the play is Claudius. The juice he pours into the ear of the elder Hamlet is a combined poison and disease, a "leperous distilment" that curds "The thin and wholesome blood" (1.5.64). From this fatal center, unwholesomeness spreads out till there is something rotten in all Denmark. Hamlet tells us that his "wit's diseased" (3.2.308), the queen speaks of her "sick soul" (4.5.17), the king is troubled by "the hectic" (4.3.65) in his blood, Laertes meditates revenge to warm "the sickness in [his] heart" (4.7.54), the people of the kingdom grow "muddied, Thick and unwholesome in their thoughts" (4.5.81); and even Ophelia's madness is said to be "the poison of deep grief" (4.5.75). In the end, all save Ophelia die of that poison in a literal as well as figurative sense.

But the chief form in which the theme of mortality reaches us, it seems to me, is as a profound consciousness of loss. Hamlet's father expresses something of the kind when he tells Hamlet how his "seeming-virtuous queen," betraying a love which "was of that dignity That it went hand in hand even with the vow I made to her in marriage," had chosen to "decline Upon a wretch whose natural gifts were poor To those of mine." "O Hamlet, what a falling off was there!" (1.5.46). Ophelia expresses it again, on hearing Hamlet's denunciation of love and woman in the nunnery scene, which she takes to be the product of a disordered brain:

> O what a noble mind is here o'erthrown!
> The courtier's, soldier's, scholar's, eye, tongue, sword;
> Th' expectancy and rose of the fair state,
> The glass of fashion and the mould of form,
> Th' observed of all observers, quite, quite, down!
>   (3.1.150)

The passage invites us to remember that we have never actually seen such a Hamlet—that his mother's marriage has brought a falling off in him before we meet him. And then there is that further falling off, if I may call it so, when Ophelia too goes mad—"Divided from herself and her fair judgment, Without the which we are pictures, or mere beasts" (4.5.85).

Time was, the play keeps reminding us, when Denmark was a different place. That was before Hamlet's mother took off "the rose From the fair forehead of an innocent love" (3.4.43) and set a blister there. Hamlet then was still "Th' expectancy and rose of the fair state" (3.1.152); Ophelia, the "rose of May" (4.5.157). For Denmark was a garden then, when his father ruled. There had been something heroic about his father—a king who met the threats to Denmark in open battle, fought with Norway, smote the sledded Polacks on the ice, slew the elder Fortinbras in an honorable trial of strength. There had been something godlike about his father too: "Hyperion's curls, the front of Jove himself, An eye like Mars ... , A station like the herald Mercury" (3.4.57). But, the ghost reveals, a serpent was in the garden, and "The serpent that did sting thy father's life Now wears his crown" (1.5.39). The martial virtues are put by now. The threats to Denmark are attended to by policy, by agents working deviously for and through an uncle. The moral virtues are put by too. Hyperion's throne is occupied by "a vice of kings" (3.4.99), "a king of shreds and patches" (3.4.103); Hyperion's bed, by a satyr, a paddock, a bat, a gib, a bloat king with reechy kisses. The garden is unweeded now, and "grows to seed. Things rank and gross in nature Possess it merely" (1.2.136). Even in himself he feels the taint, the taint of being his mother's son; and that other taint, from an earlier garden, of which he admonishes Ophelia: "For virtue cannot so inoculate our old stock but we shall relish of it." "Why wouldst thou be a breeder of sinners?" "What should such fellows as I do crawling between earth and heaven?" (3.1.117).

"Hamlet is painfully aware," says E. M. W. Tillyard, "of the baffling human predicament between the angels and the beasts, between the glory of having been made in God's image and the incrimination of being descended from fallen Adam."[61] To this we may add, I think, that Hamlet is more than aware of it; he exemplifies it; and it is for this reason that his problem appeals to us so powerfully as an image of our own.

6

Hamlet's problem, in its crudest form, is simply the problem of the avenger: he must carry out the injunction of the ghost and kill the king. But this problem, as I ventured to suggest at the outset, is presented in terms of a certain kind of world. The ghost's injunction to act becomes so inextricably bound up for Hamlet with the character of the world in which the action must be taken—its mysteriousness, its baffling appearances, its deep consciousness of infection, frailty, and loss—that he cannot come to terms with either without coming to terms with both.

When we first see him in the play, he is clearly a very young man, sensitive and idealistic, suffering the first shock of growing up. He has taken the garden at face value, we might say, supposing mankind to be only a little lower than the angels. Now in his mother's hasty and incestuous marriage, he discovers evidence of something else, something bestial—though even a beast, he thinks, would have mourned longer. Then comes the revelation of the ghost, bringing a second shock. Not so much because he now knows that his serpent-uncle killed his father; his prophetic soul had almost suspected this. Not entirely, even, because he knows now how far below the angels humanity has fallen in his mother, and how lust—these were the ghost's words—"though to a radiant angel linked Will sate itself in a celestial bed, And prey on garbage" (1.5.55). Rather, because he now sees everywhere, but especially in his own nature, the general taint, taking from life its meaning, from woman her integrity, from the will its strength, turning reason into madness. Hamlet is not the first young man to have felt the heavy and the weary weight of all this unintelligible world; and, like the others, he must come to terms with it.

The ghost's injunction of revenge unfolds a different facet of his problem. The young man growing up is not to be allowed simply to endure a rotten world, he must also act in it. Yet how to begin, among so many enigmatic surfaces? Even Claudius, whom he now knows to be the core of the ulcer, has a plausible exterior. And around Claudius, swathing the evil out of sight, he encounters all those other exteriors, as we have seen. Some of them already deeply infected beneath, like his mother. Some noble, but marked for infection, like Laertes. Some not particularly corrupt but infinitely corruptible, like Rosencrantz and Guildenstern; some mostly weak and foolish like Polonius and Osric. Some, like Ophelia, innocent, yet in their innocence still serving to "skin and film the ulcerous place" (3.4.148).

And this is not all. The act required of him, though retributive justice, is one that necessarily involves the doer in the general guilt. Not only because it involves a killing; but because to get at the world of seeming one is impelled to use its weapons. He himself, before he finishes, has become a player, has put an antic disposition on, has killed a man—the wrong man—has helped drive Ophelia mad, and has sent two friends of his youth to death, mining below their mines, and hoisting the engineer with his own petard. He had never meant to dirty himself with these things, but from the moment of the ghost's challenge to act, this dirtying was inevitable. It is the condition of living at all in such a world. To quote Polonius, who knew that world so well, men become "a little soiled i' th' working" (2.1.40). Here is another matter with which Hamlet has to come to terms.

Human infirmity—all that I have discussed with reference to instability, infection, loss—supplies the problem with its third phase. Hamlet has not only to accept the mystery of man's condition between the angels and the brutes, and not only to act in a perplexing and soiling world. He has also to act within the human limits—"with shabby equipment always deteriorating," if I may adapt some phrases from T. S. Eliot's *East Coker*, "In the general mess of imprecision of feeling, Undisciplined squads of emotion." Hamlet is aware of that fine poise of body and mind, feeling and thought, that suits the action to the word, the word to the action; that acquires and begets a temperance in the very torrent, tempest, and whirlwind of passion; but he cannot at first achieve it in himself. He vacillates between undisciplined squads of emotion and thinking too precisely on the event. He learns to his cost how easily action can be lost in "acting," and loses it there for a time himself. But these again are only the terms of every man's life. As Anatole France reminds us in a famous apostrophe to Hamlet: "What one of us thinks without contradiction and acts without incoherence? What one of us is not mad? What one of us does not say with a mixture of pity, comradeship, admiration, and horror, Goodnight, sweet Prince!"

7

In the last act of the play (or so it seems to me, for I know there can be differences on this point), Hamlet accepts his world and we discover a different man. Shakespeare does not outline for us the process of acceptance any more than he had done with Romeo or was to do with Othello. But he leads us strongly to expect an altered Hamlet, and then, in my opinion, provides him. We must recall that at this point Hamlet has been absent from the stage during several scenes, and that such absences in Shakespearean tragedy usually warn us to be on the watch for a new phase in the development of the character. It is so when we leave King Lear in Gloucester's farmhouse and find him again in Dover fields. It is so when we leave Macbeth at the witches' cave and rejoin him at Dunsinane, hearing of the armies that beset it. Furthermore, and this is an important matter in the theater—especially important in a play in which the symbolism of clothing has figured largely— Hamlet now looks different. He is wearing a different dress—probably, as Granville-Barker thinks, his "seagown scarfed" about him, but in any case no longer the disordered costume of his antic disposition. The effect is not entirely dissimilar to that in *Lear*, when the old king wakes out of his madness to find fresh garments on him.

Still more important, Hamlet displays a considerable change of mood. This is not a matter of the way we take the passage about defying augury. It is a matter of Hamlet's whole deportment, in which I feel we may legitimately see the deportment of a man who has undergone some form of insight or self-discovery in the tragic sense. Bradley's term for it is fatalism, but if this is what we wish to call it, we must at least acknowledge that it is fatalism of a very distinctive kind—a kind that Shakespeare has been willing to touch with the associations of the saying in St. Matthew about the fall of a sparrow, and with Hamlet's recognition that a divinity shapes our ends. The point is not that Hamlet has suddenly become religious; he has been religious all through the play. The point is that he has now learned, and accepted, the boundaries in which human action, human judgment, are enclosed.

Till his return from the voyage he had been trying to act beyond these, had been encroaching on the role of Providence, if I may exaggerate to make a vital point. He had been too quick to take the burden of the whole world and its condition upon his limited and finite self. Faced with a task of sufficient difficulty in its own right, he had dilated it into a cosmic problem—as indeed every task is, but if we think about this too precisely we cannot act at all. The whole time is out of joint, he feels, and in his young man's egocentricity, he will set it right. Hence he misjudges Ophelia, seeing in her only a breeder of sinners. Hence he misjudges himself, seeing himself a vermin crawling between earth and heaven. Hence he takes it upon himself to be his mother's conscience, though the ghost has warned that this is no fit task for him, and returns to repeat the warning: "Leave her to heaven, And to those thorns that in her bosom lodge" (1.5.86). Even with the king, Hamlet has sought to play at God. He it must be who decides the issue of Claudius's salvation, saving him for a more damnable occasion.

Now, he has learned that there are limits to the before and after that human reason can comprehend. Rashness, even, is sometimes good. Through rashness he has saved his life from the commission for his death, "and praised be rashness for it" (5.2.7). This happy circumstance and the unexpected arrival of the pirate ship make it plain that the roles of life are not entirely self-assigned. "There's a divinity that shapes our ends. Rough-hew them how we will" (5.2.10). Hamlet is ready now for what may happen, seeking neither to foreknow it nor avoid it. "If it be now, 'tis not to come; if it be not to come, it will be now; if it be not now, yet it will come. The readiness is all" (5.2.209).

The crucial evidence of Hamlet's new frame of mind, as I understand it, is the graveyard scene. Here, in its ultimate symbol, he confronts, recognizes, and accepts the condition of being human. It is not simply that he now accepts death, though Shakespeare shows him accepting it in ever more poignant forms: first, in the imagined persons of the politician, the courtier, and the lawyer, who laid their little schemes "to circumvent God" (5.1.75), as Hamlet puts it, but now lie here; then in Yorick, whom he knew and played with as a child; and then in Ophelia. This last death tears from him a final cry of passion, but the striking contrast between his behavior and Laertes's reveals how deeply he has changed.

Still, it is not the fact of death that invests this scene with its peculiar power. It is instead the haunting mystery of life itself that Hamlet's speeches point to, holding in its inscrutable folds those other mysteries that he has wrestled with so long. These he now knows for what they are, and lays them by. The mystery of evil is present here—for this is after all the universal grave-yard, where, as the clown says humorously, he holds up Adam's profession; where the scheming politician, the hollow courtier, the tricky lawyer, the emperor and the clown and the beautiful young maiden, all come together in an emblem of the world; where even, Hamlet murmurs, one might expect to stumble on "Cain's jawbone, that did the first murder" (5.1.73).

The mystery of reality is here too—for death puts the question "What is real?" in its irreducible form, and in the end uncovers all appearances: "Is this the fine of his fines and the recovery of his recoveries, to have his fine pate full of fine dirt?" (5.1.98). "Now get you to my lady's chamber, and tell her, let her paint an inch thick, to this favor she must come" (5.1.180). Or if we need more evidence of this mystery, there is the anger of Laertes at the lack of ceremonial trappings, and the ambiguous character of Ophelia's own death. "Is she to be buried in Christian burial when she wilfully seeks her own salvation?" (5.1.1) asks the gravedigger.

And last of all, but most pervasive of all, there is the mystery of human limitation. The grotesque nature of man's little joys, his big ambitions. The fact that the man who used to bear us on his back is now a skull that smells; that the noble dust of Alexander somewhere plugs a bunghole; that "Imperious Caesar, dead and turned to clay, Might stop a hole to keep the wind away" (5.1.200). Above all, the fact that a pit of clay is "meet" for such a guest as man, as the gravedigger tells us in his song, and yet that, despite all frailties and limitations, "That skull had a tongue in it, and could sing once" (5.1.71).

After the graveyard and what it indicates has come to pass in him, we know that Hamlet is ready for the final contest of mighty opposites. He accepts the world as it is, the world as a duel, in which, whether we know it or not, evil holds the poisoned rapier and the poisoned chalice waits; and in which, if we win at all, it costs not less than everything. I think we understand by the close of Shakespeare's *Hamlet* why it is that unlike the other tragic heroes he is given a soldier's rites upon the stage. For as William Butler Yeats once said, "Why should we honor those who die on the field of battle? A man may show as reckless a courage in entering into the abyss of himself."[62]

NOTES

60. Caroline Spurgeon, *Shakespeare's Imagery and What It Tells Us* (Cambridge University Press, 1971), 123–24.

61. E. M. W. Tillyard, *Shakespeare's Problem Plays* (University of Toronto Press, 1949), 6.

62. "Unpublished notes for a lecture," quoted in Richard Ellmann, Yeats: *The Man and the Masks* (New York, 1948), 298.

PETER WENZEL

Word and Action in the
Mad Scenes of Shakespeare's Tragedies

The mad scenes in Shakespeare's tragedies have at all times attracted the critics. But the numerous commentators on the subject have limited their perspective either to the moral and philosophical[1] or to the medical aspects[2] of these scenes, while to my knowledge no attempt has been made so far to approach them from a dramaturgical angle, asking questions like: How does Shakespeare inform his audience that from a certain time onwards, a character, having acted sanely before, has crossed over into madness? Does Shakespeare prefer to use verbal or non-verbal devices to convey this notion? How can these devices be classified? And, last but not least: Is madness in Shakespeare invariably marked by the same devices or is it indicated in different ways in order to individualize the mad characters of different plays?

What one needs to answer these questions in a methodical way is, first of all, a set of categories suitable for giving a consistent description of the verbal and non-verbal devices which mark the state of madness in each individual case. In the following I shall try to develop such a set of categories by referring to two typologies drawn from two particularly fruitful branches of modern linguistics: text linguistics and theatrical semiotics.

From *Word and Action in Drama: Studies in Honour of Hans-Jürgen Diller on the Occasion of His 60th Birthday*, edited by Günter Ahrends, Stephan Kohl, Joachim Kornelius, Gerd Stratmann, pp. 65–80. © 1994 by WVT Wissenschaftlicher Verlag Trier.

1.

The typology from theatrical semiotics will be introduced first because it is broader in scope and more widely known. In 1968, The Polish semiotician Tadeusz Kowzan[3] provided a list of thirteen theatrical sign-systems which has since then been accepted, sometimes with minor modifications, by most of the experts in the field.[4] Kowzan's categories provide a handy tool for describing the various channels through which in a modern theatre information is conveyed to the audience. In detail, Kowzan's typology includes: 1. language, 2. tone, 3. facial mime, 4. gesture, 5. movement, 6. make-up, 7. hairstyle, 8. costume, 9. props, 10. decor, 11. lighting, 12. music and 13. sound effects.

Of course, not all of Kowzan's categories are equally relevant to our project. Lighting, for instance, can be dropped because in Elizabethan times, most of the plays were written for open-air playhouses, and even in the roofed private playhouses, light effects were not yet possible for lack of the necessary technology. Likewise, decor played only a very minor role in the Elizabethan theatre and never stood in any direct relationship to the mental state of one of its characters (contrary to what we know, for instance, from modern expressionist plays). This still leaves eleven of the above-mentioned categories, but since in addition to that, some of the categories may be grouped together for simplicity's sake (as Gerhard Müller-Schwefe has shown in an earlier attempt to apply them to Shakespeare[5]), Kowzan's typology of thirteen categories can be reduced to an even handier one of only six:

1. Language or 'linguistic signs', i.e. the text of the plays itself.
2. Tone or 'paralinguistic signs', i.e. the way in which the text is articulated by the actors.
3. 'Kinesic signs', comprising facial mime, gesture and movement.
4. Make-up, hairstyle and costume.
5. Props.
6. 'Acoustic signs', comprising music and sound-effects.

Among these six sign-systems, the most complex one is, of course, that of the linguistic signs, and it therefore becomes necessary to search for further categories which may help to distinguish a sane, completely meaningful use of this sign-system from an insane one, in which meaning is at least partly blurred. In an attempt to define the concept of 'textuality', Robert de Beaugrande and Wolfgang Dressler in their *Introduction to Text Linguistics*[6] have provided a list of seven principles that are highly pertinent to this purpose. The principles include: 1. cohesion, 2. coherence, 3. intentionality, 4. acceptability, 5. informativity, 6. situationality,

7. intertextuality. Again, not all of these categories must necessarily be kept separate, because some of them overlap to a considerable extent and because it would be too difficult (and of little value) to disentangle them in the practical analyses. Thus, the principle of cohesion, defined as "the ways in which [...] the actual words we hear or see are mutually connected within a sequence",[7] and the principle of coherence, defined as "the ways in which [...] the configuration of concepts and relations which underlie the surface text are mutually accessible and relevant",[8] may both be subsumed under the principle of intentionality as "the text producer's attitude that the set of occurrences should constitute a cohesive and coherent text instrumental in fulfilling the producer's intentions".[9] This leaves five principles to be kept in mind when studying the discourse of Shakespeare's mad characters in detail, namely:

1. Intentionality, including cohesion and coherence.
2. Acceptability, which means that normally, the utterances of a discourse must be constructed in such a way that they will have some relevance for the receiver(s).
3. Informativity, which means that normally, the utterances of a discourse must not contain any recurrences, unless the recurrences have an actual communicative function.
4. Situationality, which means that normally, the utterances of a discourse must be at some level related to the situation in which they occur.
5. Intertextuality.

These five principles of textuality and the six types of sign-systems introduced before will provide the methodological framework for the following analyses. This is not to imply, of course, that insights gained without help from these categories will be excluded: Rather, the principles and types are meant to preserve our analyses from a too impressionistic approach, without blinding us to further observations gained in a less systematic way. Irrespective of the fact that there are many mad characters in the Shakespeare canon, the number of plays to be studied in this way must here be restricted to the Great Tragedies,[10] more particularly (since Othello never really goes mad[11]) to *Hamlet* (1600–01), *King Lear* (1605) and *Macbeth* (1606).

2.

For heuristic reasons, it is suitable to start, contrary to the chronology, with Shakespeare's most famous and prototypical depiction of mental, derangement: the sleepwalking scene of Lady Macbeth (*Mac.*, V,1). What is most

conspicuous in this scene is the particular care with which the dramatist
calls the attention of his audience to the abnormality of the Lady's behaviour: Even before the Lady appears herself, her doctor and a gentlewoman
have an extended discussion on her recent sleepwalks (ll. 1–17), thus establishing a frame of expectation for the Lady's aberrant behaviour. After
her appearance the Doctor and the Gentlewoman assume the function of
commentators, pointing out to the audience the various symptoms of Lady
Macbeth's mental disarray:

> *Enter* LADY MACBETH, with a taper.
> GENT
>   Lo you! here she comes. This, is her very guise; and, [18] upon
> my life, fast asleep. Observe her: stand close. [19]
> DOCT
>   How came she by that light?
> GENT
>   Why, it stood by her: she has light by her continually; 'tis her
> command.
> DOCT
>   You see, her eyes are open. [23]
> GENT
>   Ay, but their sense are shut.
> DOCT
>   What is it she does now? Look, how she rubs her [25] hands.
> GENT
>   It is an accustom'd action with her, to seem thus washing her
> hands. I have known her continue in this a quarter of an hour.
>   (V,1,18–29)[12]

Various facts deserve our attention in this passage. First, it is important to
note that in terms of our categories, the unbalanced state of the Lady's mind
is not indicated by her own speech, i.e. by linguistic signs (categ. 1), but
rather by a prop (categ. 5), namely the taper,[13] and by kinesic signs (categ.
3) such as her sleepwalking (cf. ll. 19: "fast asleep" and 23: "her eyes are
open") and the rubbing of her hands (ll. 25f.). It is true, of course, that in
accordance with the conventions of the Elizabethan theatre even these non-
verbal indicators of abnormality are integrated in the linguistic sign-system,
since they are conveyed through the dialogue of the characters serving as a
necessary compensation for the poor visibility on an Elizabethan stage, but
this does not invalidate the fact that in order to mark a character's mental
disarray, Shakespeare is here resorting to the non-verbal sign-systems first,

probably because—due to their earlier position in semiotic evolution—they are the more immediately effective means of communication.

Second, it is necessary to realize that each of the various signs employed for characterizing the Lady's mental state is carefully foregrounded with the help of a remark or a question from one of the two commentator-figures, all pointing to what the spectator should see or pay his attention to: "Lo [i.e.: Look] you! here she comes" (l. 18); "How came she by that light?" (l. 20); "You see, her eyes are open" (l. 23); and, most prominently: "What is it she does now? Look, how she rubs her hands" (ll. 25f.). Though this technique of raising the audience's attention may also be accounted for with the deeper psychological importance of the objects and actions foregrounded in this way—after all, the light of the taper is yearned for by the Lady because she is now terrified of the dark,[14] and the rubbing of her hands expresses her wish to rid herself from her guilt, there can be no doubt that in the context of an Elizabethan stage, it was its main function to guarantee that in spite of poor visibility and acoustics even the hindmost spectator would grasp the fundamental change in the Lady's mental condition.

Third, it is interesting that the comments of the Gentlewoman are used to convey the idea that the individual signs of Lady Macbeth's disturbance must not be taken as singular, unprecedented incidents but as phenomena that are typical of her recent behaviour in general: "This is her very guise" (l. 18) says the Gentlewoman, meaning according to the critical commentaries: "This is the way she has done it before".[15] The notion is stressed by her following remarks: "she has light by her continually" (l. 21f.) and (with reference to the Lady's rubbing her hands) "It is an accustom'd action with her [...] I have known her continue in this a quarter of an hour" (ll. 27–29). What is in reality visible upon the stage but for a brief moment is thus transformed in the audience's imagination into a series of repeated actions, lending Lady Macbeth's somnambulistic distraction further momentum and impressiveness.

Having caught his audience's attention in this way, the playwright is now in a position to confront it with a linguistic manifestation of Lady Macbeth's condition:

LADY M.
  Yet here's a spot.
DOCT
  Hark! she speaks. I will set down what comes from [31] her, to
satisfy my remembrance the more strongly.
LADY M.
  Out, damned spot! out, I say!—One; two: [33] why, then 'tis
time to do't.—Hell is murky.—Fie, my Lord, fie! a soldier, and

afeard?—What need [35] we fear who knows it, when none can
call our power to accompt?—Yet who would have thought the old
man to have had so much blood in him?
DOCT
  Do you mark that?
    (ll. 30–39)

Like the previous non-verbal indicators of her mental disarray, the Lady's
distracted speech is again foregrounded with the help of an introductory
comment, this time from the Doctor: "Hark! she speaks. I will set down
what comes from her" (ll. 31f.). In addition to that, the Lady's speech itself
is clearly marked as aberrant, because its linguistic structure violates almost
each of the principles of textuality outlined in my introduction: At a first
glance, the intentionality (principle 1) of the speech remains unclear, not
only because its beginning is largely made up of disconnected words and
thus lacks in grammatical cohesion, but also because due to the swift change
of its subjects (spot—clock—hell—Macbeth and the murder) the speech is
seemingly short of conceptual coherence. Moreover, it infringes upon the
principle of situationality (4) in that it is in no way related to the environment of its speaker. As the puzzled questions and exclamations with which
the Doctor and the Gentlewoman react to this and the Lady's following
speeches make sufficiently clear, the acceptability (principle 2) of her discourse is equally low. And towards the end of the scene, her utterances may
even be said to be lacking in informativity (principle 3) because they peter
out in a series of repetitions:

LADY M.
  To bed, to bed: there's knocking at the gate. Come, come, come,
  come, give me your hand. What's done cannot be undone. To bed,
  to bed, to bed.
  [Exit.]
    (ll. 62–65)

It is typical of Shakespeare's dramatic art, however, that the textuality
of Lady Macbeth's distracted speeches is only disturbed at a superficial
level—the level of the internal communication between the characters—,
while at the deeper level of the external communication between the characters and the audience, most of the above-mentioned principles of reasonable discourse are fulfilled. For it is possible, as has often been mentioned
by the critics, to link all of the seemingly disconnected parts of the Lady's
sleepwalking speeches to an intention of coming to grip with the powerful

emotions which have been haunting the Lady since the murder of Duncan. Thus, the spot to be blotted out (cf. l. 33) has an obvious connection to the pool of blood surrounding the slaughtered Duncan, the striking of the clock imagined by the Lady (cf. ll. 33f) may be associated with the bell she struck in the murder-scene (cf. II,1,61),[16] and her sudden inconsequent exclamation "Hell is murky" (l. 34) is either, as George Steevens believed, a contemptuous repetition of what her husband said in the murder-scene or, as suggested by the Clarendon edition, a guilty expression of the Lady's remorse and dread of future punishment.[17] In spite of their insufficient integration with the internal communicative situation, then, Lady Macbeth's words have an underlying, fictive situationality, which lends them conceptual coherence and an undoubted acceptability on the part of the audience. Seen from the audience's point of view, even the highly repetitive commands at the end of the Lady's distracted discourse, urging Macbeth to take her by the hand and accompany her to bed, contain a considerable degree of informativity because they can be interpreted as a desperate expression of the Lady's yearning to re-establish the broken relationship with her husband, whether mainly to dominate or to love him again.[18]

In summary, then, it can be stated that in his famous sleepwalking scene, Shakespeare succeeds in marking Lady Macbeth's discourse as clearly aberrant, while using it at the same time to inform the audience in a subtle way about this character's psychological and moral plight.

3.

In *Hamlet*, Ophelia is the character whose discourse becomes most clearly aberrant. Since contrary to Lady Macbeth's somnambulism, Ophelia's mental derangement must be understood as insanity in the full sense of the word, its oddity is marked even more clearly by particular non-verbal devices and, at the linguistic level, a violation of various principles of textuality.

Like Lady Macbeth's appearance in her sleepwalking scene, Ophelia's entrance in her mad scene (*Ham.*, IV,5) is carefully prepared through a conversation (in this case between Queen Gertrude and a gentlewoman) that draws the audience's attention to the particulars of her altered condition, such as the fact that she "hems, and beats her heart, / Spurns enviously at straws, speaks things in doubt / That carry but half sense" (ll. 5–7) and supplements her incoherent words with "winks and nods and gestures" (l. 11). Apart from the linguistic sign-system, then, the paralinguistic[19] (cf. "hems") and again the kinesic systems (categories 2 and 3) are used as effective markers of madness even before the mentally distracted Ophelia appears on the stage herself. With her appearance, two further systems—hairstyle and acoustic signs (categories 4 and 6)—are brought into play, for at least the first quarto, probably recording some contemporary staging,[20] has the scenic device that Ophelia enters "playing on a Lute, and her haire downe singing". Even more than the various indicators of Lady Macbeth's distraction, then, the indicators of Ophelia's madness cover the full range of the different sign-systems that the dramatist has at his command.

In addition to that, the audience's perception of Ophelia's madness is again carefully guided by the remarks of the commentator-figures, in this case Queen Gertrude and King Claudius. With her exclamation "Let her come in" (l. 16)—a line that is in some editions[21] ascribed to the previous speaker Horatio, which only stresses its impersonal, purely dramatic function—Gertrude prepares the audience for Ophelia's entrance. Once Ophelia has come on the stage, Gertrude repeatedly points out the oddity of Ophelia's songs and behaviour: "How now, Ophelia?" (l. 20); "Alas, sweet lady, what imports this song?" (l. 27); "Nay, but Ophelia—" (l. 34); and, addressing herself to Claudius, "Alas, look here, my lord" (l. 37). In the next part of the scene, this commenting function is adopted by Claudius, whose utterances alternate between unsuccessful attempts to establish communication with Ophelia ("How do you, pretty Lady?", l. 41, and "Pretty Ophelia ", l. 56) and imparting and asking for information about her disturbing condition ("Conceit upon her father", l. 45, and "How long hath she been thus?", l. 67, a question which, similar to some of the remarks of the Gentlewoman on Lady Macbeth, serves to inform the audience that Ophelia's madness is a permanent rather than a temporary phenomenon).

Interestingly enough, Ophelia's second appearance later in the scene (ll. 154ff.) is again announced with the set phrase "Let her come in" (l. 152), which can again be given to almost any speaker or speakers of this scene.[22] Moreover, there is again a commentator—Laertes in this case—who maps out the audience's response by first expressing his bewilderment about Ophelia's condition ("O heat, dry up my brains. Tears seven times salt / Burn out the sense and virtue of mine eye", ll. 155f.) and then hinting to the fact that to the audience, Ophelia's mad songs, like Lady Macbeth's distracted speeches in the sleepwalking scene, need not remain as uncommunicative and meaningless as to her fellow-characters, because there may be some hidden sense behind them: "This nothing's more than matter [. . .] / A document in madness: thoughts and remembrance fitted" (ll.172 and 176f.).

And in fact, analyzing Ophelia's songs in the light of our principles of textuality, we find that they work at two levels again: At a superficial level—the level of conscious interaction between the characters—they lack any intentionality, situationality and acceptability, as Gertrude's and Claudius's reactions to them make sufficiently clear. Being marked with repetitions, the songs seem to be restricted also in their informativity, and even their intertextuality (principle 5) is disturbed, because though they must all have been taken from contemporary popular ballads, they consist of fragments only whose actual source cannot always be identified.[23] But when they are looked at from the perspective of a critical spectator, the songs lose their deficiencies because they "most obviously connect with the recent death and burial of Polonius"[24] and with the pangs of Ophelia's rejected love for Hamlet,[25] so that at a psychologically deeper level, their intentionality and informativity can be taken for granted. Seen in this context, their incoherent intertextuality becomes quite functional, too, because the fragmentary nature of Ophelia's songs fits in well with her broken love relationship to Hamlet. Last but not least, even the principle of situationality seems to be preserved in the different mad songs, since, as Harold Jenkins has convincingly shown, each of them has a reference to the character who is nearest to Ophelia in the actual situation.[26] Likewise, the flowers that Ophelia, again combining mad words with mad action, distributes among the bystanders towards the end of the scene, are loaded with symbolic significance[27] and not without reference to the individual persons they are given to.[28]

In the history of *Hamlet*-criticism, the "antic disposition" (I,5,180) affected by the protagonist has often been taken as another instance of real madness in the play. There is, however, important historical and textual evidence to be adduced against this view—such as the convention that in an Elizabethan revenge tragedy, the avenger often feigns madness to gain time to investigate the murder and prepare his revenge[29] as well as the fact that Hamlet, when no longer in need of pretending madness (as in his soliloquies and his confidential interviews with Horatio and his mother) immediately shifts back from the use of prose marking his altered state of mind to blank verse spoken in all sincerity and sanity.[30] In addition to that, the thesis that Hamlet really falls victim to insanity can clearly be refuted with the help of the methodological tools developed in the present paper. For contrary to the change in Lady Macbeth's and Ophelia's state of mind, the change in Hamlet's is hardly marked by any non-verbal signs—all that Hamlet does is walk about with a book in his hands for hours (I,5,160f.), which may be a sign of melancholy, but certainly not of insanity.[31] And it is particularly striking that in his seemingly mad speeches, Hamlet violates the principles of textuality only in a limited and quite purposeful manner. Thus, he hardly ever ignores the principles of intentionality, informativity and situationality, but keeps infringing upon the principle of acceptability, though not in the sense that his answers and comments have no relevance for their receivers but in the sense that, lacking in what has been called by speech-act-theorists "the principle of co-operation",[32] they violate their expectations, feelings and norms of decency.[33]

The most important evidence against the thesis of Hamlet's insanity, however, is again to be found in the comments of other characters and, in this case, of Hamlet himself. In two asides clearly intended to guard the audience against misinterpreting Hamlet's behaviour as real insanity, ever the foolish Polonius realizes that "there is method" in Hamlet's madness (II,2,205) and that Hamlet's replies are "pregnant" with meaning (II,2,208f.). Likewise in the next scene of the play, when Ophelia is trapped into taking Hamlet's aberrant behaviour for real insanity ("O, what a noble mind is here o'erthrown!", III,1,152), her misinterpretation is immediately corrected by a comment from King Claudius: "[...] what he spake, though it lack'd form a little, / Was not like madness" (III,1,165f.). Most conspicuously, Hamlet himself is several times used by Shakespeare as a commentator explaining the feigned quality of his insanity to the audience, as in act III, scene 2 when he announces his relapse into madness at the end of a dialogue with his friend Horatio ("They are coming to the play. I must be idle", l. 90)[34] and in the famous closet scene (III,4) when he is in confidential conversation with his mother ("[...] I essentially am not in madness, / But mad in craft. [...]", l. 189f.).[35] Despite the critical controversies about the nature of his madness, then, it cannot be denied that even in the case of Hamlet, the text provides clear guidelines for the audience's evaluation of this character's state of mind.

4.

It is in *King Lear*, of course, that mad characters play the most important role, and it is small wonder, therefore, that in each case their madness is marked very clearly. The Fool, for instance, whose jesting has by many scholars been subsumed under the notion of madness,[36] is by means of his traditional parti-coloured costume, his cockscomb and his so-called 'marotte', a fool's head on a stick,[37] even visually set off prominently against the normal characters in the play, and the same is true of Edgar and Lear, the madmen in a narrower sense, whose pretended or real insanity requires a somewhat closer analysis.

Edgar's intention to escape the status of an outlaw by disguising himself as a so-called "Bedlam beggar", i.e. a former inmate of the famous Bethlehem madhouse in London, is at great length announced by himself in a soliloquy which covers all of act II, scene 3. In the course of this announcement, Edgar gives a detailed description of the Bedlamite make-up, hairstyle and costume he will wear as long as he is forced to conceal his identity:

> [...] my face I'll grime with filth,
> Blanket my loins, elf all my hairs in knots,
> And with presented nakedness outface

The winds and persecutions of the sky.
(II,3,9–12)

That Edgar is disguised exactly in this manner when he appears next in act III, scene 4 can be deduced from the Fool's insinuation: "he reserv'd a blanket, else we had been all sham'd" (l. 65) and from his own remark in an aside two scenes later: "My tears begin to take his [i.e. Lear's] part so much, / They mar my counterfeiting" (III,6,59f.). Apart from make-up, hairstyle and costume (categ. 4), other non-verbal signs such as the horn bottle which Bedlam beggars used in begging for a drink[38] (categ. 5: props) and, as it appears, the typical roaring and whining of their voices (categ. 2: paralinguistic signs) are employed to make Edgar's status as a madman unmistakably clear even for the hindmost spectators in a noisy Elizabethan audience.

The linguistic signs of Edgar's madness are equally striking. As Edgar is mainly in company with Lear and the Fool, two characters who also think and behave aberrantly, it is not possible to foreground his madness by merely infringing upon such less important criteria of textuality as situationality and acceptability, but only by violating the more elementary levels of intentionality and coherence so that Edgar's speeches, not unlike the mad songs of Ophelia, represent an extreme, dissociated and confused type of linguistic deviation. In addition to that, the severity of Edgar's Bedlamite madness is (again like that of Ophelia's) underlined by a haphazardly structured intertextuality, made up of fragments of popular songs, ballads, tales, nursery rhymes, hunting calls, charms and references to a current theological pamphlet,[40] Samuel Harsnett's *A Declaration of Egregious Popish Impostures* (1603), which, due to its function as a source-book of Elizabethan demonology, serves to suggest that the type of madness displayed by Edgar must be explained as a form of possession.

Lear's madness, in contrast to this, is of a completely different quality, both with respect to its causes and development and with respect to its linguistic expression. Being a consequence of psychological pressure built up gradually in a series of shocking experiences,[41] Lear's madness is carefully prepared by repeated announcements from the protagonist himself. "O! let me not be mad, not mad, sweet heaven; / Keep me in temper; I would not be mad!" (I,5,43f.); "I prithee, daughter, do not make me mad" (II,4,216); "O Fool! I shall go mad" (II,4,284); "My wits begin to turn" (III,2,67). According to the received opinion of the critics,[42] however, it is not until his encounter with the mad Edgar in act III, scene 4 (ll. 48ff.) that Lear goes really insane, but analyzing Lear's speeches in this scene with the help of our categories we see that even at this stage, his madness is still largely restricted to infringements upon the principles of situationality and acceptability. The same holds true even for Lear's verbal behaviour in the famous 'mock-trial-scene' III,6 when in a fully developed design of fictive situationality, he employs Edgar and the Fool as learned judges and tries his absent daughters for their cruelty. Only in act IV, Lear's mad speeches begin to leap quickly from one subject to another so that even their intentionality is sometimes fuzzy, and it is only at this stage that Shakespeare uses them for conveying the taboo-breaking comments on the corruptibility of authority and justice that have become known as "reason in madness". Not astonishingly, this new quality of Lear's madness is again underpinned by the use of a non-verbal sign-system, for in act IV, scene 6, Lear appears "fantastically dressed with wild flowers" (11. 80/81). And similar to what has been stated with respect to the mad entrance of other characters, the audience is well prepared for this change in Lear's outer appearance, because it was announced in detail by Cordelia two scenes before:

> [...] he was met even now
> As mad as the vex'd sea; singing aloud;
> Crown'd with rank fumiter and furrow-weeds,
> With hardocks, hemlock, nettles, cuckoo-flowers,
> Darnel, and all the idle weeds that grow
> In our sustaining corn.
>   (IV,4,1–6)

5.

In summary, I would suggest, three conclusions are to be drawn from the preceding analyses: First, there can be no doubt that non-verbal sign-systems, especially hairstyle, paralinguistic and kinesic signs, but occasionally also costume, props and acoustic signs, play an essential role for conveying the notion that a particular character has crossed over into the sphere of madness. Second, the linguistic devices Shakespeare uses for marking mad discourse are by no means always the same, but vary considerably from character to character, ranging from the deliberate infringements upon the principle of acceptability in Hamlet's feigned madness over a much more deeply disturbed textuality in the sleepwalking scene of Lady Macbeth and the final entrances of King Lear to the extreme disturbances in the speeches of Ophelia and Edgar, whose madness is also foregrounded by a strange, haphazardly structured intertextuality. Third and most importantly, however, it can be stated that whatever type of madness Shakespeare is going to present, he is always at pains to prepare his audience for it as carefully as possible, whether by previous announcements or by running commentaries from characters discussing those features of madness the audience is intended to perceive. This conspicuous clarity, with which Shakespeare differentiates mad from sane discourse, points to a particular firmness in his direction of the responses of his audience and should make us sceptical of the far-spread tendency in modern criticism to read his texts against the grain, doubting even their obvious meanings in all too subtle 'ironical' and 'deconstructive' interpretations. In fact, the study of even as complex a phenomenon as madness in Shakespeare's tragedies shows that with respect to his technique of directing responses, Shakespeare is still much closer to the definiteness of Medieval drama than to the openness of Postmodern plays.

NOTES

1. Cf., for instance, with reference to *King Lear* as the play with the longest and most important mad scenes: Robert Bechtold Heilman, *This Great Stage: Image and Structure in King Lear* (Baton Rouge, La., 1948; repr. Washington, 1963), 173–222: "Reason in Madness: The Madness Pattern"; Kenneth Muir, "Madness in *King Lear*", *Shakespeare Survey* 13 (1960): 30–40; Josephine Waters Bennett, "The Storm Within: The Madness of Lear", *Shakespeare Quarterly* 13 (1962): 137–155; and, arguing against the tendency of these earlier critics to regard Lear's madness as a psychic corrective for his intellectual and moral blindness: Lillian Feder, *Madness in Literature* (Princeton, N.J., 1980), 120–146.

2. Cf., for instance, as an early example of this direction in the study of Shakespeare's mad scenes H. Somerville, *Madness in Shakespearian Tragedy* (London, 1929; repr. Folcroft, Pa., 1969), and as two recent examples Clara Claiborne Park, "Canst Thou Not Minister to a Mind Diseas'd?", *American Scholar* 56 (1987): 219–234, and Derek Russell Davis, *Scenes of Madness: A Psychiatrist at the Theatre* (London, 1992), esp. 34–46.

3. Tadeusz Kowzan, "The Sign in the Theatre" (trans.), *Diogenes* 61 (1968): 52–80.

4. Cf. Keir Elam, *The Semiotics of Theatre and Drama* (London, 1980), 50/51; and Erika Fischer-Lichte, *Semiotik des Theaters: Eine Einführung*, 3 vols., I, 25–28, who adds the form of the stage as a further item to Kowzan's list.

5. Cf. Gerhard Müller-Schwefe, *Corpus Hamleticum: Shakespeares 'Hamlet' im Wandel der Medien* (Tübingen,1987), 8–19.

6. Robert-Alain de Beaugrande/Wolfgang Ulrich Dressler, *Introduction to Text Linguistics* (London, 1981), passim

7. De Beaugrande/Dressler, *Introduction*, 3.

8. De Beaugrande/Dressler, *Introduction*, 4.

9. De Beaugrande/Dressler, *Introduction*, 7.

10. Important Shakespearian characters driven to madness outside the tragedies are, above all, Constance (in *King John*) and Titus Andronicus.

11. It is true, of course, that Othello has sometimes been charged by the critics with being mad with jealousy, but it is quite clear that in these cases, madness is only used as a metaphorical concept.

12. All references and quotations in this article are from the Arden editions of the plays.

13. The taper is particularly suitable for this task, not only because of its direct connection to the Lady's sleepwalk, but also because it may be interpreted at a

symbolic level as the last gleam of reason surviving in an already largely 'benighted' mind.

14. Cf. Kenneth Muir's explanation in the Arden edition (1951), 138.

15. Cf. ibid.

16, Not all of the critical commentators of this line, however, are willing to accept this explanation (cf. for instance, Kenneth Muir in the Arden edition as against the commentators in the New Variorum, New Shakespeare, New Swan and New Penguin editions).

17. Both explanations are recorded in the New Variorum edition, 305.

18. Cf. Marvin Rosenberg, *The Masks of Macbeth* (Berkeley, Cal., 1978), 585.

19. Particular paralinguistic devices were certainly also used to mark the aberrant behaviour of Lady Macbeth. This becomes clear towards the end of the sleep-walking scene, when the Doctor, reacting to Lady Macbeth's triple "oh!" (V.1.49), exclaims: "What a sigh is there!" (l. 50). Correspondingly, most actresses in the stage history of *Macbeth* have tried to give the Lady's distracted speeches particular paralinguistic qualities (cf. Rosenberg, *The Masks of Macbeth*, 572 and 578).

20. Cf. Harold Jenkins's remark in the Arden edition of *Hamlet* (1982), 348.

21. Cf. for instance, Holger M. Klein's decision in the Reclam edition, vol. 1, 234 and his commentary on the problem in vol. 2, 478/479.

22. Thus, the second quarto gives it to Laertes (which is hardly plausible because this clashes clearly with Laertes's ensuing question), Reclam, New Cambridge and Oxford editions ascribe it to the Danish crowd waiting outside, and the Arden edition attaches it to the preceding speech of King Claudius.

23. Cf. the extended discussion of the songs by Harold Jenkins in the Arden edition, 529–536.

24. Ibid., 530.

25. This point is greatly stressed by Carroll Camden, "On Ophelia's Madness", *Shakespeare 400*, ed. James G. McManaway (New York, 1964), 247–255.

26. Cf. his commentary in the Arden edition, 530: "The appropriateness of the person to whom the songs are sung may also be more than coincidence [. . .]: the first, about a dead but unmourned lover, is sung to Gertrude; the second, a song of seduction, to the seducer Claudius; the third, a funeral elegy, to the son of the man just buried."

27. For a detailed discussion of these significances, cf. Bridget Gellert Lyons, "The Iconography of Ophelia", *ELH* 44 (1977): 60–74.

28. Cf. the long discussion in the Arden edition, 536–542.

29. Cf., for instance, Maurice Charney, *Hamlet's Fictions* (New York and London, 1988),139.

30. Cf. Harry Levin, *The Question of Hamlet* (New York, 1959), 116.

31. For the view that Hamlet falls victim to melancholy but not to insanity, cf. for instance Jerome Mazzaro, "Madness and Memory: Shakespeare's *Hamlet* and *King Lear*", *Comparative Drama* 19 (1985): 97–116, esp. 104.

32. Cf. the maxims of conversation worked out by Paul Grice, as quoted in de Beaugrande/Dressler, *Introduction*, 118.

33. This is made quite plain by the reactions of Ophelia, the character who is most deeply afflicted by Hamlet's strategy of feigning madness: "You are merry, my lord"; "You are naught, you are naught"; "You are keen, my lord, you are keen" (III.2.120; 143; 243).

34. It is true that the line, as is mentioned in the Arden (293) and in the Oxford edition (252), could possibly also be interpreted as "I must be unoccupied", but most editors take it to mean "I must be foolish, act the madman" (cf. New Swan, Reclam and New Cambridge editions).

35. In an extended commentary on the problem of Hamlet's sanity, Holger M. Klein in the Reclam-edition (vol. 2, 151, note 172) also takes these two remarks by the protagonist as a proof against his madness.

36. For lack of space, this cannot be done in the present article, although no clear borderline was drawn in Elizabethan times between folly and madness; cf. Vanna Gentili, "Madmen and Fools are a Staple Commodity: On Madness as a System in Elizabethan and Jacobean Plays", *Cahiers Elisabéthains* 34 (Oct. 1988): 11–24.

37. For a detailed account of the Fool's costume, cf. David Wiles, *Shakespeare's Clown: Actor and Text in the Elizabethan Playhouse* (Cambridge, 1987), 182–184 and 190/191.

38. Cf. Edgar's remark in III.6.73: "Poor Tom, thy horn is dry".

39. Cf. II.3.14 (and note 20 on II.3.20 in the Arden edition of *King Lear*, 1952), as well as Gloucester's later remarks (after Edgar has dropped his role as a madman): "Methinks thy voice is alter'd [. . .] Methinks you're better spoken" (IV.6.7 and 10).

40. Particularly helpful for identifying the intertextual references in Edgar's mad speeches are Russell Fraser's annotations in the Signet Classic Shakespeare edition of *King Lear*.

41. Cf. Muir, "Madness in *King Lear*", 34/35, and Davis, *Scenes of Madness*, 45.

42. Cf., for instance, Muir, "Madness in *King Lear*", 35, and Mazzaro, "Madness and Memory", 109.

NANCY CLUCK

The Fearful Summons: Death in the Opening Scenes of Shakespearean Tragedy

The opening scenes of Shakespearean tragedy typically contain a death, a near-death, or a reference to death. These intrusions of mortality prepare thematically and structurally for fatal confrontations that occur later. First scenes carry an image of death unique to the circumstances of each drama and each hero. Although heroes do not always appear in the opening scenes, a person important to them does, and this person undergoes an experience of mortality which is brought to the major characters) later in the play. The simple fact that death presents itself in the beginning is not so important as the manner in which it occurs and provides the seed of later death.[1]

In the early *Titus Andronicus* the particular images of death in I.i clearly figure the omnipresence of mortality and the mode of dying for the entire drama. Throughout the opening scene the tomb of the Andronici looms as an immediate reminder that even great heroes and rulers are not immortal. Even as Titus enters, crowned with the laurel wreath of victory, he is accompanied by the coffin of his sons; the triumphal march is at once a funeral procession. As it is opened to receive the newly dead, Titus addresses the tomb in words that suggest its relationship to a womb which will produce no more life:[2] "O sacred receptacle of my joys, / Sweet cell of virtue and nobility, / How many sons hast thou of mine in store, / That thou wilt never render to me morel" (I.i. 95–98).

From *Entering the Maze: Shakespeare's Art of Beginning*, edited by Robert F. Willson Jr., pp. 133–43. © 1995 by Peter Lang.

The central image of the tomb reappears as a pit in II.iii. The pit gapes throughout this scene as the tomb did in the opening scene. Replacing Titus burying his sons, Aaron prepares the pit to capture Titus's other sons and to implicate them in the death of the emperor's brother Bassianus. Aaron first buries gold near the pit, then engineers the capture of Lavinia and the murder of Bassianus before leading Titus's sons Quintus and Martius to the pit. After falling in, Martius discovers the body of Bassianus and realizes that the hole indeed serves as a grave. As Quintus reaches into it to try to rescue his brother, his words echo those of Titus in the first scene as they call up the image of the devouring womb: "Reach me thy hand, that I may help thee out; / Or, wanting strength to do thee so much good, / I may be pluck'd into the swallowing womb / Of this deep pit, poor Bassianus' grave" (II.iii. 237–240). Although they are hauled out of the pit, the brothers cannot escape; the womb of death yields them only temporarily before they are taken to prison and executed as punishment for the death of Bassianus.

The grave in the form of the pit and the tomb appears once again in the final act. In his last instructions, Lucius commands that a funeral procession bear the bodies of Titus and Lavinia to the Andronici tomb for proper burial; the tomb opens and closes the play, then. Lucius's instructions for the death and burial of Aaron recall the pit devised in II.iii. He is to be buried "breast-deep in the earth" and allowed to starve to death.

The open tomb is not the only image of death to be carried from I.i throughout the drama. The other major death motif stems from the murder and dismemberment of Tamora's son, Alarbus, by the three sons of Titus. After they have killed Alarbus, Lucius brags, "See, lord and father, how we have perform'd / Our Roman rites. Alarbus' limbs are lopp'd, / And entrails feed the sacrificing fire, / Whose smoke, like incense, doth perfume the sky" (I.i. 145–148). This type of revenge occurs several more times in the play. Even after his daughter is mutilated and Titus has cut off his own hand as appeasement for his sons, he prostrates himself in the street of Rome at the opening of Act III while his two sons are marched to the place of execution. His pleas do not prevail, and the heads of his sons, along with his own hand, are sent to him.

The culminating image of dismemberment and sacrifice issues from the rage of Titus in the final act. Having murdered, dissected, and cooked her sons, Titus explains to Tamora before killing her, "Why there they are, both baked in this pie, / Whereof their mother daintily hath fed, / Eating the flesh that she herself hath bred" (V.iii. 60–62). Even here Titus' words recall his language of I.i in which he suggests the tomb is an unnatural womb which will yield no more sons. The flesh of the dismembered and baked sons repeats the sacrificial fire arising from Alarbus' body in I.i.

The image of dismemberment again joins with the tomb and the pit in Lucius' final orders. Tamora is not to be buried. Rather, "As for that ravenous tiger, Tamora, / No funeral rite, nor man in mourning weed, / No mournful bell shall ring her burial, / But throw her forth to beasts and birds to prey" (V.iii. 195–198). Tamora herself will undoubtedly be dismembered and eaten as her sons have been.

The death motif in *Romeo and Juliet* stems from the figure of the duel, as many critics have noted. In the opening scene, though, it is the specific duel between Benvolio and Tybalt that carries the death of both Romeo and Juliet. The fight which breaks out among the servants, and even the frustrated struggles of the two old men, Montague and Capulet, have little direct bearing on the future lovers. As Joan Hartwig has pointed out in another context, " . . . the servants have not cause but habit to fight. In that instance, the feud has lost its content and has become merely repetition of the formula."[3] Because they are directly involved with Romeo and Juliet, Benvolio and Tybalt bring with them to their duel the ominous future looming before the two major characters. Unlike the servants and even the fathers, Benvolio appears not to want to fight; on the contrary, he strives to quell the servants. The hot-headed Tybalt, though, forces the issue with: "Turn thee, Benvolio, and look upon thy death" (I.i. 67). In taking the fight to Benvolio, Tybalt initiates Romeo's later encounter with mortality and his final death. The agony of Tybalt and Benvolio becomes the death agony of Romeo and Juliet. Tybalt and Benvolio are the carriers of death.

The motif set up by the Benvolio/Tybalt fight occurs again in III.i, IV.iii, and, finally, in V.iii. These scenes form analogues to the opening scene and structure the growth of Romeo and Juliet toward the recognition and acceptance of mortality and death. Act III, scene i opens with Benvolio again attempting to keep the peace. He urges Mercutio to go to a tavern with him in order to avoid the Capulets in the heat of the day. Once again he fails as peacemaker as Tybalt enters and begins a quarrel with Mercutio in the absence of Romeo. When Romeo enters, Tybalt turns his attention to taunting him. Rather than accepting Tybalt's challenge, Romeo tries, like Benvolio, to be a peacemaker. His attempts fail, though, and he ironically becomes an accomplice in his friend's death. Mercutio represents Romeo in Tybalt's mind, and he receives his death blow under Romeo's arm. Like Benvolio before him, failing as peacemaker, Romeo brings death to Mercutio. Benvolio's earlier fight with Tybalt, then, is mirrored in the Mercutio/Tybalt duel which, in turn, brings the knowledge of mortality to Romeo and Juliet. It is interesting to note that Benvolio disappears from the play after this scene.

Juliet muses on her mortality in IV.iii as she contemplates taking the potion which will bring apparent death. Her speech, in the *memento mori* tradition, conjures up horrible images of madness and death which culminate in her fantasy that she may awaken and "pluck the mangled Tybalt from his shroud." Her fears and hesitation end only when she sees Tybalt's ghost seeking out Romeo. In death Tybalt hastens Juliet's action which ultimately leads to her death, as he had in life carried death or the knowledge of death to Benvolio, Mercutio, and Romeo.

Finally, Tybalt figures in Romeo's last musings in V.iii. His attention momentarily diverted from the apparently dead Juliet, Romeo sees Tybalt's body, asks forgiveness, and promises to kill himself:

> Tybalt, liest thou there in thy bloody sheet?
> O, what more favor can I do thee
> Than with that hand that cut thy youth in twain
> To sunder his that was thy enemy.
> Forgive me, cousin!
>   (V.iii. 97–101)

Tybalt does not directly cause Romeo's death, of course, but his presence at all the deaths in the play works out the figure initiated in his struggle with Benvolio in the opening scene. Benvolio, who has transferred the agony to Mercutio, Romeo, and, indirectly, to Juliet, has disappeared from the play, but his absence, as the dead Tybalt's presence, plays out the death motif of I.i.

The image of death in the opening of *Julius Caesar* is more impersonal than in the two earlier tragedies, but it acquires cosmic proportions. Rather than an actual death or a physical conflict, the earliest warning of mortality comes from an angry tribune, who reminds a fickle crowd of a leader they had earlier celebrated. As the people prepare for the feast of Lupercal and decorate statues of the victorious Caesar, Marullus admonishes the revelers, recalling that Pompey died violently when he was at the height of his power:

> O you hard hearts, you cruel men of Rome,
> Knew you not Pompey? Many a time and oft
> Have you climb'd up to walls and battlements,
> To tow'rs and windows, yea, to chimney-tops,
> Your infants in your arms, and there have sat
> The livelong day, with patient expectation,
> To see great Pompey pass the streets of Rome.
> And do you now strew flowers in his way
>
> . . . .
> That comes in triumph over Pompey's blood?
>   (I.i. 36–51)

The reference to the rise and fall of Pompey is to be played out in Caesar's life and death. As he achieves his greatest power he falls to assassins at the foot of Pompey's statue. Bathing his hands in Caesar's blood in Act III, Brutus notes the proximity of Caesar and Pompey: "How many times shall Caesar bleed in sport, / That now on Pompey's basis lies along / No worthier than the dust"(III. i. 114–16). The references to Pompey both by the tribune and by Brutus provide an emblem of mortality and a warning against pride and ambition.

The opening scene is reflected in its counterpart, III.iii. With Caesar dead, Brutus is now the undisputed center of the play. But in this scene, it is the citizenry again who act out the death warning. While in the opening of the tragedy death entered as a simple reference to Pompey, in this later analogue scene the plebeians actually carry Cinna the poet away to his death. The action should warn the new leaders, particularly Brutus, of the dangers of power and the omnipresence of death. Killed because his name is the same as one of the conspirators, Cinna serves as a substitute only temporarily for the assassins who are soon to meet their own deaths.

In I.ii, the continuation of the opening scene, the death image takes on cosmic proportions. The soothsayer links supernatural omens directly to Caesar as he warns, "Beware the ides of March." The intrusion of the seer upon the festivities suggests that the life and death of Caesar are linked with metaphysical forces. Signs from beyond the everyday world precede every major death in the drama. As Calpurnia reminds Caesar, "When beggars die, there are no comets seen; / The heavens themselves blaze forth the death of princes"(II.ii. 30–31).

On the day of his death Caesar initially decides not to go to the capitol because Calpurnia tells him of the horrible things reportedly witnessed by the watch:

A lioness hath whelped in the streets,
And graves have yawn'd and yielded up their dead;
Fierce fiery warriors fight upon the clouds,
In ranks and squadrons and right form of war,
Which drizzled blood upon the Capitol.
    (II.ii. 17–21)

The augurers, too, urge him not to go, for "Plucking the entrails of an offering forth, / They could not find a heart within the beast" (II.ii. 39–40). Caesar's power and ambition have grown to such an extent, however, that he seems not to believe himself mortal. Decius's appeal to his vanity succeeds where the supernatural events do not, and Caesar goes to the Capitol and death.

The dead Caesar, in turn, becomes an emissary from the supernatural realm, appearing as a ghost to Brutus. Only the frightened Brutus sees the "monstrous apparition" and questions its identity, "Art thou some god, some angel, or some devil, / That mak'st my blood cold and my hair to stare?" (IV. iii. 279–80). The ghost responds by warning Brutus that he will see him at Philippi. That the ghost is an omen of death becomes evident in V.v when Brutus urges Volumnius to hold his sword: "The ghost of Caesar hath appear'd to me / Two several times by night; at Sardis once, / And, this last night, here in Philippi fields. / I know my hour is come" (V.v. 17–19).

Although the lives and deaths of the rulers of Rome are bound up with the supernatural, Caesar and Brutus never introspectively consider their own mortality or grow from the knowledge of death. In *Hamlet*, though, the contemplation of death stands at the heart of the drama. The opening scene of *Hamlet* prepares for the ongoing struggle with questions of death. Like the earlier Benvolio, Horatio serves as a stand-in for Hamlet and initiates the pattern for his friend's confrontation with the ghost and with his own mortality. As Robert Willson has noted, this scene shows Horatio's conversion from one who will not "let belief take hold in him" to one who is convinced that the ghost of Hamlet's father exists. His transformation from skeptic to believer is a model for Hamlet's later conversion.[4] It is Horatio and not Hamlet who first meets the ghost, just as it is Benvolio and not Romeo who first meets Tybalt in the earlier tragedy. The friends of the heroes encounter death first and provide the motif to be replayed. Hamlet encounters death in the form of a ghost and spends much of the drama debating with himself on the meaning of both life and death and on his proper role in the face of his father's death.

Hamlet's actual conversion occurs at sea, but the audience learns of it when he returns to Denmark. In V.i Shakespeare provides an analogue *memento mori* scene similar to I.i. The somber tone of the opening of I.i changes to one of black comedy as the gravediggers "replace" the sentinels. Horatio and Hamlet appear together this time, but their jokes are interrupted by the entrance of the funeral procession with the corpse of Ophelia. As his father's ghost had earlier interrupted the sentinels, now Ophelia's body intrudes into the opening scene of the final act. Unwittingly, Hamlet has once again returned from abroad for a funeral.

The resemblance does not end here, however, for Ophelia's experience mirrors Hamlet's earlier struggle with life's meaninglessness in the face of death. Ophelia has suffered the same kind of despair as a result of Hamlet's spurning her. Unlike Hamlet, who has only feigned madness and contemplated suicide, Ophelia actually goes mad and commits suicide.

Hamlet's conversion becomes evident in the way he emerges from his second experience with the death of one close to him. No longer questioning and brooding, the returned Hamlet in V.ii. has resolved to act. He explains to Horatio his uncovering of the plot against his own life; he has, while at sea, come face to face with his own mortality, and as a result can now act. Like Horatio before him, he has been converted from skepticism and passivity to belief and action. As a result he sees himself joined with higher purposes. He no longer feels that he is acting entirely alone, for "Our indiscretion sometimes serves us well / When our deep plots do pall, and that should learn us / There's a divinity that shapes our ends, / Rough hew them how we will" (V.ii. 8–11). Hamlet has consigned himself to higher powers, realizing that "readiness is all." His conversion is complete; he can die a hero's death.

Hamlet's change plays out Horatio's conversion in I.i, but it comes more slowly as a result of a series of deaths and of questions concerning life's meaning in the face of death. After Hamlet's most immediate experience of mortality at sea, Shakespeare creates a scene analogous to I.i. Now in V.i Hamlet stands with Horatio as witness to the appearance of another ghost in Ophelia. Hamlet has gone beyond Ophelia and beyond his questioning to align himself with other powers and to achieve heroism.

In *Antony and Cleopatra*, the death motif is no longer carried by friends of the heroes but by the prototypical messenger. Unlike the earlier plays, the opening scene of *Antony and Cleopatra* seems not to contain death; the messenger is refused and with him the possibility of mortal news. Antony's denial is reinforced by Cleopatra's taunts which refer to his relationship with Caesar and Fulvia:

> Nay, hear them, Antony.
> Fulvia perchance is angry; or who knows
> If the scarce-bearded Caesar have not sent
> His powerful mandate to you: "Do this, or this;
> Take in that kingdom, and enfranchise that;
> Perform't, or else we damn thee."
>   (I.i. 19–24)

The messenger can be refused only once, though; messengers of one sort or another return with news of death in I.ii, IV.xiv, and in IV.xv. Death finally cannot be denied in the play, either by Cleopatra's actions and taunts or Antony's dotage. As the characters begin to accept the news of death, they begin to move toward heroism.

Two messengers come to Antony in I.ii, one bringing battle news and the other bringing the news of Fulvia's death. Antony's lack of grief sets off more taunts from Cleopatra, "Now I see, I see, / In Fulvia's death, how mine receiv'd / shall be" (I.ii. 126–27). Her words bear great irony, for the news of her death drives Antony to his own. Yet, she is correct at this juncture; Antony grieves little because he cares little for others. Only after he suffers humiliation in battle with Caesar does he realize that he has "fled myself" and has led his men to cowardice. Not until his self-indulgence receives a death blow can he begin to have compassion for others.

The second messenger of death comes to Antony after the defeat in battle. In IV.xiv, Cleopatra's messenger, Mardian, comes to Antony with the news of her "death." Antony's reaction in this scene should be compared to his behavior in the first two scenes of the drama when he first refuses to receive the messenger and then fails to grieve over his wife's death. The humbled Antony of IV.xiv has gained compassion, and chooses death rather than life without Cleopatra. Ironically, he does not succeed in dying immediately but must himself become the messenger of death to Cleopatra. As the first messenger is refused, as Cleopatra's first death is a sham, so Antony's attempt initially falls short.

Cleopatra's attendant, Diomedes, precedes Antony to the monument with news of his impending death. Cleopatra's real grief attests to her growth during the play. Her verbal taunts in I.i having become an active ploy in her mock death vanish in the face of his death. Upon hearing the message and seeing the dying Antony she cries, "O sun, / Burn the great sphere thou mov'st in! darkling stand / The varying shore of the world" (IV.xv. 14–12).

The refused messenger in the opening scene, then, becomes a motif in the drama as he is transformed into the messenger of death in later scenes. The way the hearers receive his news reveals their growth from doting, taunting, game-playing lovers to mature individuals who have learned compassion and accepted mortality.

The opening scenes of these five tragedies suggest a structure characteristic of other Shakespearean tragedies. The unique death motif for each drama is sounded first in the opening scene. The motif may be most obvious in analogous scenes which show the growth of the heroes as a result of their confrontations with mortality and death. The image may present a *memento mori* in the form of a grave or tomb or the recollection of others who have died. Another character, such as Benvolio or Horatio, may carry death and bring the recognition of mortality to others. In myriad forms, death lurks in the opening scenes and becomes the agent by which many of the characters reach heroic stature.

NOTES

1. In his *Shakespeare's Opening Scenes* (Salsburg, Austria: Institut für Englische Sprache und Literatur, 1977), Robert F. Willson, Jr. discusses such scenes as keynote scenes.

2. C. L. Barber and Richard P. Wheeler, *The Whole Journey: Shakespeare's Power of Development* (Berkeley: University of California Press, 1986), pp. 129, 143.

3. Joan Hartwig, *Shakespeare's Analogical Scene* (Lincoln: University of Nebraska Press, 1983), p. 88.

4. Willson, pp. 116–118.

Othello

If we are to believe the latest Arden editor, *Othello* is closer in date to *Hamlet* than we used to think, for he says it was composed in "late 1601." At any rate, there is a cluster of plays near this date, a year or two after *Hamlet* and probably close to *Twelfth Night* and *Troilus and Cressida*.[1] Others prefer a date nearer 1604; that would twin the play with *Measure for Measure*, the plot for which derives from the collection of stories by Giraldo Cinthio. The issues are very complicated, and there is little certainty in any of the results.

The existence of two texts (the Quarto of 1622 and the Folio of 1623) creates problems different from those encountered in *Hamlet* or *King Lear* but no less difficult. They remain unlikely to be solved in such a way as to command anything approaching editorial consensus, and I do not in any case aspire to assist the editors in their enquiries, but with *Othello* as with *Hamlet* it is necessary on occasion to say where a particular reading originates and why one has chosen it. Textual scholars, loving their trade, will not agree, but critics hoping to comment on the language of the plays must think it unfortunate that the texts of three of the greatest of them should present these virtually intractable textual problems. Fortunately the plays remain for the most part intelligible, and susceptible to comment on their greatly varying styles.

What is extraordinary is the extent of the differences between plays written, one after another, in the first years of the new century. The style of

From *Shakespeare's Language*, pp. 165–82. © 2000 by Frank Kermode.

Othello we may think of as having been formed while Shakespeare was reading for the task—mostly of Cinthio's novella, which he handles with notable skill and freedom, but also current books about the Mediterranean world.

Since the principal characters of the story were soldiers, the setting couldn't be other than military in character. Shakespeare had plenty of experience doing the military—the life of various kinds of soldier is amply recorded in the History plays and *All's Well*, and is not absent from *Hamlet*—but he had not hitherto attempted that almost invariant type, the foul-mouthed N.C.O. I myself have memories, happily remote, of Iago-like warrant officers, sycophantic self-seekers, the main difference being that Iago has a surprisingly educated vocabulary. At its core, however, is filth.

The first word of the play is Roderigo's "Tush," and Iago's reply begins with an oath: "'Sblood." His first word to Brabantio is "'Zounds" (85), repeated at line 107. None of these expletives is to be found in the Folio text. Honigmann counts fifty cases where the profanities of Q are deleted or modified in F probably because the latter, dependent on a manuscript written by the scribe Ralph Crane, was produced after 1606, when the Act to Restrain the Abuses of the Players forbade the use of oaths or the name of God.[2] "Tush" and "pish" may sound like Rosalind's "pretty oaths that are not dangerous" (*As You Like It*, IV.1.189), but their elimination along with others more shocking makes a considerable difference to the tone of the play, and especially to the characterisation of Iago. The profanities occur not only in soldierly contexts, where they could be taken simply as appropriate to the language of the camp, but more significantly in the context of sexual disgust to which Iago's thoughts repeatedly refer themselves.

The opening scene, as always with Shakespeare carefully excogitated, never simple narrative exposition, is here worth particularly close attention. It does provide some necessary exposition but also describes an evil soldierly prank: you may think Roderigo must be half drunk to be seduced into the noisy demonstration outside Brabantio's house—as dangerous to him as it is useful to Iago. There have been critics, led by Dr. Johnson, who have wished away the first act of the play, and indeed Boito eliminated it when writing the *Otello* libretto for Verdi. But this move, however correct Johnson might think it and however economical in terms of lyric theatre, would not be sufficient compensation for its cost.

This opening scene outside Brabantio's house, with the subsequent interruption of the wedding night of Othello and Desdemona, seems to me a version of charivari. Charivari was an old custom: if you disapproved of a match as being incongruous in some way, for instance if you deplored a disparity in age (or in colour) between bride and bridegroom, you could call your neighbours and make a disturbance outside their dwelling. The practice was at one time reflected in the clamorous reaction to eclipses, also instances of order disrupted, as Othello remembers in V.ii.99–101, "Methinks it should be now a huge eclipse / Of sun and moon, and that th' affrighted globe / Did yawn at alteration."

Iago will use the noise of the charivari, this "rough music," to his own ends. In the passage before they start making a row, while he and Roderigo are still whispering in the street, we judge the violence of his emotion by his vocabulary: if I don't hate Othello "Abhor me … Despise me" (1.1.6, 8), with a hint that, since he knows his own foulness, these are indeed the proper responses to him. Unlike Roderigo, he need not make himself known to Brabantio, and can use what sexual insults he pleases: "Even now, now, very now, an old black ram / Is tupping your white ewe" (88–89) is Iago's way of informing the senator that his daughter has eloped, and this voyeuristic and disgusted attitude to sex is constant in him. They are at it at this very moment! Imagine it! And the man is black, a devil: the senator's daughter is being "cover'd with a Barbary horse" (111), is "making the beast with two backs" (116). Brabantio recognises the speaker as a "profane wretch" (114), "a villain" (117), but Iago has disappeared before the senator has made ready to hurry with Roderigo to the Sagittary, there to continue the process of charivari and disturb the wedding night of Othello and Desdemona.

Iago's onslaught on Brabantio's susceptibilities is kept up by his pupil Roderigo ("the gross clasps of a lascivious Moor" [126]); but he is required to be somewhat civil, as Iago is not. One striking aspect of the scene is that there are echoes of *Hamlet*'s habitual hendiadys. As George T. Wright demonstrated, Othello comes second only to *Hamlet* in the frequency of its use of hendiadys, though it offers less than half as many instances;[3] Shakespeare's enthusiasm for the device was waning, as one can see as *Othello* proceeds. But the habit of expansive doubling continues at the outset of this new one: "as loving his own pride and purposes," "trimm'd in forms and visages of duty," "The native act and figure of my heart," "by night and negligence," "your pleasure and most wise consent," "play and trifle with your reverence," "an extravagant and wheeling stranger / Of here and every where," "flag and sign of love;" "the property of youth and maidhood"—all these occur in the first 170 lines. Othello's opening speech in the next scene carries it on. "my life and being," "my unhoused free condition / Put into circumscription and confine" (I.ii.21, 26–27). Brabantio continues the habit in his protest to the Duke:

> my particular grief
> Is of so flood-gate and o'erbearing nature
> That it engluts and swallows other sorrows …
> (I.iii.55–57)

And:

> I therefore apprehend and do attach thee.
> For an abuser of the world, a practicer
> Of arts inhibited and out of warrant.
>   (I.4.77–79)

There is another trace of the device in the senators' war council ("Neglecting an attempt of ease and gain / To wake and wage a danger profitless" II.iii.29–301). Later instances are Brabantio's "a judgment main'd and most imperfect" (99), "thin habits and poor likelihoods" (108), "indirect and forced courses" (111). The Duke calls the proposed expedition "stubborn and boist'rous" (228) and Othello refers, in Hamletian vein, to "the flinty and steel couch of war" (230), asking for Desdemona "such accommodation and besort / As levels with her breeding" (238–39); and, in a very strained expression, referring to his sight as "My speculative and offic'd instruments" (270). Desdemona, addressing the Senate, catches the habit in her speech proclaiming her part in the wooing: "That I did love the Moor to live with him, / My downright violence, and storm of fortunes. / May trumpet to the world" (I.iii.248–50). Here her own sense that the unconventionality of her choice amounts to a kind of social violence is emphasised by hendiadys ("My downright violence, and storm"). Later we have "quality and respect," "honesty and trust" (I.iii.282, 284), "worldy matter and direction" (299), and so on. The habit has spread to almost every character, but examples become harder to find as the play discovers and develops its own dialect, becomes less fond of semantic collision and contraction.

Hamlet can be coarsely bawdy, and seems to mean to offend Ophelia by being so, but although in future plays Shakespeare was to be capable of rendering deep sexual disgust (for example in *Troilus and Cressida*, *Timon of Athens*, and *The Winter's Tale*, and in one or two sonnets) Iago is probably his most disgusted and disgusting character, claiming precedence over Thersites and Apemantus by virtue of his centrality to an action of which he is indeed the sole agent. Mention of Desdemona having sex is all that is needed to make him talk dirty: Othello "hath boarded a land carract" (I.ii.50) means that he has gone aboard her, almost as an act of piracy or rape, as if any other explanation of the relationship were out of the question. The scene ends with a prose discussion between Iago and Roderigo, and here Iago offers the young man he means to push deeper into corruption an account of his beliefs and habits. Although it may suggest a similar self-hatred, this confession in no way resembles the Credo written by Boito for Verdi, which makes of Iago a gloomy nineteenth-century atheist. Yet it does offer a kind of philosophy.

Roderigo is in love with Desdemona, and Iago cannot think of love as anything but lust: the beloved object is a guinea hen, a loose or worthless woman; the lover is behaving like a baboon. Roderigo claims that it is not in his "virtue" or nature to stop being "fond," whereupon Iago delivers an extraordinary speech comparing the body to a garden, considered as a piece of coarse nature that the gardener, or human will, can amend. The fluency and power of this speech are remarkable—the persuasiveness of the analogy and the conceptual clarity of the conclusion drawn:

> If the beam of our lives had not one scale of reason to poise another
> of sensuality, the blood and baseness of our natures would conduct
> us to most prepost'rous conclusions. But we have reason to cool our
> raging motions, our carnal stings, our unbitted lusts . . .
>
> (I.iii.326f.)

Iago's opening exclamation ("Virtue? a fig! 'tis in ourselves that we are thus or thus" [319]) ensures that the speech begins with the equivalent of an obscene gesture, but the argument that the will should have "power and corrigible authority" is perfectly conventional. This is good doctrine, the reason controlling the senses, the lower powers of the soul. Roderigo's admission that he cannot wield such control, his will being presumably unequal to the task, is met with another piece of advice: love "is merely a lust of the blood and a permission of the will" (334–35), which means that love is possible only because the will has abdicated its power over the senses. Iago's deception of Roderigo depends on the young man's willingness to believe that Desdemona is sexually corruptible, that he can buy her with presents, taking comfort meanwhile from the thought that the violent beginning of Desdemona's love for Othello will surely be followed by a movement of revulsion, as Iago's philosophy of lust would lead him to expect. And for good measure Othello will surely, in his turn, grow sick of Desdemona. "The food that to him now is as luscious as locusts, shall be to him shortly as acerb as the coloquintida" (347–49). The locust was a very sweet fruit, the food of John the Baptist in the wilderness; coloquintida was bitter and used as a purge. Iago can look about quite widely for his similes. The union of the lovers is a match between "an erring barbarian and a super-subtle Venetian" (355–56), a black man and a well-born Venetian lady; they had, at least among the vulgar, reputations, the black man for superior sexual powers, the Venetian lady for love affairs.

The aptness of this talk, and its lexical resourcefulness, display a mind, almost the mind of a poet, made formidable and alien by the context of corruption, a mind capable of seeming honest when honesty is called for but soured with its own baseness. Iago's baseness is more fundamental than a mere desire for revenge against Cassio and Othello; it is darker than Edmund's in *King Lear*. The whole point of the dialogue between Desdemona and Iago on the wharf at Cyprus (II.i) is to demonstrate that Iago, though apparently willing to pass the time of day with women, cannot quite manage to keep suppressed his loathing of them; he hates them for being sexed. That Cassio delights in touching them, smiling, taking their hands, and so forth makes him a man whom Iago hates less for his lieutenancy than for his sexual freedom, his ease with women:[4] "a most profane and liberal counsellor," he calls him (163–64); and although there is here a tinge of puritanical contempt for the libertine, Iago's next exchange with Roderigo, which follows hard upon the rapture greeting Othello's safe arrival, again dwells on the image of Desdemona engaged in "the act of sport" (227). He knows that she is to be credited with a "delicate tenderness" (232), but he uses that knowledge only to persuade Roderigo that she will come to "disrelish and abhor" the Moor—"very nature will instruct her" to do so (233–34). Her flirting with Cassio is lechery, and after it copulation must inevitably follow: "hard at hand comes the master and main exercise, th' incorporate conclusion. Pish!" (261–63 [F]). (Othello, infected by Iago's corruption, echoes this "Pish!" in IV.i.42.)

     In the course of the play this kind of talk is contrasted with the innocently excessive courtesies of Cassio, the secret rebelliousness of Emilia, and of course the honesty of Othello himself, before his fall. Cassio's language is so near the extreme of doting admiration that Iago can profess to believe that his "civil and humane seeming" is only a cover for his "salt and most hidden loose affection" (II.i.239–41). Of course his immediate intention is to gull Roderigo; the art of the play is to make his claim seem not quite implausible. Cassio's extravagances, however disinterested, may sometimes go over the top, as when he expresses his hopes that Othello will arrive safely in Cyprus, and "Make love's quick pants in Desdemona's arms" (II.i.80); here he uses a trope from erotic poetry, to be found also in Thomas Carew's poem "A Rapture": "Yet my tall pine shall in the Cyprian strait / Ride safe at anchor, and unlade her freight." Cassio has a touch of the libertine, and his relationship with Bianca is important to the plot, but he is incapable of the language of Iago; he combines a politely seductive way of talking[5] with a matter-of-fact attitude to sexual satisfaction, a not unusual combination.

     A dialogue in Act II is carefully inserted to make plain this capital difference between Iago and Cassio. Iago says Othello has left early to be with Desdemona: "He hath not yet made wanton the night with her; and she is sport for Jove."

CAS.

She's a most exquisite lady.

IAGO.

And I'll warrant her, full of game.

CAS.

Indeed she's a most fresh and delicate creature.

IAGO.

What an eye she has! Methinks it sounds a parley to provocation.

CAS.

An inviting eye; and yet methinks right modest.

IAGO.

And when she speaks, is it not an alarum to love?

CAS.

She is indeed perfection.

IAGO.

Well—happiness to their sheets!

(iii.18ff.)

This keenly written passage (some of which F tries to render as verse) contrives a social encounter that can only make Cassio uneasy; his position is such that despite his being the superior officer he cannot reprove Iago, only withhold assent to his slyly voyeuristic propositions and provide more courtly alternatives. When Iago invites him to drink to the health of "black Othello" (32), he tries to decline the invitation, such toasts being a courtesy he disapproves of because, as he explains, he has a weak head for drink. This is candid, but Iago seems to have known about this weakness already. Cassio makes a mistake when, having himself been addressed as "lieutenant" (13), he replies with "good Iago" (33), a patronising form of address like "honest," a word which from now on becomes central to the play. Iago resents it, for it is a word normally used of inferiors, but he makes use of it, since a reputation for good-humoured servile reliability suits his ends.[6] Cassio indeed loses this match, since it is as if he were explaining or defending his more delicate sexual attitudes by deriving them from his higher rank and class, a certain coarseness in these matters being exactly what one would expect of a social inferior.

Iago naturally has no use for the language of courtship; all love-making for him is merely the submission of the will to the base passions of the body. He assumes that Othello is a "lusty Moor" (II.i.295), perhaps because he is black, and the ideas of blackness and sexual potency were already twinned, or perhaps because he just assumes that all men are lusty. Othello himself has explained to the Duke that he wants Desdemona to come to Cyprus with him, "Nor to comply with heat (the young affects / In me defunct) and proper satisfaction; / But to be free and bounteous to her mind" (I.iii.264–66). (Here "affects" means "passions," "defunct" means not "dead" but "spent, a matter of the past," and "proper" means "personal" or even, in this context, "selfish."[7]) Othello is to him a gross and grossly privileged body, so deficient in the cunning of intellect that he is easily duped. Iago doesn't seem to be particularly lustful himself; he may take that to be a source of strength, while still envying others who are.

     All this we infer only from the language of the individual characters. As it happens, Iago's is least interesting when he is thinking in verse; his soliloquy at the end of II.i is unconvincing, almost an admission of confusion in the author as well as the character, a muddle of implausible motives where none was needed other than the established foulness of the man's imagination.[8] Even when Othello asks him to explain the reason for the brawl (II.iii.176ff.) he speaks of the peaceful merriment that preceded it as being "in terms like bride and groom / Devesting them for bed." His obsession gets uninhibited play when he later tells Othello what he experienced when sharing a bed with Cassio (III.iii.413–26)[9] and again expresses his obsessive interest in what people do in bed ("kiss me hard ... laid his leg / Over my thigh"). When Boito rewrote this for Verdi ("*Era la notte, Cassio dormia*"), he had to leave this kind of thing out, as too strong for a polite late-nineteenth-century audience; Verdi supplied the feeling with eery music, giving the speech the air of an erotic dream.[10]

     The pivotal scene of the play is III.iii, which from the outset, with Iago's "I like not that" as Cassio withdraws, to the end, when Othello has accepted the charge against Desdemona and planned her death and Cassio's, is fewer than five hundred lines long, probably less than half an hour of stage time. It is extraordinarily bold. Desdemona aids the process, twice commending Iago's honesty, a conviction of which in the other characters is now essential to his design; at her exit Othello speaks of his love for her and the chaos that will follow if his love should ever cease. It is at exactly this point (93) that Iago goes to work, sowing doubts about Cassio. The dialogue is spare, at first sounding almost like casual chat between a superior, who calls his interlocutor "thou," and a subordinate, who must use "you" but who, without ceasing to be deferential, can count on his boss's trust and on a long acquaintance:

IAGO.
 My noble lord—
OTH.

What dost thou say, Iago?

IAGO.

  Did Michael Cassio, when you woo'd my lady,
  Know of your love?

OTH.

  He did, from first to last. Why dost thou ask?

IAGO.

  But for a satisfaction of my thought,
  No further harm.

OTH.

  Why of thy thought, Iago?

IAGO.

  I did not think he had been acquainted with her.

OTH.

  O yes, and went between us very oft.

IAGO.

  Indeed!

OTH.

  Indeed? ay, indeed. Discern'st thou aught in that?
  Is he not honest?

IAGO.

  Honest, my lord?

OTH.

  Honest? ay, honest.

IAGO.

  My lord, for aught I know.

OTH.

  What dost thou think?

IAGO.

  Think, my lord?

OTH.

  Think, my lord? By heaven, thou echo'st me,
  As if there were some monster in thy thought
  Too hideous to be shown . . .

  . . .

  If thou dost love me,
  Show me thy thought.
  (93–116)

In the first exchange the pentameters are broken up, giving the passage a peculiar uneasiness, which is reinforced by the triple "honest" and the triple "think," especially where two usages collide. "What didst not like?" asks Othello, seventy-five lines after Iago planted the expression. The question whether Cassio is or merely "seems" honest (unlike Iago, whom Othello accepts as honest all through) is now adroitly raised. "I dare be sworn I *think* that he is *honest*." "I *think* so too. . . . Why then I *think* Cassio's an honest man":

Nay, yet there's more in this.
I prithee speak to me as to thy thinkings,
As thou dust ruminate, and give thy worst of thoughts
The worst of words.
    (130–33)

At which point Iago expresses moral indignation, again with sound doctrine, explaining that even a slave can keep his thoughts to himself, and that one may have "uncleanly apprehensions" (139) without revealing them. But Othello insists that if Iago *thinks* him wronged he should make known his "thoughts" (143–44); "By heaven, I'll know thy thoughts" (162).

Here we are only at the beginning of a storm; no high colours, no blasts of rhetoric; the words "honest" and "think," "thinking," "thoughts" have to do all the work. After a while Iago, who has spoken of his own "jealousy" (147), meaning something like "envy" or "undue curiosity," but without sexual implication, uses the word again, now with full sexual reference and direct application to Othello's case: "O, beware, my lord, of jealousy! / It is the green-ey'd monster which doth mock / The meat it feeds on" (165–67). The seventy or so lines of verse that have elapsed before there is any direct accusation of Cassio and Desdemona have brought Othello to "misery" (171). He soon asserts that he could never suffer cuckoldry, adding that Desdemona's infidelity, if it existed, could not be attributed to any weakness in himself: "For she had *eyes*, and chose me" (189). And now the insistence is on eyes: "I'll *see* before I doubt" (190) . . ."*Look* to your wife, *observe* her well with Cassio, / Wear your *eyes* thus, not jealous nor secure" (197–98) (not suspicious but not overconfident); "In Venice they do let God *see* the pranks / They dare not show their husbands" (202–3) . . ."She that so young could give out such a seeming / To seel her father's *eyes* up" (209–10) . . ."If more thou dost *perceive*, let me know more; / Set on thy wife to *observe*" (239–40). This string of words will culminate in Othello's demand for "the ocular proof . . . Make me to *see*'t" (360–64). A passage of high tension, generated by all the words that have been in play: "honest," "think," "see":

OTH.
I do not *think* but Desdemona's honest.

IAGO.
>
> Long live she so! and long live you to *think* so!
> (225–26)

Iago then touches on the disparity or disproportion between Othello and his Venetian wife, already become, through his assiduity, a credible cause of concern:

IAGO.
>
> To he direct and honest is not safe.
>
> OTH.
>
> Nay, stay. Thou shouldst be honest.
>
> IAGO.
>
> I should be wise—for honesty's a fool . . .
> (378–82)

> I *think* my wife be honest, and *think* she is not;
> I *think* that thou art just, and *think* thou art not.
> I'll have some proof.
> (384–86)

"I see, sir, you are eaten up with passion . . . You would be satisfied? . . . but how? How satisfied, my lord? / Would you, the supervisor, grossly gape on? / Behold her topp'd?" (391–96) (here he uses to Othello himself the word Roderigo had used to Brabantio in the opening scene: "the gross clasps of a lascivious Moor" [126] and "Your daughter . . . hath made a gross revolt" [133–34], as well as "top," a variant of the word "tupping" in line 89).

> It were a tedious difficulty, I *think*,
> To bring them to that prospect, damn them then,
> If ever mortal eyes do see them bolster
> More than their own. What then? How then?
> What shall I say? Where's satisfaction?
> It is impossible you should see this,
> Were they as prime as goats, as hot as monkeys . . .
> (397–403)

The only "satisfaction" available is Iago's account of his night with Cassio.

It becomes clear, in this masterly dialogue, that Iago's interest in sex is to watch others doing it, or at least to think about them doing it. It was important therefore to develop these ideas of seeing, these increasingly coarse

descriptions and conjectures. The tone has grown calculatedly immodest—
"damn them then"—and this is achieved before the story about Cassio in
bed, and before the handkerchief provides what looks like satisfactory ocular
evidence. For the tactician Iago has correctly guessed Othello's reaction even
to the possibility of his wife's unfaithfulness, and at first with all the hesita-
tions proper to an honest man (and an inferior) communicating such a suspicion, he infects Othello with his own disgust. Following the uses of "honest,"
"think," and "see," with their derivatives, one begins to understand how compact and fierce this writing is. Even after the account of Cassio's dream, when
Othello is ready to tear his wife to pieces, the honest man can admit "yet we
see nothing done; / She may he honest yet" (432–33)—which is the moment
to introduce the handkerchief, something which can be seen, something with
which Iago can claim to have seen Cassio wiping his beard. And the scene
ends with the pair swearing a joint oath of loyalty and vengeance.

Considering the scantiness, or absence, of incriminating evidence, and
the completeness of Othello's collapse, it would be easy to read this scene as
an allegory of demonic possession, a reading Othello himself for a moment
considers but dismisses in the last scene of the play: "I look down towards his
feet; but that's a fable. / If that thou be'st a devil, I cannot kill thee" (V.ii.286–
87). The success of Iago is "diabolic" only in the sense that his temptation
has discovered in Othello a horror of his tempter's apparent knowingness
about sex. Once more the effect is got by reiteration: "honest," "think," etc.
The magical force of this rhetoric is what makes the scene possible.

Soon the handkerchief, the false substitute for "ocular proof," becomes
itself the means of equally terrible reiteration. Othello credits it with an occult
power that has now become appropriate to the occasion. The Egyptian or
gipsy who gave it to his mother "could almost read / The thoughts of people"
(III.iv.57–58). It had the power of controlling his father's love for his mother;
if she lost it he would loathe her. He is talking about his own love for Desdemona: "there's magic in the web of it" (69).

The ensuing dialogue with Desdemona—she lying about the handkerchief and crazily resuming her plea for Cassio, while he says almost nothing
but "handkerchief"—is as brilliantly conceived as the Othello–Iago dialogue,
and it is hard to imagine a dramatic poetry more minimally perfect:

OTH.
  Is't lost? Is't gone? Speak, is't out o' th' way?
DES.
  Heaven bless us!
OTH.
  Say you?

DES.

It is not lost; but what and if it were?

OTH.

How?

DES.

I say, it is not lost.

OTH.

Fetch't, let me see't.

DES.

Why, so I can, sir, but I will not now.

This is a trick to put me from my suit.

Pray you let Cassio be receiv'd again.

OTH.

Fetch me the handkerchief, my mind misgives.

DES.

Come, come;

You'll never meet a more sufficient man.

OTH.

The handkerchief!

DES.

I pray talk me of Cassio.

OTH.

The handkerchief!

DES.

A man that all his time

Has founded his good fortunes on your love,

Shar'd dangers with you—

OTH.

The handkerchief!

DES.

I' faith, you are to blame.

OTH.

'Zounds![11]

(III.iv.79–98)

It has often been remarked, by G. B. Shaw with derogatory intent, that Othello is the most operatic of Shakespeare's tragedies; think, for example, of the duet at the end of III.iii (where Verdi has the advantage of Shakespeare that he can make Iago and Otello swear their oath together instead of having to do it one at a time). This intense Shakespearian scene, too, is in its way equally musical. This kind of writing, by quasi-musical, quasi-magical

means, achieves a rawness of passion, a conflict between innocently suicidal enquiry and a rage almost beyond words. Rage beyond words was not
something the early Shakespeare would have even thought of aiming at.
Here, as in Hamlet, a long experience of theatre has taught him a new way
of writing poetry.

The strangest line in Desdemona's part comes in IV.iii. Othello has just
grossly insulted and struck her in the presence of Lodovico, the Venetian
envoy. Now he orders her to bed. Talking with Emilia, she remembers the
maid Barbary and her song, but before she sings it she says, with apparent inconsequence, "This Lodovico is a proper man" (35). None of this passage (30–52) is included in Q. There must have been some good reason to
exclude the Willow Song (perhaps the temporary unavailability of a boy actor
who could sing), and the line about Lodovico was lost along with the song.
Some modern editors, including Honigmann, give the line to Emilia, but
only because it seems "out of character" for Desdemona.[12] Despite his treatment of her, she has continued submissive and loving to Othello, even when
he acted out his horrible pretence that she was a whore and Emilia her bawd.
After Othello's aria "Had it pleas'd heaven / To try me with affliction . . ." (IV.
ii.47ff.) she hardly complains: "I hope my noble lord esteems me honest," and
"Alas, what ignorant sin have I committed?" (65, 70). Even at her boldest, as
when she insists on going to Cyprus, she has deserved Lodovico's compliment,
"Truly, an obedient lady" (IV.i.248). Yet now, at a moment of intense marital
distress, her thoughts wander momentarily to another man. Very shortly she
listens with amazement to Emilia's avowal that she would be unfaithful to
her husband if the reward was great enough. Desdemona says she would not
behave so "For the whole world" (IV.iii.79). The fine speech (not in Q) in
which Emilia stands up for women's right to sensual life against the restric-
tions imposed by tyrannical men is not the sort of thing Desdemona would
ever have spoken (IV.iii.84–103). Yet she is rather taken by Lodovico, and at
a very odd moment.

It is true that she can say unexpected things; she is represented as suffering a kind of loss of attention: after the horrible brothel scene when cast
as "that cunning whore of Venice / That married with Othello" (IV.ii.89–90),
she declares herself "half asleep" (97) and hardly understands what Emilia
says next. These moments may contribute to any secret disposition in an audience to agree that it was less than seemly of this young woman, ignoring the
"curled darlings of her nation," to marry a man so alien and so much older, an
"extravagant and wheeling stranger" (I.i.136), a general whose social standing,
though high, depends entirely upon his military rank in an embattled state.
(As Auden remarks, Brabantio was happy enough to have Othello to supper
and hear his tales, but that was another matter from having him as a son-

in-law.[13]) And she is made to lie[14]—about the handkerchief, and about the identity of her murderer. Many of these traits may be attributed to a strain of feminists in the play, a hint of the ways in which women might sometimes escape the regime imposed by their husbands—a little quiet talk with another woman, a venial fib or two. Yet the fact remains that there is a faint ambiguity in her character as we try to see it as a whole, and this is notoriously true also of Othello's.

There have been some celebrated criticisms of Othello's generally orotund way of speaking, which may be regarded as a sort of innocent pompousness or, if you dislike it, a self regard that is not so innocent. It is easy enough to explain the choice for Othello of this particular mode of speech. He is meant to be a man whose sole reason for existence is command—after all, he is responsible for the security of an empire, Cyprus being a province that must be defended. The self-esteem of such a man can be rendered in the naturally hyperbolical terms of military glory. It has been observed that Londoners of the time were familiar with the idea of magnificent North African potentates. "The black, or tawny, soldier-hero was a figure in festivals long before he reached the Elizabethan stage . . . These Moorish shows were resplendent, soldierly and sensual . . . the role of the Moor in public spectacle was to enrich the public conception of power and sexual potency in the early stages of Tudor empire."[15]

The example of Marlowe's Tamburlaine was fairly recent, but Othello does not have his out-and-out bombast, and there is a touch of modesty and courtesy in his speech. His first line, "'Tis better as it is" (I.ii.6), is intended to promote calm in the face of Iago's pretended anger on his behalf; he has nothing to fear from Brabantio, he says, because of his services to the state. Here he claims royal birth, like a sultan in a Lord Mayor's Show; he will not boast of it except by mentioning it, but the final effect is not quite modest. When he speaks of his "demerits," the word (as in *Coriolanus*, I.i.275) means "merits." It is an odd word since it can also, mean its opposite; but I think the point of it is to have Othello use a strange word rather than a familiar one—something he does on a good many other occasions. Its oddness makes it stand out against the bustling language of the messages concerning the military crisis, and his character is already pretty firmly established as calm, grandiloquent, unaware of his vulnerability, by the famous line "Keep up your bright swords, for the dew will rust them" (I.ii.59). This invulnerability is founded in a soldier's courage, and it does not, as he supposes, extend to the dangers of civilian life.

Arriving in the Senate House, where all the talk is practical, he utters an oration on the topic of his marriage ("Most potent, grave, and reverend signiors" [I.iii.76ff.]) and on his wooing of Desdemona, "Wherein I spoke of most disastrous chances: / Of moving accidents by flood and field, / Of hairbreadth scapes i' th' imminent deadly breach, / Of being taken by the insolent foe / And sold to slavery" (134–38)—a speech of forty-one lines celebrated for their grandeur, which is enhanced by the tinkling couplets and plain prose of the following speeches by the Duke and Brabantio. The speech is completely successful; the Duke is proud that his warrior deputy talks exactly as he would be expected to fight, superbly. And the grandeur depends partly on Othello's use of unusual words like "demerit" and "agnize" and "indign." The one word he finds no synonyms for is "honest," twice applied to Iago in this scene (284, 294) and repeatedly in later scenes. And it is the honest Iago who will, in the course of the play, reduce Othello's language as well as his honour.

Before the temptation scene it is impossible to imagine Othello using the vocabulary of Iago; indeed, he rarely uses language appropriate to prose. It is essential to the character that until he collapses he speaks grandly. Later come the anguished repetitions of "handkerchief," the questioning of the sense in which Iago uses the word "lie," the pathetic stress on "honesty," the unaccustomed *langue verte* picked up from Iago, and the vile berating of Desdemona, whom he calls a whore, which suits his action in striking her.

Othello's final speech has been much commented upon. In a famous essay T. S. Eliot noted that in his self-pitying grandeur, his boasting about his weapon and his past achievements, he stresses his claim to be serving the state but makes no mention whatever of Desdemona. "Humility is the most difficult of all virtues to achieve; nothing dies harder than the desire to think well of oneself . . . I do not believe that any writer has exposed this *bovarysme*, the human will to see things as they are not, more clearly than Shakespeare."[16] This view has been much attacked, but it has not lost all its force. Eliot does not support his observation by comment on the language of the speech, which has some resemblance to that of Othello's speech to the Senate at the outset. It repeats the point made in I.ii.18 about the respect he has won by "My services which I have done the signiory," but important differences arise from the fact that he cannot now allow himself to speak of "My parts, my title, and my perfect soul" (1.6.31). Instead, he compares himself to Judas ("the base Indian") who "threw a pearl away / Richer than all his tribe" (V.ii.347–48).[17] He claims not to be jealous except when "wrought." He cannot confess to weeping without explaining that it isn't his usual practice. And he ends with a recollection of one more notable service to the state.

We need not suppose that Shakespeare was contemptuous; only that, as his language suggests, Othello was human, the victim of long habit, and wanting, as he ended his life, to enter a plea for merciful interpretation. That he did not get it in the play, and has not always had it subsequently, merely shows how variable interpretation must be when it has to work on language as complex as that of *Othello*.

NOTES

1. *Othello*, ed. E.A.J. Honigmann (Arden edition, 1997). The date is discussed in Appendix I, pp. 344–50, the text in Appendix 2, pp. 351–67, which summarises the arguments in Honigmann's book on the subject, *The Texts of "Othello"* (1996).

2. On the cleaning up of F. see Honigmann. p. 352.

3. "Hendiadys and *Hamlet*," *PMLA* 96, pp. 168ff.

4. W. H. Auden thought otherwise, arguing that Cassio is easy only with "women of his own class." "The Joker in the Pack," in *The Dyer's Hand* (1963), p. 262.

5. Auden speaks of Cassio's "socialized eroticism," p. 262.

6. See Empson's essay "Honest in *Othello*," in *The Structure of Complex Words*, pp. 218–49. The preceding chapters, "Honest Man" and "Honest Numbers" (pp. 185–217), are also relevant.

7. See the discussion of "defunct" in Hulme, *Explorations in Shakespeare's Language*, pp. 153–54. I think the best of her suggestions is that it means "past danger." The sense of "proper" seems to be misunderstood by Honigmann ("in conformity with rule").

8. Auden, who describes Iago as a practical joker, goes so far as to say that he ought to act brilliantly when being all the varieties of himself as presented to Othello, Cassio, Desdemona, etc., but badly in the soliloquies: "He must deliver the lines of his soliloquies in such a way that he makes nonsense of them" ("The Joker in the Pack," p. 258).

9. On the importance in the play of the word "bed," which occurs more than twenty times, see R. R. Heilman, *Magic in the Web* (1956).

10. *Otello* is not only the finest of Shakespearian operas but in certain respects offers an intelligent commentary on its source. It has been remarked that Boito underlined certain passages in the play, for example Iago's description of love as "merely a lust of the blood and a permission of the will," but Verdi did not set them; I take these to indicate that Boito saw the importance of the lines but, feeling he could not use them, indicated that the music must somehow convey their sense. See James A. Hepokoski, *Otello* (1987), for a study of Boito's dealings with Shakespeare.

11. F weakens this exit by substituting "Away" for "'Zounds."

12. This is the reason why some editors transfer Miranda's excoriation of Caliban (*The Tempest*, I.ii.351–62) to Prospero. But the motive is not a good one, for it assumes that editors already know all they need to about the limits of the character.

13. "The Joker in the Pack," p. 263. Auden remarks that in a mercantile and warlike society like Venice there was need of foreign soldiers and also of usurers, the latter being Jews and socially unacceptable despite their utility. "No Venetian would dream of spitting on Othello as on Shylock, but a line was drawn nevertheless, and it excluded marriage to a high-born Venetian woman."

14. "Lie" is another reiterated word; "lie/lies" occurs twenty-five times in the play. It provides the theme of Desdemona's talk with the Clown (III.iv), a scene which prepares us for Iago's casual and obscene punning in the horrible IV.i: "Lie—With her? / With her? On her; what you will . . . / Lie with her? lie on her? We say lie on her, when they belie her" (34–37)—at which point Othello has his fit. This device of hammering away at certain words is, as we have seen, a habit of the mature Shakespeare.

15. Philip Brockbank, "The Theatre of *Othello*," in *On Shakespeare* (1989), p. 200. Brockbank's information comes from *The Calendar of Dramatic Records in the Books of the Livery Companies of London, 1485–1640*, eds. D. J. Gordon and Jean Robertson (1954).

16. "Shakespeare and the Stoicism of Seneca," in *Selected Essays* (1932), pp. 131–32.

17. "Judean" is the reading of F; Q (and F2) read "Indian." The arguments for and against are summarised by Honigmann in the Arden edition, p. 342.

WERNER VON KOPPENFELS

Laesa Imaginatio, *Or Imagination Infected by Passion in Shakespeare's Love Tragedies*

The Pathology of Fancy

A far too frequently quoted passage from *A Midsummer Night's Dream* places lovers in the disreputable company of poets and madmen, all of them fired and driven by fancy or imagination (both terms are largely synonymous in those pre-Coleridgean times):

> Lovers and madmen have such seething brains,
> Such shaping fantasies, that apprehend
> More than cool mason ever comprehends.
> The lunatic, the lover, and the poet
> Are of imagination all compact.
>   (5.1.4–8)[1]

What is being stated here, in the final phase of an Elizabethan comedy, and with more than a pinch of authorial irony, is the pathological character of "strong" imagination so suspiciously tied up with the furor of erotic, melancholic, and poetic passions. But no sooner has the equation been set up in the name of male rationality during the prenuptial chitchat of warlike Theseus and his not entirely tamed bride Hippolyta than it is questioned by the female voice of the duo. Fancy's challenge to the reality principle clearly

From *German Shakespeare Studies at the Turn of the Twenty-first Century*, editd by Christa Jansohn, pp. 68–83. © 2006 by Rosemont Publishing and Printing.

has some powerful compensation in store for its followers. The ambivalence of its nature in theory and Shakespearean practice is worth looking into.

According to Aristotle, human imagination occupies an important middle ground between sense perception and notional thought, *aisthesis* and *noesis*.[2] What the great systematist regards and describes in a neutral way, can be seen from a different—e.g., moralist—angle as a dangerous border-crossing activity, or an unwholesome mixture of incompatible elements; as manic delusion manifesting itself in milder form among lovers (witness the Roman tag *amens amens*, lovers are out of their wits) and disastrously in the different stages of madness. The poetic dimension of delusive fancy refers us back to the Platonic archetype of the poet as "enthusiast" ("the poet's eye in a fine frenzy rolling"), as someone overwhelmed—in view of Aristotle's masculine reason one is tempted to say "unmanned"—by the force of fancy. An unmanning cf reason is the common denominator of Theseus's three categories of delusion. The potential productivity, though, of the imagination so brilliantly slandered by him is more than hinted at in the, example of the poet. The warrior and statesman who sweeps away, as his kind is wont to do, in the name of reality the supposed chimeras of the imagination, is but a figment of fancy himself.

The productive side of the imagination is duly taken note of in classical rhetoric, where it is made to serve the *evidentia* or graphic quality of each specific subject treated by the orator, in order to vivify the merely factual and thereby "move" the audience.[3] The poetic output of an excited fancy will be one of the leitmotifs for the following reflections on the relationship between passion and imagination in Shakespeare's love tragedies.

But first of all the notion of fancy as a menace to reason and a disease of the spirit calls for discussion. This concept was widely propagated by European moralism with its insistence on the delusions of *homo sapiens* in view of his inability to rule his unruly passions. Montaigne, the father of modern skepticism, approaches the topic in his own personal manner: "I am one of those that feele a very great conflict and power of imagination. All men are shockt therewith, and some overthrowne by it. The impression of it pierceth me, and for want of strength to resist her [sic], my endeavour is to avoid it" (I, xx).[4] Montaigne's artful surrender to the forces of fancy recommends the tactics of flight against the attacks of an irresistible enemy. On the other hand, an infectious imagination might appear as the moralist's natural ally, since it drastically reveals the impotence of reason and willpower. As the essayist goes on to expound in great detail, the emasculating effect of fancy sometimes cause's sexual failing, or—thus in the late essay III,xii—turns men into cowards through fear of death.

Early modern philosophy will intensify this charge in the name of its most sacred principles. Descartes and Pascal both denounce the imagination as a deadly adversary to reason, but from different points of view. For Descartes, it is the ruin of pure thought unclouded by prejudice, while for Pascal it embodies the supreme power of self-deception which prevents man from recognizing his need of salvation.[5] Malebranche calls it, or her, in a nicer gendered formula, "la folle du logic," the fool (or madwoman) in the house of reason; and Hobbes, who sees it as one of the main causes for religious enthusiasm and civil war, honors it with the deeply ambiguous definition of "decaying sense."[6] Thus its Aristotelian middle position between body and soul/spirit/reason is changed into what amounts to a betrayal of the spirit, and its Greek and Latin etymologies are given a pejorative twist: *phantasia* is reduced to a mere phantom, and *imaginatio* to a distorted image.

An aspect of the imagination that seems especially uncanny to rational thought is the fact that this ambivalent agent of body and soul, in an act of mirror-like inversion, tends to subject the mind to the external objects that set it afire. Bacon speaks about "this *Ianus of Imagination*" and continues: "Neither is the *Imagination* simply and onely a Messenger, but is invested with, or at least wise usurpeth no small authoritie in it selfe."[7] The senses, when overexcited by strong impressions (says Robert Burton, to whom we owe the epoch's most detailed psychosomatic study of the imagination), act forcefully on the mind, and this infection in its turn leads on to pathological states of the body, to "this thunder and lightning of perturbation, which causeth such violent and speedy alterations in this our microcosm, and many times subverts the good estate and temperature of it. For as the body works upon the mind ... so, on the other side, the mind works upon the body, producing by his passions and perturbations miraculous alterations, as melancholy, despair, cruel diseases, and sometimes death itself."[8] What Theseus announced but jokingly, Burton, as a physician of body and soul, confirms with scholarly authority: an infected imagination, or *laesa imaginatio* in his medical terminology, is the common cause of both mental and erotic derangement, since it distorts and blows up ("misconceiving or amplifying") the true proportion of things.[9] Among those particularly susceptible to the force of fancy, artists and writers are explicitly included: "In poets and painters imagination forcibly works, as appears by their several fictions, antics, images" (I, 159).

Thus Burton's discourse on melancholy diagnoses a *circulus vitiosus* between body and mind: a melancholy disposition makes the fancy prone to infection, and an infected fancy may derange the balance of bodily humors to the point of madness. Burton treats love melancholy as a particular species of corrupted imagination, whose cruelty surpasses the Spanish Inquisition (III, 141), and jealousy as its subspecies, "a bastard branch or kind of love-melancholy" no less infernal. Revealing as to the gender aspect of fancy is his statement that the passion of love "turns a man into a woman" (III, 142).

The heroes of the Shakespearean love tragedy bear out this diagnosis quite openly:

ROMEO.
  O sweet Juliet, / Thy beauty hath made me effeminate
  (*Romeo and Juliet*, 3.1.113–14)

TROILUS.
  I am weaker than a woman's tear
  (*Troilus and Cressida*, 1.1.9)

ANTONY.
  My sword, made weak by my affection . . .
  (*Antony and Cleopatra*, 3.11.67)

To an Elizabethan audience this insight would imply a dangerous topsy-tur-vydom in the hallowed hierarchy of the sexes: the "Herculean hero" Antony enslaved and "unsexed" by Omphale! For the specifically female manifesta-tions of melancholy Burton quotes several authorities who attribute this disease to corrupt vapors arising from the menstruous blood to cloud the brain ("that fuliginous exhalation of corrupt seed, troubling the brain, heart and mind"; I, 414), and therefore regard it as a "natural" evil. The *weaker vessel*,[10] runs the—commonplace—argument, is more or less at the mercy of its bodily passions; its physical delicacy makes the imagination a convenient gate of access, left invitingly open to every disturbing impression. Male fancy infected by erotic passion entails an infringement of mental sovereignty, and therefore the danger (or chance?) of a certain loss of manliness.

The Case in Point of Infected Imagination: Othello

The protagonist of one Shakespearean love tragedy, it is true, loudly and before the highest witnesses claims the immunity of his warlike nature to this debilitating passion:

OTHELLO
  No, when light wing'd toys
  Of feather'd Cupid seel with wanton dullness
  My speculative and offic'd instruments,
  That my disports, corrupt and taint my business,
  Let housewives make a skillet of my helm,
  (1.3.268–72)

So much hubris must go before a fall, which it announces by way of dramatic irony, and which will actually take place as a visual shock in 4.1. There we see Othello literally overthrown by the sexual fantasies Iago's words have sadistically implanted in his mind. He loses not only his manly but also his manlike carriage, writhing on the ground in a fit that Iago diagnoses as epilepsy or falling sickness (line 43). Iago cynically assumes the role of a doctor who notes with satisfaction the effect of his well-dosed drug: "Work on, / My medicine!" (4.1.44–45) But what he administers is the poison, not the antidote—a black parody of the true physician like Burton, whose analysis of love melancholy is at the same time a therapeutic offer.

Burton calls jealousy "a most violent passion . . . , an unspeakable torment, a hellish torture, and infernal plague," raging especially among Africans and Italians, for "southern men are more hot, lascivious, and jealous than those as live in the north" (III, 264). With characteristic animation he goes on to describe the symptoms of an imagination attacked by jealousy: "strange gestures of staring, frowning, grinning, rolling of eyes, menacing ghastly looks, broken pace, interrupt precipitate half-turns" (III, 280)—as if he were coming straight from a performance of *Othello*. The following relation seems to be aimed directly at Desdemona's intercession for Cassio: "at home, abroad, he is still the same, still inquiring, maundering, gazing, listening . . . Why did she smile, why did she pity him, commend him? . . . a whore, a whore, an arrant whore . . ." (III, 281).

Within the canon of Shakespeare's tragedies, *Othello* is the classical case of *laesa imaginatio*, a corruption of fancy induced by jealous love that will prove a sickness unto death. The stages of this disease are dramatized as an inescapably fatal process, and at the same time as a diabolic manipulation of the hero by his hidden antagonist—the prehistory, the initial moment presented with tremendous compression in 3.3, the gradual overpowering of Othello's mind and soul, and the deadly conclusion. An essential aspect of Othello's status as an exotic outsider in overcivilized Venice is, from the very beginning, his noble and expansive use of imagery, which gives a seductive quality to his speech. When asked by the Duke to reveal the magic tricks that won Desdemona's heart, his witchcraft turns out to have been a natural art of rhetoric whose native urgency appealed directly to the listener's fancy: "She'd come again, and with a greedy ear / Devour up my discourse" (1.3.149–50).

To Iago this inner realm of emotional linguistics, this interface of adventuring and imagination in his master, is a hostile territory asking to be occupied and devastated; for it expresses a kind of nobility that he perceives as a negation of his own being. When talking to his follower Roderigo he dismisses Othello's high rhetoric as a distortion of reality, mere high-flown "conceit" in the twofold sense of arrogance and swollen metaphorics: "Mark me with what violence she first lov'd the Moor, but for bragging and telling her fantastical lies" (2.1.222–24). Iago's cynicism is an anti-imaginative, though by no means realistic, outlook—his own obsession with corrupt sexual fantasies being too much in evidence. He is bent on "untuning" the Othello music, on taking down his master's high erotic imagination ("I'll set down the pegs that make this music," 2.1.200) in order to turn this amorous idealism, so profoundly alien and menacing to his nature, into his own vision of "goats and monkeys." Iago's imagination, as far as we can tell, is naturally corrupt, i.e., fundamentally distinguished from Hamlet's or Lear's erotic disillusion which is the result of intense suffering.

In *Othello* the close connection between imagination and imagery is made use of as a dramaturgic point. The "monster in thy thought," the "horrible conceit," whose half-hidden outline Othello discovers in his ensign's mind, as soon as Iago's poison has begun to affect his vision (3.3.107; 115), makes itself felt like some foreign matter in his mind. "Dangerous conceits are in their nature poisons" (3.3.326), is Iago's knowledgeable comment. His quasi Pavlovian expertise in stimulus and response causes his victim repeatedly to fall into a frenzy, in response to certain words calculated to unleash his murderous rage. The way Othello regards and treats his wife as a whore, first in front of the Venetian ambassador and next in the "intimate" scene following, shows him as the object of his own "horrible conceit," which shortly afterwards will drive him to the complementary acts of murder and suicide. In the first case a man alienated from himself destroys his own better self in the guise of the woman he loves, while in the second one he condemns and executes the slanderer and miscreant within himself: "a malignant and a turban'd Turk" (5.2.353). The final cure of his *laesa imaginatio is* a lethal operation performed on his own body.

Female Imagination as Proleptic Fantasy: Juliet

As image-creating force of human consciousness, the imagination invariably keeps a metaphorical distance from reality, transforming its elements by an amplifying or shrinking process. The era's variable perspectives of love, from vertiginous idealism to sexual cynicism—acted out in black-and-white contrast in Shakespeare's *Sonnets* and incomparably shaded off in Donne's *Songs and Sonnets*—offer ample scope for the conceits of fancy and of metaphorics. In *Othello* for instance we watch the denigration of "high" love as a process of semantic inversion, set off by a tempter with diabolic traits; and we see an image of this in the great warrior's surrender to his antagonist of the psychomachia, due to his loss of faith in his own heroic stature.

In Shakespeare's first love tragedy things are rather different. Here the absolutism of Romeo's and Juliet's love remains intact in the face of enormous challenges. The cynics in love, Mercutio and the nurse, are not enemies but allies. Their erotic naturalism serves as a dramatic foil to the great passion, nor are they unimaginative themselves, as the Queen Mab speech goes to show.[11] They are merely part of an environment whose lack of understanding will prove fatal to "high" love. While Romeo's enflamed imagination takes the initiative at the first meeting, with elaborate conceits to which Juliet responds in kind, she will later on, having outgrown childhood all at once, make herself visionary in order to anticipate, and as it were stage, future events in her own mind.

The first of these proleptic fantasies is the ironic sequel to the killing of Mercutio and Tybalt which leads to Romeo's banishment. Unaware of these events, Juliet anticipates her approaching wedding night in a surge of feverish joy. In a prothalamion soliloquy she equates the longed-for coming of night with the bridegroom's embrace, since both will take away all girlish sense of shame from the wife-to-be:

> Come, civil night,
> And learn me how to lose a winning match,
> Play'd for a pair of stainless maidenhoods.
> Hood my unmann'd blood, bating in my cheeks,
> With thy black mantle; till strange love grow bold,
> Think true love acted simple modesty.
> Come, night, come, Romeo, come, thou day in night,
> (3.2.10–17)

Here Juliet, who ironically compares herself to an impatient child at the end of the passage, in her state of excited erotic imagination voices female desire in a way that is without parallel among Shakespeare's contemporaries. The rhythm of this unchildlike apostrophe suggests anticipated fulfillment through its imaginative sensuousness. But hardly has this passionate expectation of happiness been conjured up in a theater of fantasy that turns the longed-for future into immediate present, when it is cruelly disclaimed; and from now on Juliet's proleptic fantasy will project scenarios of terror that prepare herself, and the audience, for the final catastrophe. This happens when, after the couple's one and only night of love, she looks down from her balcony and sees Romeo below "As one dead in the bottom of a tomb" (3.5.56). But her most tormenting fantasy of terror is to be found in her second soliloquy, before drinking the fatal sleeping draught, in her moment of utter desolation. It culminates in the "horrible conceit" (Othello's formula!)

of her awakening among the corpses in the vault of the Capulets, where she feels herself going mad as the body of Tybalt rises to meet her: "Stay, Tybalt, stay!" (4.3.57). Her imagination tainted by darkest melancholy makes Juliet resemble at this juncture those crazed melancholics, who—Burton tells us—are "more like dreams than men awake, they feign a company of antic, phantastical conceits . . . and sometimes think verily that they hear and see present before their eyes such phantasms or goblins" (I, 394).

At such moments of crisis that seem to put the very existence of love at hazard, the distressed imagination projects a dramatic image of its suffering into the future, a device frequently found in that most Shakespearean of love poets, John Donne.[12] As the speaker of his poems is both lover and poet, the lover's imagination quite naturally engenders poetic conceits. In "The Apparition," for instance, the spurned suitor sees himself posthumously visit his lady's chamber, where he will have her, bathed in the sweat of terror, and left unprotected by her drained lover of the moment, at his mercy. In Donne's Elegy XVI the speaker, who is about to leave for the continent, tries to dissuade his beloved from her plan (worthy of a Shakespearean heroine) to follow him on his dangerous ways in the disguise of a page. No, let her be sure of his unwavering faithfulness, and await his return in patience. By no means must she frighten her nurse at night—like Juliet, the girl seems to be underage—with nightmarish fantasies, and give away their secret bond of love:

> nor in bed fright thy nurse
> With midnight's startings, crying out, "Oh, oh
> Nurse, O my love is slain, I saw him go
> O'er the white Alps alone; I saw him, I,
> Assailed, fight, taken, stabbed, bleed, fall, and die."

Like Juliet's imagined awakening in the vault, this disaster scenario is a compact little drama in itself. Moreover, in Donne the lover's fantasy is raised, as it were, to the second power, since the speaker is picturing the way his lady might imagine his own death! By this device the male "authority" of love and its poetic rendering can keep the situation under control, and persuasively prophesy a happy ending to the crisis; whereas Juliet's black forebodings will come true, though in a different way than she imagines—after the law of tragedy, and according to Burton's prognosis for the advanced states of love melancholy: "death is the common catastrophe to such persons" (III, 187). In this context, one out of only two unambiguous Shakespearean quotes in *The Anatomy of Melancholy*[13] recapitulates the final words of the play: "Who ever heard a story of more woe, / Than that of Juliet and her Romeo?" (III, 187).

Awakening from the Dream of High Love: Troilus

Like *Romeo and Juliet*, *Troilus and Cressida* is the tragedy of two young lovers who are drawn to each other in a world of old men and old conflicts. They have to spend their "wedding night" furtively, to be torn apart as "fortune's fools" in the cold grey light of the following dawn by the so-called force majeure, the brutal impact of external circumstances. While in Shakespearean comedies like *A Midsummer Night's Dream* the well-earned wedding night after the final scene promises lasting happiness to the well-assorted couples, in the love tragedies the discords of the world outside invade the moment of erotic fulfillment. In *Othello*, no less than two nights of love are severely disturbed in this way. The Venetian wedding night comes to an abrupt end, due to the Turkish menace and Iago's machinations, and the first night on Cyprus is fatally interrupted by Roderigo's staged brawl with Cassio. The anticlimactic nature of the "tragic" night of nights, perhaps the dramatic equivalent to the notorious postcoital sadness, holds a mirror up to the dialectics of high expectation and disillusion, of sublime erotic fantasy and the troublesome realities of love. In this respect, *Troilus and Cressida* contains a more telling lesson than *Romeo and Juliet*.

For the differences between the two plays are so prominent that they largely conceal the similarities. Even the tragic character of the Trojan drama about love and war has been in dispute from the beginning. How can a play lay any claim to tragic dignity, whose two plots end with a foul and unexpiated betrayal, and which pursues with merciless consequence the debunking of *heros* and *eros*? Yet Shakespeare's tragedy is by no means incompatible with satire—see *Hamlet*—, and his Hector is not the only heroic warrior who falls victim to a cowardly cabal—see *Coriolanus*. Even more decisive for the question of genre is the clearly marked dramatic instant in which the passion of love tilts over into a passion of suffering. In *Troilus and Cressida* there are two such moments of terrible isolation and intensity, set off by the relentless onward march of events: Cressida's outburst of despair in 4.2.96–103, and Troilus's mental torture while he watches Cressida's infidelity in the eavesdropping scene (5.2.137–60).

The play's analogy with *Romeo and Juliet* is deceptive in other respects, too, for the love—passionate, by all means—of the Trojan couple is quite unlike the fierce erotic absolutism of the Veronese lovers. In Troy the lovers are no longer immune from the cynical view of love surrounding them, so obtrusive in the lewdness of Pandarus, in the sexual pragmatism of Diomed, and in the obscene foaming of Thersites. The violent oscillations of feeling in Shakespeare's final love tragedy seem to cast their shadows before, as if Troilus and Cressida were, in spite of their youth, lovers of advanced age like Antony and Cleopatra.[14]

Shakespeare's dramatic art draws a discreet but inexorable parallel between Cressida and Helen. The greatest beauty of the world and cause of the Ten Years' War is granted only an incidental scene of utmost triviality that serves as distorting mirror to the hollow heroics of the play. Neither apotheosis nor tragic dignity can be allotted to the exploits of Hector and the soon-to-be-consummated love of Troilus in a world whose symbol of love and chivalry is a dallying Helen, fawned upon by an effeminate Paris and amused with a smutty song by Pandarus. In this drama of contrasting perspectives, where all sublime certainties dissolve in the opposition of inflating fantasy and deflating satire, Troilus during the council scene is made to carry his point against his brother Hector, whose advice is to send Helen back to the Greeks:

> HECTOR
> Brother, she is not worth what she doth cost
> The keeping.
> Troilus
> What's aught but as 'tis valued?
> . . . .
> Why, she is a pearl,
> Whose price hath launch'd above a thousand ships,
> And turn'd crown'd kings to merchants.
>   (2.2.51–83)

Things and men have no absolute worth—imagination fixes their market value: "La raison a beau crier, elle ne peut mettre le prix aux choses" (Pascal).[15] Kings are merchants, and women mere commodities in a male-dominated world. Cressida, who keeps her erotic fantasy under strict control, sees herself with masculine eyes: "Women are angels, wooing; / Things won are done" (1.2.286–87). The love duet of Troilus and Cressida before their bodily union is ironically undercut not only by the pander's prose but even more by their own doubts and premonitions. Troilus, who had described himself as "mad in Cressida's love" even in the first scene, feels literally unmanned by his proleptic erotic imagination as Pandarus is about to lead his niece into his arms:

> I am giddy; expectation whirls me round;
> Th' imaginary relish is so sweet
> That it enchants my sense; what will it be,
> When that the wat'ry palates taste indeed
> Love's thrice-repured nectar? Death, I fear me,
>   (3.2.18–22)

The anticlimax to this excess of imagination comes gradually, with Pandarus's innuendoes on the morning after and Cressida's ill-humored reaction to them, with Troilus's fainthearted worry about his good name as soon as he learns about Cressida's repatriation, and most incisively during the eavesdropping scene in the Greek camp.

This scene, one of the most outrageous in the Shakespeare canon, has an interesting parallel in *Othello* 4.1. There Iago arranges an eavesdropping for his master in order to provide him with "ocular proof" and drive him inextricably into his mania of jealousy. While the hidden observer is writhing with agony, Desdemona's handkerchief, material center of Iago's plot, actually changes hands under his eye. Iago himself appears both as actor and commentator of the scene, which is real as well as illusory. By analogy—and contrast—a worldly-wise Ulysses presents the young Trojan, for whom he seems to feel a certain sympathy, with the very real betrayal of his beloved and the ocular proof of its performance in guise of the "sleeve" Cressida surrenders to Diomed, again a textile piece of evidence. The *evidentia* of the presentation, true to the rules of rhetoric, affects the observer and listener strongly in both cases, even to near-madness. "You are moved, Prince," is Ulysses' comment (*Troilus and Cressida* 5.2.36), with the very words Iago will use to describe the effect of his insinuations on Othello's mind: "My lord, I see y' are mov'd" (*Othello* 3.3.224).

But of course Ulysses, who sees through the conceit of his Greek warriors no less than through Cressida's erotic opportunism, is no Iago—though also an expert manipulator of men. That he accompanies the young Trojan on his ill-starred quest must be more than a gesture of politeness. It is his way of sobering down Troilus, an attempt to cure his diseased imagination. But the task fails, like so many reasonable initiatives that remain powerless against the general delusion. It fails, because it succeeds all too well, for the treatment leaves the patient traumatized. It will turn the noble youth from the other side into a savage next day on the battlefield.

"'Tis mad idolatry / To make the service greater than the god" (2.2.56–57), Hector had told his brother Troilus when the latter was defending Helen and the cost of her keeping. Troilus's own love had been idolatrous, and his service greater than his goddess, an imbalance that demands painful correction. His emotional outburst after witnessing Cressida's betrayal expresses a bitter reaction against the epoch's cult of high love with its well-worn Platonic and Petrarchan trappings; but also a nagging doubt about the sublimation of eros in general which is perfectly in key with the antiheroic bias of the play. This radical distrust of the sublime—a problematic element in tragedy—is echoed in the moralist skepticism of Montaigne and in the poetry of Donne. Donne's "Farewell to Love" stages the change from inflation to deflation of

the amorous imagination in shocking conceits that make no bones about
their analogy to sexual tumescence and its sequel:

> Whilst yet to prove,
> I thought there was some deity in love
>   So did I reverence, and gave
> Worship . . .
>   Thus when
> Things not yet known are coveted by men,
>   Our desires give them fashion, and so
> As they wax lesser, fall, as they size, grow.
>
> But, from late fair
> His highness sitting in a golden chair,
>   Is not less cared for after three days
> By children, than the thing which lovers so
> Blindly admire, and with such worship woo;
> Being had, enjoying it decays . . .
>   (p. 56f, 1–16)

The extreme tension between Donne's complex stanzaic form and his
brutally chopped-up syntax is comparable to what Shakespeare does to
the inner form of tragedy in *Troilus and Cressida*: he deconstructs it with a
vengeance.

Fluctuating Fantasies of Love: Antony and Cleopatra

In his last love tragedy Shakespeare performs a miracle. He not only succeeds in giving a new dramatic pattern to the dialectics of high and low
eros, of heaven-bound love fantasy and the infernal downfall of its—tragic
or satiric—disillusion, but finally raises the poetic potential of the pattern to
unsurpassable heights. The protagonists' will to transfigure their autumnal
passion alternates with suspicions of its fragility and hollowness. The amplifying and reductive quality of imagination both in the observers and in the
lovers themselves imposes its peculiar fluctuating rhythm on the structure
of the whole play.

When in the initial scene Antony sees himself as monarch of a realm of
love much greater than the Roman empire, he recalls some of Donne's lovers
who, in poems like "The Good-Morrow" or "The Sun Rising," feel in possession of a world set apart for them, way above external reality, a world whose
superiority is "proved" by the conceits of their image-creating fantasy. But
only a little later Antony will be quite ready to invert the proportions, and to

place his political duties above the love bond celebrated as a wonder of the world just a dramatic moment ago. And after losing the dominion over the world—partly through Cleopatra's fault—at Actium, he sees his loss made up for by a single tear of hers (3.11.69–70), only to revile her, a few scenes later, in the harshest of terms for betraying him to the enemy. In Donne's "Valediction: Of Weeping," we may remember, a lover's tear is made to assume the dimension of the globe, to be dissolved, one stanza later, in an equally metaphoric deluge.

In its thirst for infinity, the great passion soon reaches its limits; the eternity it loves to invoke is a matter of the past, not the present: "Eternity was in our lips and eyes . . ." (1.3.35).[16] In his moments of doubt and imaginative detumescence the great conqueror's huge appetite for life and love shrinks to his revulsion from the stale remnants of a sexual meal:

> I found you as a morsel, cold upon
> Dead Caesar's trencher; nay, you were a fragment
> Of Cneius Pompey's . . .
>   (3.13.116–18)

Troilus used exactly the same images at the nadir of his love experience:

> The fractions of her faith, orts of her love,
> The fragments, scraps, the bits and greasy relics
> Of her o'er-eaten faith, are given to Diomed.
>   (*Troilus and Cressida*, 5.2.158–60)

In Donne's poetry, such conceits mark the opposite pole to the superiority over the boundaries of time and space claimed by the ecstatic lovers—the banal physics of love as opposed to its metaphysics:

> He that but tastes, he that devours,
>   And he that leaves all, doth as well:
> Changed loves are but changed sorts of meat . . .
>   ("Community")

In Donne as in Shakespeare, the enormous span that leads to the sublime transfiguration of the erotic passion begins (or ends) at the low point of sexual cynicism with its negative hyperbolics of a thoroughly disenchanted fantasy. It is to this span that *Antony and Cleopatra* owes its triumphant finale. When Cleopatra stages her suicide in a hopeless situation as a supreme act of love, the sublime actress of her own death gains the evidence of this transformation from the force of her erotic fantasy which turns defeat into apotheosis. It is her first meeting with Antony on the river Cydnus which she performs again, transcending—like Othello in his final speech—the miserable here-and-now to live up, for the last time, to the heroic image of herself. The royal costume is of utmost importance for this play within the play, this end which acts out a beginning:

> Show me, my women, like a queen; go fetch
> My best attires. I am again for Cydnus
> To meet Marc Antony
> . . . .
> Give me my robe, put on my crown, I have
> Immortal longings in me . . .
>   (5.2.227–81)

Just at the moment that proves it mortal, love reaches out imperiously for immortality.[17] The power of their imagination may make the lovers appear as fools or madmen to their sober or cynical contrasting figures—Enobarbus, Caesar—, but to the audience they are the moving poets of their own passion. And in this the female imagination surpasses the male one. In her ability to compel even the unimaginative to pay homage to her spell, Cleopatra is clearly her maker's mouthpiece. Thus Enobarbus invokes, in uncharacteristically luminous images, her Egyptian magic in the cold Roman atmosphere; later on, after his "reasonable" defection, a last magnanimous gesture of Antony's makes him die of a broken heart. And the final reflection of Cleopatra's posthumous triumph strikes a spark of imagination even from that cool expert in realpolitik, Octavius Caesar:

> she looks like sleep,
> As she would catch another Antony
> In her strong toil of grace.
>   (5.2.346–48)

Among Shakespeare's dramatis personae, only those gifted with an idealizing imagination are capable of love passion in the double sense of the word, and only they seem able to fully engage our compassion for their suffering. An imagination susceptible and vulnerable to high erotic passion is both hazard and distinction; just as, according to Burton and his many forerunners, the melancholic's laesa imaginatio is a disease as well as a creative potential, since the special sensitivity of the patient puts him above the more callous of soul. If an essential historical condition for the birth of Elizabethan tragedy was the transitional stage from a metaphysical to a more secular consciousness, by analogy Shakespeare's love tragedy may be positioned between faith and doubt, between an extreme idealization and sublimation of secular love and the materialist lowlands of sexual disenchantment.

To pass the voice of disillusion off as Shakespeare's ultimate message, and to take Thersites for his spokesman in these matters, would undo the incomparable drama of love and imagination in some of his greatest plays. Such "shrinking imagination" is disabling for readers, critics, and producers alike.

NOTES

1. All quotations are from *The Riverside Shakespeare*, ed. G. Blakemore Evans (Boston: Houghton Mifflin Company, 1974).

2. Cf. Silvio Vietta, *Literarische Phantasie* (Stuttgart: Metzler, 1986), 45–46.

3. Cf. John L. Halio, "The Metaphor of Conception and Elizabethan Theories of the Imagination," *Neophilologus* 50 (1966): 454–61; for the context of rhetoric, see Vietta, *Literarische Phantasie*, 49–56; and Heinrich Lausberg, *Handbuch der literarischen Rhetorik* (Munich: Hueber, 1960), 810–19.

4. Michel de Montaigne, *Essays*, tr. John Florio, 3 vols. (London: Dent, 1946), I: 92.

5. For Descartes, see Vietta, *Literarische Phantasie*, 25–31; Pascal, *Pensées*, fr. 82, ed. Ch.-M. den Granges (Paris: Garnier, 1955), 95: "C'est cette partie décevante dans l'homme, cette maitresse d'erreur et de fausseté . . ."

6. Nicole Malebranche, *De la Recherche de la vérité*, ed. G. Rodis-Lewis (Paris: Bordelet, 1962), pt. II; Thomas Hobbes, *Leviathan*, I, ii; ed. B. Crawford Macpherson (Harmondsworth: Penguin, 1968), 88.

7. Francis Bacon, *The Advancement of Learning*, ed. Michael Kiernan (Oxford: Clarendon Press, 2000), 106.

8. *The Anatomy of Melancholy*, ed. Holbrook Jackson (London: Dent, 1964), I: 250. All Burton quotations are from this edition.

9. Burton, I: 252. Cf. Pascal, *Pensées*, 99 (fr. 84): "L'imagination grossit les petits objets jusqu' à en remplir notre âme, par une estimation fantastique; et, par une insolence téméraire, elle amoindrit les grands." The menacing nature of this distortion of reality is of central importance for the moralists' distrust of the imagination from Montaigne to Malebranche.

10. Biblical term for the "weaker sex" after 1 Pet. 3:7. Cf. Malebranche, 267: " . . . parte que les moindres objets produisent de grands mouvements dans les fibres délicates de leur cerveau . . ."

11. Cf. Jerome Mandel, "Dream and Imagination in Shakespeare," *Shakespeare Quarterly* 24 (1973): 61–68, 62; the author reads this famous passage as a critique of the *imagination* ("Mercutio voices the arch-sceptic's position"), but is it not also its exuberant *vindication*?

12. Cf. Patrick Cruttwell, *The Shakespearean Moment (London*: Chatto and Windus, 1954), chs 1–3. All Donne quotations from *The Complete English Poems*, ed. A. J. Smith (Harmondsworth: Penguin, 1971).

13. Cf. *The Anatomy of Melancholy*, ed. Nicolas K Kiessling et al., 6 vols. (Oxford: Clarendon Press, 1989–2000), index of VI: 419, s.v. "Shakespeare."

14. "Something in the climate of the play has aged both lovers, not as persons but as lovers, and before their time as it were" (Arnold Stein, "*Troilus and Cressida*: The Disjunctive Imagination," *Journal of English Literary History* 36 [1969]: 145–67, 149).

15. Pascal, *Pensées*, 95 (fr. 82).

16. This is pointed out by Robert Ornstein, "The Ethic of the Imagination: Love and Art in *Antony and Cleopatra*," *Stratford-upon-Avon Studies* 8 (1966): 31–46; Ornstein terms even Cleopatra's sexuality "an emotion recollected" (35).

17. "To some degree every aspect of her imagination is ironic"; Sidney R. Homan, "Divided Response and the Imagination in *Antony and Cleopatra*," *Philological Quarterly* 49 (1970): 460–68, 465.

Chronology

1564	William Shakespeare christened at Stratford-on-Avon on April 26.
1582	Marries Anne Hathaway in November.
1583	Daughter Susanna born, baptized on May 26.
1585	Twins Hamnet and Judith born, baptized on February 2.
1587	Shakespeare goes to London, without family.
1589–90	*Henry VI, Part 1* written.
1590–91	*Henry VI, Part 2* and *Henry VI, Part 3* written.
1592–93	*Richard III* and *The Two Gentlemen of Verona* written.
1593	Publication of *Venus and Adonis*, dedicated to the Earl of Southampton; the *Sonnets* probably begun.
1593	*The Comedy of Errors* written.
1593–94	Publication of *The Rape of Lucrece*, also dedicated to the Earl of Southampton. *Titus Andronicus* and *The Taming of the Shrew* written.
1594–95	*Love's Labour's Lost*, *King John*, and *Richard II* written.
1595–96	*Romeo and Juliet* and *A Midsummer Night's Dream* written.
1596	Son Hamnet dies.

1596–97	*The Merchant of Venice* and *Henry IV, Part 1* written; purchases New Place in Stratford.
1597–98	*The Merry Wives of Windsor* and *Henry IV, Part 2* written.
1598–99	*Much Ado About Nothing* written.
1599	*Henry V, Julius Caesar,* and *As You Like It* written.
1600–01	*Hamlet* written.
1601	*The Phoenix and the Turtle* written; father dies.
1601–02	*Twelfth Night* and *Troilus and Cressida* written.
1602–03	*All's Well That Ends Well* written.
1603	Shakespeare's company becomes the King's Men.
1604	*Measure for Measure* and *Othello* written.
1605	*King Lear* written.
1606	*Macbeth* and *Antony and Cleopatra* written.
1607	Marriage of daughter Susanna on June 5.
1607–08	*Coriolanus, Timon of Athens,* and *Pericles* written.
1608	Mother dies.
1609	Publication, probably unauthorized, of the quarto edition of the *Sonnets.*
1609–10	*Cymbeline* written.
1610–11	*The Winter's Tale* written.
1611	*The Tempest* written. Shakespeare returns to Stratford, where he will live until his death.
1612	*A Funeral Elegy* written.
1612–13	*Henry VIII* written; The Globe Theatre destroyed by fire.
1613	*The Two Noble Kinsmen* written (with John Fletcher).
1616	Daughter Judith marries on February 10; Shakespeare dies April 23.
1623	Publication of the First Folio edition of Shakespeare's plays.

Contributors

HAROLD BLOOM is Sterling Professor of the Humanities at Yale University. He is the author of 30 books, including *Shelley's Mythmaking, The Visionary Company, Blake's Apocalypse, Yeats, A Map of Misreading, Kabbalah and Criticism, Agon: Toward a Theory of Revisionism, The American Religion, The Western Canon,* and *Omens of Millennium: The Gnosis of Angels, Dreams, and Resurrection. The Anxiety of Influence* sets forth Professor Bloom's provocative theory of the literary relationships between the great writers and their predecessors. His most recent books include *Shakespeare: The Invention of the Human,* a 1998 National Book Award finalist, *How to Read and Why, Genius: A Mosaic of One Hundred Exemplary Creative Minds, Hamlet: Poem Unlimited, Where Shall Wisdom Be Found?,* and *Jesus and Yahweh: The Names Divine.* In 1999, Professor Bloom received the prestigious American Academy of Arts and Letters Gold Medal for Criticism. He has also received the International Prize of Catalonia, the Alfonso Reyes Prize of Mexico, and the Hans Christian Andersen Bicentennial Prize of Denmark.

A.D. NUTTALL was a professor of English at Oxford University. He was the author of numerous books, including *Shakespeare the Thinker* and *Two Concepts of Allegory: A Study of Shakespeare's* The Tempest.

E.A.J. HONIGMANN taught English literature at the Shakespeare Institute (University of Birmingham), University of Glasgow, and at the University of Newcastle upon Tyne. He is the author of several works on Shakespeare as well as the editor of several of his plays. Among his texts are *Shakespeare: Seven Tragedies—The Dramatist's Manipulation of Response* and *Shakespeare's Impact on His Contemporaries.*

ARTHUR KIRSCH is a professor of English, emeritus, at the University of Virginia. He has written extensively on Shakespeare as well as on Auden and has edited a new edition of Auden's *The Sea and the Mirror: A Commentary on Shakespeare's "The Tempest."*

NICHOLAS GRENE is a professor at Trinity College, Dublin. He has written *Shakespeare, Jonson, Moliere: The Comic Contract* and *Shakespeare's Serial History Plays* and has written and edited other titles as well.

MAYNARD MACK is a professor at the University of Maryland. His books include *Killing the King: Three Studies in Shakespeare's Tragic Structure* and *King Lear in Our Time.* He is the co-editor of *The Norton Anthology of World Literature* and has edited various editions of some of Shakespeare's plays.

PETER WENZEL is a professor at RWTH Aachen campus, Germany. He has published a book on Shakespeare and been on the advisory board for Bochum publications in evolutionary cultural semiotics.

NANCY CLUCK was a professor at the University of Texas–Dallas, where she taught Shakespeare and Renaissance drama. She authored *Literature and Music: Essays on Form.*

FRANK KERMODE has taught at many universities, notably University College, London, and Cambridge University, and has been a visiting professor at several others. He has written and edited numerous works, among them *The Sense of an Ending* and *Shakespeare, Spenser, Donne.*

WERNER VON KOPPENFELS is emeritus professor at the University of Munich. He has published numerous works on the English Renaissance, the Enlightenment, and literature in its European context. He is a translator and is editor and co-translator of anthologies of English and French poetry.

Bibliography

Baldo, Jonathan. *The Unmasking of Drama: Contested Representation in Shakespeare's Tragedies.* Detroit, Mich.: Wayne State University Press, 1996.

Bell, Millicent. *Shakespeare's Tragic Skepticism.* New Haven: Yale University Press, 2002.

Bloom, Harold. *Shakespeare: The Invention of the Human.* New York: Riverhead Books, 1998.

Bradshaw, Graham. *Misrepresentations: Shakespeare and the Materialists.* Ithaca, N.Y.: Cornell University Press, 1993.

Bratchell, D.F., ed. *Shakespearean Tragedy.* London: Routledge, 1990.

Bulman, James C. *The Heroic Idiom of Shakespearean Tragedy.* Newark; London: University of Delaware Press; Associated University Presses, 1985.

Cahn, Victor L. *The Heroes of Shakespeare's Tragedies.* New York: Peter Lang, 1988.

Coronato, Rocco. "Hamlet and Infinite Interpretation." In *Paper Bullets of the Brain: Experiments with Shakespeare,* edited by Shaul Bassi and Roberta Cimarosti, pp. 55–66. Venice, Italy: Cafoscarina, 2006.

Cunningham, James. *Shakespeare's Tragedies and Modern Critical Theory.* Madison, N.J.: Fairleigh Dickinson University Press; London; Cranbury, N.J.: Associated University Presses, 1997.

Deats, Sara Munson, ed. Antony and Cleopatra: *New Critical Essays.* New York: Routledge, 2005.

Dillon, Janette. *The Cambridge Introduction to Shakespeare's Tragedies.* Cambridge, England: Cambridge University Press, 2007

Einersen, Dorrit. *Shakespeare's* Troilus and Cressida: *Tragedy, Comedy, Satire, History or Problem Play?" Angles on the English-Speaking World* 5 (2005): 45–55.

Everett , Barbara. *Young Hamlet: Essays of Shakespeare's Tragedies*. Oxford [England]: Clarendon Press; New York: Oxford University Press, 1989.

Ghose, Zulfikar. *Shakespeare's Mortal Knowledge: A Reading of the Tragedies*. New York: St. Martin's Press, 1993.

Guilfoyle, Cherrell. *Shakespeare's Play within Play: Medieval Imagery and Scenic Form in* Hamlet, Othello, *and* King Lear. Kalamazoo: Western Michigan University, Medieval Institute Publications, 1990.

Hall, Michael. *The Structure of Love: Representational Patterns and Shakespeare's Love Tragedies*. Charlottesville: University Press of Virginia, 1989.

Hamlin, William M. *Tragedy and Scepticism in Shakespeare's England*. Basingstoke, Hampshire; New York: Palgrave Macmillan, 2005.

Hunt, Marvin W. *Looking for Hamlet*. New York: Palgrave Macmillan, 2007.

Hutson, Lorna. *The Invention of Suspicion: Law and Mimesis in Shakespeare and Renaissance Drama*. Oxford, England: Oxford University Press, 2007.

Kahan, Jeffrey, ed. King Lear: *New Critical Essays*. New York: Routledge, 2008.

Kinney, Arthur F., ed. Hamlet: *New Critical Essays*. New York: Routledge, 2002.

Knight, George Wilson. *The Imperial Theme: Further Interpretations of Shakespeare's Tragedies Including the Roman Plays*. London; New York: Routledge, 2002.

———. *Shakespeare's Dramatic Challenge: On the Rise of Shakespeare's Tragic Heroes*. London; New York: Routledge, 2002.

Krims, Marvin Bennett. *The Mind According to Shakespeare: Psychoanalysis in the Bard's Writing*. Westport, Conn.: Praeger, 2006.

Lawrence, Sean. *The Difficulty of Dying in* King Lear." *English Studies in Canada* 31, no. 4 (December 2005): 35–52.

Leggatt, Alexander. *Shakespeare's Tragedies: Violation and Identity* . Cambridge, England: Cambridge University Press, 2005.

Levy, Eric P. *Hamlet and the Rethinking of Man*." Madison, N.J.: Fairleigh Dickinson University Press, 2008.

Liebler, Naomi Conn. *Shakespeare's Festive Tragedy: The Ritual Foundations of Genre*. London; New York: Routledge, 1995.

Mangan, Michael. *A Preface to Shakespeare's Tragedies*. London; New York: Longman, 1991.

Margolies, David. *Monsters of the Deep: Social Dissolution in Shakespeare's Tragedies*. Manchester, UK; New York: Manchester University Press; New York: distributed exclusively in the USA and Canada by St. Martin's Press, 1992.

McEachern, Claire, ed. *The Cambridge Companion to Shakespearean Tragedy*. Cambridge, England: Cambridge University Press, 2002.

Mooney, Michael E. *Shakespeare's Dramatic Transactions*. Durham: Duke University Press, 1990.

Moschovakis, Nick, ed. Macbeth: *New Critical Essays*. New York: Routledge, 2008.

Murakami, Ineke. "The 'Bond and Privilege of Nature' in *Coriolanus*." *Religion and Literature* 38, no. 3 (Autumn 2006): 121–36.

Nordlund, Marcus. *Shakespeare and the Nature of Love: Literature, Culture, Evolution*. Evanston, Ill.: Northwestern University Press, 2007.

Reid, Robert Lanier. *Shakespeare's Tragic Form: Spirit in the Wheel*. Newark: University of Delaware Press; London: Associated University Presses, 2000.

Romm, Joseph J. "Why Hamlet Dies." *Hamlet Studies: An International Journal of Research on The Tragedie of Hamlet, Prince of Denmarke* 10, nos. 1–2 (Summer–Winter 1988): 79–94.

Rosenberg, Marvin. *The Masks of Anthony and Cleopatra*. Newark: University of Delaware Press, 2006.

Sadowski, Piotr. *Dynamism of Character in Shakespeare's Mature Tragedies*. Newark : University of Delaware Press; London; Cranbury, N.J.: Associated University Presses, 2003.

Smith, Emma, ed. *Shakespeare's Tragedies*. Malden, Mass.: Blackwell, 2004.

Taylor, Neil, and Bryan Loughrey, ed. *Shakespeare's Early Tragedies:* Richard III, Titus Andronicus *and* Romeo and Juliet: *A Casebook*. Basingstoke: Macmillan, 1990.

van Oort, Richard. "Shakespeare and the Idea of the Modern." *New Literary History* 37, no. 2 (Spring 2006): 319–39.

Willson, Robert F., Jr. *Shakespeare's Reflexive Endings*. Lewiston: Edwin Mellon Press, 1990.

Wilson, Richard. "'Blood Will Have Blood': Regime Change in *Macbeth*." *Shakespeare Jahrbuch* 143 (2007): 11–35.

Young, David. *The Action to the Word: Structure and Style in Shakespearean Tragedy*. New Haven: Yale University Press, 1990.

Zamir, Tzachi. *Double Vision: Moral Philosophy and Shakespearean Drama*. Princeton: Princeton University Press, 2007.

Zimmerman, Susan, ed. *Shakespeare's Tragedies*. New York: St. Martin's, 1998.

Acknowledgments

A.D. Nuttall, "Shakespeare's Imitation of the World: *Julius Caesar* and *Corio-lanus*." From *A New Mimesis: Shakespeare and the Representation of Reality*. Copyright © 1983 by A.D. Nuttall; 2006 by A.D. Nuttall for the preface to the Yale edition. All rights reserved by the Estate of A.D. Nuttall, c/o Writers' Representatives LLC, New York, NY.

E.A.J. Honigmann, "The Uniqueness of *King Lear*: Genre and Production Problems." From *Myriad-minded Shakespeare: Essays on the Tragedies, Problem Comedies and Shakespeare the Man*. Published 1989, 1998 by St. Martin's Press. Reproduced with permission of Palgrave Macmillan.

Arthur Kirsch, "For He Was Great of Heart." From *The Passions of Shakespeare's Tragic Heroes*, pp. 1–20, 147–48. Copyright © 1990 by the Rector and Visitors of the University of Virginia. Reprinted by permission of the University Press of Virginia.

Nicholas Grene, "*Antony and Cleopatra*." From *Shakespeare's Tragic Imagination*. Published 1992 by St. Martin's Press. Reproduced with permission of Palgrave Macmillan.

Maynard Mack, "'The Readiness Is All': *Hamlet*." From *Everybody's Shakespeare: Reflections Chiefly on the Tragedies*. Published by University of Nebraska Press. Copyright © 1993 by Maynard Mack.

Peter Wenzel, "Word and Action in the Mad Scenes of Shakespeare's Tragedies." From *Word and Action in Drama: Studies in Honour of Hans-Jürgen Diller on the Occasion of His 60th Birthday,* edited by Günter Ahrends, Stephan Kohl, Joachim Kornelius, and Gerd Stratmann. Copyright © 1994 by WVT Wissenschaftlicher Verlag Trier.

Nancy Cluck, "The Fearful Summons: Death in the Opening Scenes of Shakespearean Tragedy." From *Entering the Maze: Shakespeare's Art of Beginning,* edited by Robert F. Willson, Jr. Copyright © 1995 by Peter Lang.

Frank Kermode, "*Othello.*" From *Shakespeare's Language.* Copyright © 2000 by Frank Kermode. Reprinted by permissions of Farrar, Straus and Giroux, LLC.

Werner von Koppenfels, "Laesa Imaginatio, or Imagination Infected by Passion in Shakespeare's Love Tragedies." *From German Shakespeare Studies at the Turn of the Twenty-first Century,* edited by Christa Jansohn. Copyright © 2006 by Rosemont Publishing and Printing. Reprinted by permission.

Every effort has been made to contact the owners of copyrighted material and secure copyright permission. Articles appearing in this volume generally appear much as they did in their original publication with few or no editorial changes. In some cases, foreign language text has been removed from the original essay. Those interested in locating the original source will find the information cited above.

Index